THE MODERNISM OF EZRA POUND

THE MODERNISM OF EZRA POUND

The Science of Poetry

Martin A. Kayman

St. Martin's Press   New York

First published in the United States of America in 1986

Printed in Hong Kong

ISBN 0–312–54295–X

Library of Congress Cataloging-in-Publication Data
Kayman, Martin A., 1953–
The Modernism of Ezra Pound.
Includes index.
1. Pound, Ezra, 1885–1972–Criticism and
interpretation.   2. Modernism (Literature)   I. Title.
PS3531.O82Z69   1986   811'.52   85–26237
ISBN 0–312–54295–X

Contents

Preface

Since Hugh Kenner inaugurated modern Pound criticism with *The Poetry of Ezra Pound* (London: Faber, 1951), well over seventy major studies of the poet have been published in English, not to mention the thousands of specialised articles and doctoral dissertations in near-constant production. With the centenary in 1985, one can expect further proliferation. To come upon the public with yet another work requires *some* sort of justification other than evangelical zeal or the personal conviction of illumination.

The general justification for the enormous activity of the 'Pound industry' is most certainly not a massive popular interest in Pound. Rather perhaps the opposite: the need felt by scholars to express Pound's objective importance for the writing of poetry, for literary history and theory to an audience who continue to recognise his significance but who are disinclined by his apparent esotericism to read him, or about him.

This phenomenon would be of immediate interest only to a sociology of literary studies did it not indicate something about Pound's work itself, and were it not symptomatic of the relations between literary modernism in general and the modern reading public. The paradox of Pound's reputation as an important modernist – much praised and studied 'professionally', but little read in popular terms – points not only to his notorious (and often, in the event, overrated) 'difficulty', but specifies that difficulty in terms of his simultaneous centrality and eccentricity in relation to modern literary culture, the idiosyncratic place in a literary tradition Pound made for himself by a calculated distance from the mainstream, yet from which he continues to exercise a major influence on the writing of, and about, poetry.

At the outset of his career, Pound displays the conviction that poetry was losing its seriousness for the modern audience in an increasingly disadvantaged competition with other discursive and aesthetic practices. As severe as he felt the crisis was, so radical had to be the restatement of the art which would reinstitute its seriousness. In order to launch a modern poetry which would not be a second-rate philosophy, painting, music or narrative in verse, Pound felt himself forced to dislocate the poetic tradition which, according to him, was responsible for the crisis, and to construct a new beginning against orthodoxy.

If Pound has some responsibility for the apparently deliberate obscurity of the resources and techniques of much modernist verse, it is not from a spirit of perversity. His difficulty may be viewed rather as a reflection of the radical nature of his gesture, corresponding to the extremity of the crisis and the radicality of his ambition: no less than a much-needed renaissance for poetry. Thus what is experienced by the reader as difficulty or obscurity in Pound is most often a consequence of his heterodoxal eccentricity: his going to the margins in order to relocate poetry in the centre.

The problems of complexity and innovation consequent on this radicality against inherited convention are then in large part responsible for the proliferation of explanatory material about the poet, his work and his ideas. Of this exegesis, explication and popularisation there is more than enough, and the present text does not mean to offer itself as yet another revision of Poundian theory, let alone another interpretation of the thematic unity (or not) of the work. For this, the classics of Pound scholarship are quite sufficient. This book not only has nothing as such to add to their explanations and the fund of Poundian information they contain, but also cannot help – and would not seek to avoid – its dependence on them.

Yet I encounter in these indispensable texts a major problem: the manner in which, as Ian F. A. Bell has recently argued in *Critic as Scientist: The Modernist Poetics of Ezra Pound* (London: Methuen, 1981), their explications and popularisations tend to reproduce the lines and values of Pound's own discourse. For example, Hugh Kenner's use of Buckminster Fuller's 'knot' theory, and Donald Davie's 'forma' or 'ontwerp' (adapted from Pound himself and from Allen Upward, respectively) may both paraphrase principles of Poundian technique (in this case, the 'vortex'), but they are not instruments for its analysis. The reader ends up elucidated but not necessarily wiser.

In this way, the creation of a school of Poundian criticism characterised by such repetitions – which itself contributes to the sealing-off of Pound's eccentricity – may be seen as a further consequence of that eccentricity. Given the nature of his deliberate dislocation from the conventional tradition, it is to an extent inevitable that explications of Pound's work should have problems in translating it into more familiar theoretical concepts and so characteristically end up exhibiting a tendency to a sympathetic esotericism.

So it is that Pound's own radical exclusion of such traditional elements as Descartes, Kant, Marx and Freud, and its loyal repetition in the explicators who seek to honour his self-defined difference, has not only failed to relocate Pound in a tradition other than his own, but has also kept his work for a long time immune from critical traditions which have otherwise dominated areas of literary theory.

However, since the mid 1970s, and especially since the founding of the British (now International) Ezra Pound Conference at the University of Sheffield in 1976, a new generation of largely European scholars have begun to introduce new strategies for reading into the area of Pound studies in such a way that Pound is beginning to be discussed and analysed in terms less of his own making and increasingly in relation to major theoretical developments of our period. See, in particular, the essays collected in *Ezra Pound: Tactics for Reading*, ed. Ian Bell (London: Vision, 1982), and *Ezra Pound and History*, ed. Marianne Korn (Maine: National Poetry Foundation, 1985), as well as the monographs by the editors themselves, Ian Bell's *Critic as Scientist* and Marianne Korn's *Ezra Pound: Purpose/Form/Meaning* (London: Pembridge Press, 1983).

Such an exercise is not of course entirely new, nor have all such attempts to make Pound answer to the sort of questions which have for some time been directed at writers such as James Joyce and Paul Valéry, for example, avoided their predecessors' traps of inappropriate and reductive readings of the continually recalcitrant and unorthodox Poundian paradigm. The problem continues to be that of respecting the specificity of the paradigm whilst making its analysis intelligible to historical and theoretical debate. However, this new scholarship, distinguished by its more thorough knowledge of Pound's work and its greater theoretical sophistication, is, to my mind, pulling Pound out of his ghetto and into a context which enables us to discuss his position in relation to modernism as a whole without having either to reduce Pound to the status of an inconvenient eccentric or, alternatively, to subordinate modernism to his figure – as in Hugh Kenner's symptomatic title for his study of modernism, *The Pound Era* (London: Faber, 1975).

It is in this sense that the present work claims its (always relative) originality, locating itself very much in the recent context of Pound studies. I should thus like gratefully to acknowledge my debt to my colleagues at the Ezra Pound Conference. In trying to combine historical and formal analysis of the Poundian discourse and to relate it to central issues of modernism, I am far from abnegating Pound's centrality. The text remains concerned to establish his importance as a modernist, representative of a tradition that he himself propagated. However, I pose the question of Pound's significance not only in terms of his achievement and influence, but also in terms of the sorts of theoretical questions that are posed by the very attempt to *read* Pound. It seems to me, in short, that the difficulty and inconvenience of Pound's work is related to the fact that the act of reading him in itself demands reflections and, more importantly, *decisions* about the nature of the poetic text and its relations to the discourses that surround it, threaten it, and may be used to justify it.

In my own experience, I have always found that the primary question that picking up a book by Pound effectively poses strikes at a decisive crisis of modernism: the relation between art and politics – a question that we cannot help putting in personal terms: how comes it that we enjoy or value the poetry of a fascist? My first, introductory chapter seeks to sketch Pound's importance with particular reference to this question and its centrality in Pound and for us, as readers.

The body of the text analyses Pound's modernist techniques, centred on the theory and practice of metaphor which he developed in his formative years in London (1908–20), prior to embarking on *The Cantos*, and which were intended to resolve the crisis of the rupture between the poet and his inheritance and the poet and his audience which may be seen as characteristic of the predicament of the modern poet.

Thus the second chapter concentrates on the first central moment of crystallisation of Pound's poetics of metaphor in the practice and history of Imagisme. Here I attempt an analysis and theorisation of the poetic technique of the Image in relation to the critical problem it seeks to resolve. At the same time, I seek to show the political effects of Imagiste techniques in the production of history: in this case, the history of Imagisme as a literary movement itself.

The most important constant in this period of the formation of Pound's poetic theory is the use of a scientific discourse to mediate the technical project and to present the role of the poet in the contemporary world, by modernising his aesthetic function in scientific terms. My analysis of this discourse is indebted and complementary to that of Ian Bell, and tries to show in what way this discourse parallels and is informed by the contemporary scientific discourse of empirio-criticism (also known as phenomenalism).

An analysis of the second major crystallisation of Pound's poetics, *The Chinese Written Character as a Medium for Poetry* (1919–20), shows, at the theoretical level, how Pound's theory corresponds to what we might call a phenomenalist theory of language. Identifying the paradigm in this way enables us to revise the orthodox Poundian criticism, which is perceived as symptomatic of the epistemological closure that such a poetic implies. Once again this is not to detract from Pound's importance but to relocate its terms: a reflection not of a contemporary scientific reality, but of a specific and in itself considerably influential scientific discourse about reality.

In a work of this sort, it is not possible to provide any kind of complete account of *The Cantos*, but it is important to demonstrate the consequences of this poetic in practice. Thus, in Chapter 4, I analyse a selection of metaphorical strategies as we find them conveying important values in *The Cantos*.

A central element which emerges in the discussion of Imagisme and Pound's metaphorical technique in his earlier poems and in *The Cantos*, as much as in his use of scientific discourse and in *The Chinese Written Character*, is the pursuit of primitive linguistic energies and a theory of myth as the basis for a poetic project expressed not in mystical but in scientific terms. In the analysis of poetic technique in some elements of *The Cantos*, I seek to relate the metapoetics of myth in technical and theoretical terms to more local devices of Pound's 'objective' poetics of phenomenalism.

This leads into the final chapter, where I try once more to relate my argument about Pound to larger questions of modernism. Pound's attempt to regenerate poetry by a return to primitive linguistic and mythic energies and his justification of this in terms of a revolutionary scientific reality is seen as not only typical but also exemplary of many modernist projects. The text concludes with a critique of this specific project, using Pound's courageous and rigorous confrontation of the aesthetic and the political in the field of poetry and the authoritarian consequences of his historically conditioned options as both the justification of his importance and the starting-point for a reassessment of the modernist crisis.

Some of the material presented here has appeared in different forms in papers for the International Ezra Pound Conference (1981, 1982), in articles in *Paideuma* (Maine), *Biblos* (Coimbra, Portugal) and the *Revista da Universidade de Coimbra*, and in *Ezra Pound: Tactics for*

Reading, ed. Ian Bell, and my own *Alguns dos nossos melhores poetas são fascistas: uma introdução a Ezra Pound* (Coimbra: Fenda Edições, 1981).

The text has a somewhat long history, which is in effect the story of its debts: first, to my doctoral supervisor, David Howard, and to the colleagues at the University of York who helped at the time, especially in the areas of literary theory and epistemology: Geoffrey Wall, Baudoin Jourdant and Michael Hay; secondly, to my colleagues at the University of Coimbra, whose constant feedback to my lectures and classes on Pound advanced my thinking considerably; thirdly, as I have already indicated to my colleagues at the Ezra Pound Conference, and particularly to Ian Bell, Eric Mottram, Marianne Korn and Stephen Wilson. Naturally, all errors are mine, despite their best efforts to correct them.

M. A. K.

Acknowledgements

The author and publishers are grateful to all the copyright-holders who have given permission to reproduce material in copyright.

The extracts from the following works by Ezra Pound are reprinted here by permission of the Ezra Pound Literary Property Trust and Faber & Faber Ltd, London, and New Directions Publishing Corporation, New York:

The Literary Essays of Ezra Pound (edited by T. S. Eliot), copyright 1935, 1954 by Ezra Pound;

Selected Prose, 1909–1965 (edited by William Cookson), copyright © 1973 by the Estate of Ezra Pound;

Selected Letters of Ezra Pound 1907–1941 (edited by D. D. Paige), copyright 1950 by Ezra Pound;

Translations, copyright 1953 © 1954, 1963 by Ezra Pound (all rights reserved);

Gaudier-Brzeska, copyright 1916 © 1970 by Ezra Pound (all rights reserved);

The Cantos: Cantos 1–41 copyright 1934, Cantos 42–51 copyright 1937, Cantos 52–71 copyright 1940, Cantos 72–84 copyright 1948, Cantos 85–95 copyright 1956, Cantos 96–109 copyright 1959, Cantos 110–117 copyright 1962, all copyright by Ezra Pound;

The Chinese Written Character as a Medium for Poetry, edited with notes by Ezra Pound, copyright 1920 by Ezra Pound;

Collected Shorter Poems (US title *Personae*), copyright 1926, 1952 by Ezra Pound;

Collected Early Poems, copyright © 1976 by the Trustees of the Ezra Pound Literary Trust (all rights reserved);

Jefferson and/or Mussolini, copyright 1935 by Ezra Pound;

the extracts from 'The Book of the Month', *Poetry Review*, vol. I, no. 3 (March 1912) and from 'Status Rerum', *Poetry*, vol. I, no. 4 (January 1913), and the letter published originally in *The Pound Era* by Hugh Kenner, copyright © 1985 by the Ezra Pound Literary Property Trust.

The extracts from the following works by Ezra Pound are reprinted by permission of New Directions Publishing Corporation, New York, and Peter Owen Ltd, London:

Guide to Kulchur, copyright © 1970 by Ezra Pound, all rights reserved;

The Spirit of Romance, copyright © 1968 by Ezra Pound, all rights reserved.

The extract from 'A Note on War Poetry' is reprinted from *Collected Poems 1909–1962* by T. S. Eliot, copyright 1936 by Harcourt Brace Jovanovich, Inc; copyright 1963, 1964 by T. S. Eliot; reprinted by permission of the publisher.

The extract from *Is 5?* by e. e. cummings, reprinted by permission of Liveright Publishing Corporation.

The extracts from *Epoch and Artist* by David Jones, reprinted by permission of Faber and Faber Ltd.

The extract from 'The Young Housewife' by William Carlos Williams is reprinted from *The Collected Earlier Poems* by William Carlos Williams, copyright 1938 by New Directions Publishing Corporation; reprinted by permission of New Directions.

A Note on the Text

All references to *The Cantos* are to the Faber & Faber edition (London, 1975). Location of passages will be given in the main text, Canto numbers preceding page number.

1 Introduction: Some of our Best Poets are Fascists

In 1934, Ezra Pound published a collection of essays entitled *Make it New*, including a long and important piece called 'Cavalcanti: Medievalism', which is subsequently dated '1910–1934'. Making it new out of the medieval: 'I hadn't in 1910 made a language, I don't mean a language to use, but even a language to think in.'[1] Pound had arrived in Europe in 1908, aged twenty-three, with a small collection of poems which he published privately in Venice under the title *A Lume Spento*. In London he produced selections from this work, adding new texts in a series of volumes: *A Quinzaine for this Yule* (1908), *Personae* and *Exultations* (1909) and *Canzoni* (1911), from which the title *Personae* was recovered in 1926 as the generic title for Pound's collected shorter poems. Referring to the earlier *Personae*, Pound wrote in 1914 that it represented the beginning of a ' "search for oneself" ', for ' "sincere self-expression" ', a 'search for the real'.[2] The voices and techniques experimented with in his first works constitute, then, a double project for both a 'language' and a poetic 'self', which then become the base for his collected shorter poems and the major work, *The Cantos*. His main resources in this first period (1908–11) were those writers discussed technically and historically in his *Spirit of Romance* (1910) – the Troubadours of Provence, the Tuscan poets, their contemporaries and successors: making it new out of the medieval.

Amongst them we find François Villon, who is contrasted with the more central Dante ('in some ways one of the most personal of poets'[3]): 'Dante's vision is real, because he saw it. Villon's verse is real, because he lived it.'[4] One of Pound's two 'Villonauds' of 1910 is 'The Ballad of the Gibbet':

Skoal!! to the gallows! and then pray we:
God damn his hell out speedily
And bring their souls to his 'Haulte Citee'.[5]

Almost forty years later, the irony implicit in the dramatic imitation of the poet who 'lived it' in his Parisian prison works itself out as Pound recovers a form of identifying and restoring voice in a cage on death row at Pisa Disciplinary Training Centre: 'As a lone ant from a broken ant-hill / from the wreckage of Europe, ego scriptor' (76/458) – a poetic self restored, discovering the personal and historical irony that 'Le paradis n'est pas artificiel, / l'enfer non plus' (76/460); 'a man on whom the sun has gone down' (74/430), his political dream in ruins, holding the ideal city he had sought to construct 'now in the mind indestructible' (74/430).

This voice is found in the Pisan Cantos, written in the cage. In 1949, they were awarded the Bollingen Prize for poetry by the Library of Congress: the first major public recognition of Pound's talent by his native country, at the same moment as that State was accusing him of treason for his active support of the Axis during the war.

The discussion aroused by this award may appear to have been the last serious occasion for debate on the relation between politics and poetry in the West, which has left us now only with the more smug polemics of the Pasternak and Solzhenitsyn affairs. It is to be noted however that the award was given in explicit despite of the political context, as the citation made clear: 'To permit other considerations than that of poetic achievement to sway the decision would destroy the significance of the award and would in principle deny the validity of that objective perception of value on which civilized society must rest.'[6] Hence Donald Davie has written of the award that it

> was enormously to the credit of American society, but it did nothing to vindicate the exalted reality of living the poet's life (something William Carlos Williams claimed for Pound). For what it meant in effect was that American society accepted and recognised an absolute discontinuity between the life of the poet and the life of the man.[7]

This distinction between 'objective' aesthetic value and political activity has given the poet in the West an impotent freedom. 'And for much of this,' Davie writes, 'Pound is to blame.'

But it is hard to 'blame' Pound for this, precisely because it is inappropriate to treat him thus. The fundamentally political project of 'The Serious Artist' (1913), which governs his entire career as poet and pamphleteer, is not abandoned even in Pisa: 'Here error is all in the not done, / all in the diffidence that faltered . . .' (81/522).[8] As Pound sought to develop a modern poetic capable of responding to what he perceived as the responsibility of the artist, so does his art demand to be read.

'The Pisan Cantos' differs from the preceding sections of the major work largely in terms of a relative relocation of the poetic self in relation to the historical and political references which are a major characteristic of the entire poem. Whereas, in the previous sections of *The Cantos*, the dominant tendency had been towards an attempted 'impersonal' presentation of a public reference frame (not, of course, without major problems), the explicit discovery here is 'that the drama is wholly subjective' (74/430), and thus that

> nothing matters but the quality
> of the affection –
> in the end – that has carved the trace in the mind
> dove sta memoria
>
> (76/457)

In Pisa, without a library, the historical vision which in large part constitutes *The Cantos* is filtered through an apparently personal act of memory.

Of course, the imperatives, as well as the conditions of composition, are different. Whereas previously the ambition had been to build the city, the defeat of the Axis and Pound's own arrest determined the need for some sort of shift in the poem. Here it is first a matter of recuperating the coherence of the self under major pressure, and of sustaining a poem whose political ambition, expressed by a predominantly historical reference, had been defeated by real political events.

A principal element which provides the 'affection' adequate to recovery is the recollection of the sites and friends of 'our London / my London, your London' (80/516): the London of the early experimental years (1908–20), populated, as is the text, by W. B. Yeats, James Joyce, T. S. Eliot, Wyndham Lewis, Henri Gaudier-Brzeska, A. R. Orage, and so on; the London of the 'search for oneself' and for 'a language to think in' in order to 'make it new'.

Hence, at the point where the political project encounters disaster, the poem returns to the site from which it distantly originated, in an affectionate recall of its background within a community of writers, at a specific place and at a specific historical moment. It is this return which, in large part, characterises the poetic power of the sequence, and hence contributes much to its so-called 'objective value'. Whether then at the level of reference, or at the level of sub-text, the 'life' is too present in the poem for us to divorce it from a book idealised as an apolitical aesthetic event.

As mediated by the text, the return appears to be personal, and the 'life' involved might therefore seem merely autobiographical. But, although 'historical' in a different sense from, say, the Malatesta Cantos (8–11), the Pisan Cantos have a significance which extends beyond that of an isolated personal career. For Pound's career is far from isolated: inasmuch at least as he is far from being an eccentric figure in modernism, and inasmuch as his trajectory from London to Pisa (and, textually, back again) is more than contingent to the events it traverses, we can say that there is more at stake here than a possible personal tragedy.

We might determine two central ironies: the relation between Pound the (prize) poet and Pound the (criminal) citizen, and between them and the Pound persona (Villon). The ironies offer a story and a tableau of a poet who indeed 'lived it': the sixty-year-old poetic innovator of first importance, the literary entrepreneur, major lyricist, epic artist; the 'serious artist', poet of history and economics, the Confucian, constitutionalist, radical anti-capitalist – arrested by the US Army and indicted for treason; writing his most accessible and publically successful poetic sequence, and being awarded a prize by a US government agency. Within this perspective, one might argue that these complex ironies have for their object modernism itself, with History as their agent.

In order to justify such a perspective, one would have to establish Pound's importance for modernism: to what extent is he in fact representative of and influential in the historical moment?

This is a question of literary history, and it may well be too early to regard modernism as, in Hugh Kenner's phrase, 'The Pound Era'.[9] But an inventory of Poundian innovation might lead us to the conclusion that Pound pioneered a great many of the techniques which most of us now take for granted in modern poetry: free verse, juxtaposition, concision, direct presentation, the rejection of didacticism, the use of allusion and quotation, 'imagisme', the 'objective correlative',[10] and techniques of 'impersonality'. Similarly, many of the criteria which we now use to judge modern verse were propagandised and put into practice by Pound: the primacy of rhythm and of the image, modern standards of translation, economy of expression, the 'concrete', 'objectivity'. Furthermore, in more direct terms, Pound was a technical and professional hub. During his lifetime he assisted – technically, personally and/or financially – W. B. Yeats, James Joyce, T. S. Eliot, Robert Frost, H. D. (Hilda Doolittle), and others. Amongst those claiming kinship, influence or discipleship were William Carlos Williams, Charles Olson, Louis Zukofsky, e. e. cummings, George Oppen, Basil Bunting and Allen Ginsberg – not to mention hundreds of lesser imitators, beneficiaries and devotees. The travelling was by no means all one way; but Pound was certainly very much at its centre. There is also a 'third generation' who express their debt to his initiatives – poets such as Robert Creeley, Robert Duncan, Edward Dorn, Jonathan Williams, among many others. 'Open-field' poetry, 'concretism', 'objectivism', 'projective verse' all owe much to Pound's experiments and achievements. Indeed, one might say that there is a 'Poundian tradition' which, while not exclusive in terms of modern poetry, is arguably dominant. It is probable that in not one instance did Pound originate the technique or the critical value – there were people writing free verse before Pound – but it was he who popularised and most consistently exemplified them, provided them with a critical discourse, and it is in his work that we find them all coherently put to productive use.

Pound enthusiasts, as I have indicated, may tend to exaggerate what is already a gigantic-enough stature to the extent of ranking Pound with Homer and Dante, as one who 'changed the means of expression'. Whether one wishes to go that far or not, one must at the very least assert that Pound is, if not the major figure in modernism, one of its most radical and influential innovators in verse. As Eliot, who knew of what he spoke at first hand, from the revisions that Pound made to *The Waste Land*, wrote in testimony, 'It is on his total work for literature that he must be judged: on his poetry, *and* his criticism, *and* his influence on men and on events at a turning point in literature.'[11] In these terms, Pound is to be judged as major – not necessarily as unique or original, but by the same token as absolutely not peripheral. Pound is representative of a tradition – a tradition he himself promulgated. It is in such a capacity that we should regard him and his story: in a radical modernist tradition, in very large measure that out of which our contemporary poetic scene grew. It is not an exaggeration to argue that Pound is a father and leading representative of Anglo-American modernism.

As a technician he is almost incomparable – few contemporaries enter the contest: in a direct context, perhaps Eliot himself, Paul Valéry, David Jones and Wallace Stevens. Pound's *ABC of Reading* (1934) indicates the source of the achievement: an arduous training in world literature. His ideology was to 'take the best' from whatever culture, whatever period, and learn to do it himself. He sought, in the early years, to 'bring poetry up to the level of prose',[12] and to do this according to a '*Weltlitteratur*' standard.[13] It is the ideology of the poet as artisan; for Pound, 'technique is the test of a man's sincerity'.[14] The *sine qua non* of a poet's claim to be read is his ability to write well, rather than the exquisiteness of his sensibility.

Hence we find Pound's enthusiasm for translation and imitation (forms of writing which he also succeeded in transforming). His translations are usually (and sometimes provocatively) 'inaccurate', but somehow they often seem more authentic than doggedly precise renderings. Thus Pound first really caught public attention with his rendering of the Anglo-Saxon poem 'The Seafarer' in 1911,[15] making the Old English rhythms 'new' in a way that he was also to exploit in Canto 1. In this early period, we find him translating, imitating and learning from the Provençal Troubadours (Arnaut Daniel, Bertrans de Born, Bernart de Ventadour, Arnaut de Marvoil, Cino, Pierre Vidal), from Guido Cavalcanti (*Sonnets and Ballate of Guido Cavalcanti*, 1912), from the French of Villon and Jules Laforgue, the Chinese of Rihaku and others, the Latin of Horace, Ovid and Sextus Propertius, and the German of Heine. All this was less a matter of assimilating sensibilities than of a training in technique: how to produce specific literary effects, since 'technique is the means of conveying an exact impression of exactly what one means in such a way as to exhilarate'.[16]

His more 'orthodox' masters were Dante, Flaubert, Browning, Yeats, Swinburne, Henry James and Ford Madox Ford (Hueffer) – plus a continually problematic relation with Walt Whitman. His first period sees him experimenting with the techniques of Browning and of Yeats and the poets of the 1890s – dramatic monologues and mystical or psychological experience, often using the Troubadours as context.[17] Then, around 1912, under the influence of Ford, came the first major step towards modernism: the movement known as Imagisme.

Towards and through the First World War, Pound allied his Imagisme to the art movement known as Vorticism, developing the theory of the Image into that of the Vortex, and writing largely short, terse lyrics and satires and experimenting with small-scale sequences (in *Ripostes*, 1912; *Lustra*, 1916). In the meantime, around 1913, he was given the papers of the sinologist Ernest Fenollosa to edit. In 1915, he published a book of poems in translation, *Cathay*; in 1916, with Yeats, some Noh plays, and in 1920, as he was beginning the definitive form of *The Cantos*, his working of *The Chinese Written Character as a Medium for Poetry* – the most coherent single statement of his poetic theory. This work on the Chinese led him into what fast became a major interest: Chinese culture, and, most of all, Confucius.

By the end of the First World War, Pound appears to have felt that he had learnt sufficient to start, as it were, the work itself: a language and a self for an epic. The longer Provençal poem 'Near Perigord' experiments with questions of history and writing. In 1917 came three experimental Cantos; then, in 1919, a version of Propertius, the *Homage to Sextus Propertius*, as a summary of and a farewell to London and what he perceived as the decadent British Empire. In 1920, in *Hugh Selwyn Mauberley*, a mini-epic of the London years, Pound experimented with another sequence in an attempt, as he put it later, to condense the novel into verse.[18]

Armed with not only a language and a persona or personae, but also with the social-credit economic theories of Major C. H. Douglas (encountered at the end of the war), Pound moved via Paris to Rapallo. The 1920s and 1930s were dedicated to *The Cantos*, the translations of Confucius, economic and political essays and books, and, finally, support for Mussolini.

That, very broadly, is the trajectory which intervenes between the London evoked at Pisa and Pisa itself. In this, the invention of Imagisme may be seen as crucial: the difference between *Canzoni* (1911), the last book before Imagisme, and *Ripostes* (1912) is more marked than any other shift in Pound's development. Imagisme is, furthermore, Pound's first and generally most lasting intervention in the public literary realm, and source of much of his influence on contemporaries and future generations. For this reason I devote a chapter to it in this book.

But, before we consider Imagisme and the Image, we have first to understand the problematic out of which it emerged as a first and influential step towards poetic modernism. We shall also see here further evidence of Pound's representative centrality – perhaps more 'symptomatic' than 'donative' in this instance[19] – leading us back to the double project for a 'language' and a 'self' in *Personae*.

II

Pound tells us that he came to London in order to learn from Yeats, since he 'thought that Yeats knew more about poetry than anybody else'.[20] Yeats, to whom Arthur Symons had dedicated his *Symbolist Movement in Literature* (1899) as 'the chief representative of that movement in our country',[21] was thus a link with the French Symbolists and the English poets of the 1890s. But, in apprenticing himself to Yeats, Pound was inevitably identifying himself with a problematic inheritance.

When he wrote of not having 'made a language', he had contrasted himself with, for example, Dante Gabriel Rossetti, who, Pound felt at the time, had 'made his own'. Writing to Lucy Masterman (wife of the Liberal politician C. F. G. Masterman) in 1912, Ford Madox Ford, who rapidly became the second part of an instructive poetic dialectic for Pound, and who was personally closer to that inheritance, disagreed:

> My father once wrote of Rossetti that he set down the mind of Dante in the language of Shakespeare. That was clever of my father, but could there have been a greater condemnation of that magic Amateur . . . for what he ought to do is to write his own mind in the language of his day.
>
> Forget about Piers Plowman, forget about Shakespeare, Keats, Yeats, Morris, the English Bible and remember only that you live in our terrific, untidy, indifferent, empirical age, where not a single problem is solved and not a single Accepted Idea from the poet that has any more magic . . . .[22]

For Ford, the poets of the 1890s belonged to an outdated age, which no longer spoke in the special conditions of the present.

Ian Bell has recently restated the problem at large: 'For the writer, the disintegration of the world into a series of markets with the rise of industrial capitalism was reflected in the more immediate problem of the disruption of his relationship with his audience.'[23] At this stage, however, the problem applied more acutely in the case of the writer as poet. The poetry of both the Symbolists and the poets of the 1890s is a poetry of and in crisis. The tone may at times have been perversely affirmative, as in Mallarmé's 'La littérature ici subit une exquise crise, fondamentale' ('Crise de vers', 1896), but the sense of crisis itself, and its resolution by a turning-inwards of poetry, are symptomatic of a situation of extremity. The development of industrial capitalism, which determines the crisis, had also given rise to a new genre which had, at least in its early stages, successfully accompanied the social transformation. Hence, whilst for the poet the inheritance of Hugo or Tennyson no doubt weighed heavily, an even greater symptomatic source of anxiety was probably the success of the realist novel – for that very success pointed to the transformation which presented such problems to the poet.

The novel too was on the verge of a similar crisis by the end of the century, as the material reality of industrial capitalism began to outstrip the novel's temporary ability to accompany it. This crisis was accelerated by the cinema as a mode of production and distribution through the present century.[24] None the less, as an inheritance, the realist novel had been displacing poetry from its central aesthetic position. The realist novel had marked out a territory for itself, and its techniques and construction served the evolving industrial landscape better than those of verse. Furthermore, in marking out such a territory – no less than the physical, moral and social reality of industrial capitalism – it had also marked out an audience: the bourgeoisie, petit-bourgeoisie and the higher sections of the new proletariat likewise created or expanded by that development, and now being brought into readership. Symbolism is, then, a reaction to this crisis, to the disruption of a relation to an audience and to an object.[25]

Paul Valéry, direct inheritor of Mallarmé, saw the disruption with the audience as the only common defining feature in Symbolism. In his retrospective essay 'L'Existence du Symbolisme' (1938), he starts by observing how difficult it is to find a common aesthetic quality in the Symbolists, and finally decides that what they share is an ethical, rather than aesthetic, characteristic. He distinguishes the Symbolists from previous literary 'movements' (Classical, Romantic, Realist) in terms of 'une résolution commune de renoncement au suffrage du nombre': 'Ils opèrent ainsi une sorte de révolution dans l'ordre de valeurs, puisqu'ils substituent progressivement à la notion des oeuvres qui sollicitent le public . . . celle des oeuvres qui créent leur public.'[26] At the moment when the mass market emerges, the Symbolists turn away from it in what is clearly a retreat into a self-generated exclusivity.

Broadly speaking, then, one might say that the technical advances of the novel as a discourse of physical and social reference had driven poetry into a corner within which it could only turn in upon itself. Rejecting a public audience, it denies itself public themes, in a retreat into private and largely mystical values. Hence, in Swinburne as in Mallarmé, a (dignifying) obsession with technique, with 'pure poetry', is justified by a mystification of the craft to the point of religiosity.[27] The retreat from what we symptomatically call 'the prosaic' is clear in Symons:

> Allowing ourselves, for the most part, to be but vaguely conscious of that great suspense in which we live, we find our escape from its sterile, annihilating reality in many dreams, in religion, passion, art; each a forgetfulness, each a symbol of creation; religion being the creation of a new heaven, passion the creation of a new earth, and art, in its mingling of heaven and earth, the creation of heaven out of earth. Each is a kind of sublime selfishness, the saint, the lover, and the artist having each an incommunicable ecstasy which he esteems as his ultimate achievement . . . .[28]

One might see Symbolism then as a professional crisis for the poet, reflecting a larger social crisis: the new condition that evolves through the eighteenth and nineteenth centuries, and whose first symptoms may be seen in Romanticism, is that of a new social reality/audience which appears to oppose itself to the higher 'spiritual' values. The form which generally responds most productively to and benefits from these developments is the realist novel. The poet is left with the pressing risk of alienation from the social reality which produces the audience and its concerns – negatively forced into the extreme of 'sublime selfishness', he has only himself, his own creativity, and a personal or specious mythology as subjects for writing, whilst justifying his lack of audience with an ideology of an elect or select 'created' self and audience.

Pound however is not a Symbolist, but a modernist; what he inherits is not simply the subjectivity, mysticism and self-reference of late Symbolism, but also the imperatives exhibited in the realist novel. Modernism as a whole may indeed be characterised as that moment of crisis of subjective and objective realism which, inheriting 'an apparently unresolvable cultural bifurcation between *symbolisme* and naturalism',[29] sets about trying to resolve it. In this sense, Pound is centrally representative inasmuch as he constantly demonstrates, especially in his early writings, a radical preoccupation born out of the dislocation and the desire to resynthesise it.

Pound's stated need to 'make a language' is itself symptomatic, bespeaking a rupture with an available continuous tradition or community from which he might draw a language, in which he might insert himself and distinguish himself as a poet – as we see in the 'pure' creativity of the 1908 poem 'Plotinus', from *A Lume Spento*:

> Obliviate of cycle's wanderings
>   I was an atom on creation's throne
>   And knew all nothing my unconquered own.
> God! Should I be the hand upon the strings?
>
> But I was lonely as a lonely child.
> I cried amid the void and heard no cry . . . .[30]

Both theme and community are lacking. The absence of an object or context for creation generates anxiety, resolved by what appears to be a Symbolist stance of the self-adequate creative subject:

> And then for utter loneliness, made I
> New thoughts as crescent images of *me*.

But, as we have seen, 'self-expression' is not that simple for Pound – 'and with the words scarcely uttered one ceases to be that thing'.[31] The 'me' whom Pound's personae are to image is very different from Valéry's 'persona' M. Teste, who 'avait en somme substitué au vague soupçon du Moi . . . un être imaginaire défini, un Soi-Même bien déterminé, ou éduqué, sûr comme un instrument, sensible comme un animal, et compatible avec toute chose, comme l'homme'.[32] Isolated from a defining place and a generative language – a 'traditional' poetic self and discourse – the poet's attempt to express 'images of me' on a creative void is complicated for Pound by a radical fracture of the poetic self.

Yet the multiplication of images of the self, reflected in the exercise of personae, is symptomatic not of a merely autobiographical anxiety, but rather of a crisis in the position of the poet in relation to (non-poetic) society – the issue which, Valéry suggests, was rejected by the Symbolists ('Que m'importe le "talent" de vos arbres – et des autres! Je suis chez moi, je parle ma langue, je haïs les choses extraordinaires'[33]). For the displacement and consequent multiplication of images of the poetic self is generated not from within

– it is not an uncertainty about who he is in any personal sense – but precisely by a hostile social context.

This is clearly expressed in a poem which accompanies 'Plotinus' in *A Lume Spento*, 'Masks':

> These tales of old disguisings, are they not
> Strange myths of souls that found themselves among
> Unwonted folk that spake an hostile tongue?[34]

'Masks' is a Yeatsian term with a similar function to Pound's 'personae'. It is here presented not in terms of an instrument for remedying incoherent selfhood, but rather as a *defence* against a society which is hostile to that self. The responsibility for the inability of the self to speak his 'native tongue' lies with society, not with the poet. We see this theorised in the 1912 essay 'Psychology and Troubadours': 'I believe in a sort of permanent basis in humanity, that is to say, I believe that Greek myth arose when someone having passed through delightful psychic experience tried to communicate it to others and found it necessary to screen himself from persecution.'[35] Pound later reformulated this into an important statement on myth, to which we shall be returning:

> The first myths arose when a man walked sheer into 'nonsense', that is to say, when some very vivid and undeniable adventure befell him, and he told someone else who called him a liar. Thereupon, after bitter experience, perceiving that no one could understand what he meant when he said that he 'turned into a tree' he made a myth – a work of art that is – an impersonal or objective story woven out of his own emotion, as the nearest equation that he was capable of putting into words.[36]

In this sense, if we can place 'personae' between 'masks' and 'myth', they are indices not of a personal doubt of vocation, or even of the question of 'self-knowledge', but of a position of incomprehension or hostility imposed on the would-be poet by an unsympathetic social context.

The sense of dislocation is also evidenced by the restricted usefulness of the immediate tradition. Pound's characteristic pursuit of an alternative tradition indicates the unsatisfactory nature of the inheritance of the 1890s in general and of Yeats in particular, in themselves. As we have seen, Pound's response was to seek to construct a global 'living tradition' (as he called it), searching back behind the origins of Western Renaissance Humanism. In this way, 'the undeniable tradition of metamorphoses'[37] provides a primary source for experimental personae.

Such voices are basically confident, assertive of their incomprehensible vision – as in the poem which has always opened collections of *Personae*, and which is suggested by the above quotation, 'The Tree'. This poem begins, 'I stood still and was a tree amid the wood, / Knowing the truth of things unseen before;' and ends with a muted defiance: 'Natheless I have been a tree amid the wood / And many a new thing understood / That was rank folly to my head before.'[38] One finds a similar celebration of mystical visions ('delightful psychic experience'[39]) in such poems as 'Paracelsus in Excelsis', 'Francesca' and 'Speech for Psyche in the Golden Book of Apuleius' (the first and the third revisiting Browning and Walter Pater, respectively). The less anxious the persona, the more mystical or occult the 'self' that is expressed. These are values that Pound seeks to preserve in any new 'language', and which tend at the extreme point to full metamorphosis as the most total form of poetic vision.

However, as soon as a society is invoked, one is made aware of an extreme, not to say literal, state of alienation. Thus, in the poem 'La Fraisne' (which echoes Yeats), the persona is a former 'gaunt, grave councillor' who has metamorphosed into a tree – 'Till men say that I am mad'[40] – and who is left talking to the breeze. Similarly, Piere Vidal (*sic*), 'who ran, mad as a wolf', transformed by his love for Loba of Penautier, curses,

> O Age gone lax! O stunted followers,
> That mask at passions and desire desires,
> Behold me shrivelled, and your mock of mocks;
> And yet I mock you by the mighty fires
> That burnt me to this ash.[41]

But at this point where the transformation is literalised, the poem breaks down, the fool–wolf sniffs the air and is captured. Metamorphic mysticism may serve as an expression of psychic adventure, passion or privileged vision for the poet, but it is not comprehended by society and hence 'mocked' or persecuted, to the point where 'delightful psychic experience' risks being reduced to a more pathological alienation.

For this reason we find that most of the personae that Pound experimented with between 1908 and 1911 are in various ways expressive of modes of alienation. In the 'living tradition', the great 'treasure' is the tradition of metamorphoses; its distant inheritors, according to the thesis of *The Spirit of Romance*, were the Provençal Troubadours.

As we have seen, La Fraisne and Vidal register the danger of the inheritance in their worlds. Other Troubadour personae register a less radical alienation, but are none the less expressive of the marginalisation of the poet, generally more closely in terms of his relation to his more immediate audience. 'Cino' is, in this sense, exemplary. Wandering the roads in exile, he demystifies the seductive (but unrepaid) charms of his verse:

> Bah! I have sung women in three cities,
> But it is all the same;
> And I will sing of the sun.
>
> Lips, words, and you snare them,
> Dreams, words, and they are as jewels,
> Strange spells of old deity,
> Ravens, nights, allurement . . . .[42]

The song he is professionally obliged to sing to his patroness is a tiresome and somewhat mechanical compliment to an inadequately appreciative audience. By the same token, the poet does have something of importance to say, but he is not permitted to speak it:

> And all I knew were out, My Lord, you
> Were Lackland Cino, e'en as I am,
> O Sinistro.

The poet is forced into a position and a language which he demystifies, by a society which he sees through but is prevented from publicly demasking; he can only wander the roads of exile, and 'sing of the sun'.

'Marvoil' is likewise in exile, but for different reasons. He appears to have let his language exceed his position as a poet; taking his love poetry too seriously, he overstepped his position as composer of flattering lyrics to the Countess of Beziers and actually made love to her. When Alfonso IV of Aragon appeared as a rival, Marvoil was sent into exile. He is condemned to writing love poems for his lady and burying them in a hole in a wall in a cheap tavern in Avignon. Or one might consider again Villon, addressing his fellow social outcasts in prison; or how Bertrans de Born can only revenge himself for the indifference of his lady by turning her into 'Una donna ideale' ('Na Audiart').[43]

These Troubadours, then, characteristically have professional positions and a proper conventional language, but the position is oppressive and the language ineffective in relation to real social relations. They thus become divorced from their social role and ironic towards it. These personae are expressive of an alienation of the poet's private self and language from his public position and discourse.

Another mode of alienation is the lament, and poems such as 'Threnos' or 'Planh for the Death of the Young English King' exploit what will always be a negative discourse of dislocation: the regret for a lost or vanishing past when things were different. On the other hand, the satiric tone which we find occasionally in Pound's Troubadours (such as Cino and Marvoil) becomes dominant in other poems, such as the translations and adaptations from Heine. Once again, the personae, as is suitable for a satiric voice, are confident or defiant figures dislocated from or marginalised by society, in search of a true audience:

> This is our reward for our works,
> > sic crescit gloria mundi:
> Some circle of not more than three
> > that we prefer to play up to,
> Some few whom we'd rather please
> > than hear the whole aegrum vulgus
> Splitting its beery jowl
> > a-meaowling our praises.
>
> > > ('Au Salon'[44])

Throughout these early poems one feels the pressure of the loss or rejection of a genuine audience, and the consequences the poet suffers for this absence: discontent, lament, exile (or, in Villon's case, imprisonment), 'madness' or being condemned to talking privately to no one except, perhaps, himself, the trees, a hole in the wall, or some idealised auditor.

In short, it is not the personal self that is in doubt. What is at issue is the real – political and linguistic – possibility of finding a position and a discourse in which to express the self and have it understood. Provence is a major resource because, despite all, 'Provence knew'

'Tis not a game that plays at mates and mating,
'Tis not a game of barter, lands and houses,
'Tis not 'of days and nights' and troubling years,
Of cheeks grown sunken and glad hair gone gray;
There *is* the subtler music, the clear light
Where time burns back about th'eternal embers.
We are not shut from all the thousand heavens:
Lo, there are many gods whom we have seen,
Folk of unearthly fashion, places splendid,
Bulwarks of beryl and of chrysoprase.

                                    ('The Flame'[45])

The discontinuity which exists between the privileged vision and the social universe in which it is now oppressed or reduced to eccentricity constitutes the problematic of the poet who seeks a 'self-expression', a 'language'.

The poet refuses to compromise his vision: 'I, even I, am he who knoweth the roads / Through the sky, and the wind thereof is my body'. He is ready: 'My pen is in my hand / To write the acceptable word'; but 'Who hath the mouth to receive it' ('De Aegypto')?[46] Pound's position is distinguished from one which would merely embrace the inherited mystical language by his latent or explicit dissatisfaction with a merely private audience. A language or body (self) of pure 'wind', of spirituality, is not adequate for the modern world: 'A book is known by them that read / That same' ('Famam Librosque Cano').[47] 'Your songs' (we might believe them to be Yeats's) do have an audience: 'The little mothers / Will sing them in the twilight' and 'the little rabbit folk / That some call children . . . . Will laugh your verses to each other', whilst, ironically, 'Mine' are read by an impoverished browser who, finding them 'Some score years hence' on a second-hand stall, 'analyses form and thought to see / How I 'scaped immortality'.

The desire to encounter an audience other than 'little mothers' and indigent browsers is more explicit in Pound's early prose, and is closely linked to the search for an 'acceptable word' in which to materialise the 'wind'. In 1912, Pound published a 'Credo' in which he wrote, in respect of the question of 'Symbols',

I believe that the proper and perfect symbol is the natural object, that if a man use 'symbols' he must so use them that their symbolic function does not obtrude; so that *a* sense, and the poetic quality of the passage, is not lost to those who do not understand the symbol as such, to whom, for instance, a hawk is a hawk.[48]

The private Symbolist language will not of course reach this audience. And, despite occasional attacks on the 'vulgus', Pound's prose constantly has such an 'unpoetic' audience in mind.[49] He put the problem in his first series of articles, 'I Gather the Limbs of Osiris' (1910–11):

How, then, shall the poet in this dreary day attain universality, how write what will be understood by 'the many' and lauded by 'the few'? What interest have all men in common? What forces play upon them all? Money and sex and tomorrow . . . [and the fact that] every man who does his own job really well has a latent respect for every other man who does *his* own job really well; this is our lasting bond . . . the man who really does the thing well, if he be pleased afterwards to talk about it, gets always his auditors' attention; he gets his audience.[50]

Hence first the value of *technique* as the means of reattaining an audience.

But this 'technique' is not the priestly craft of the Symbolists; it is indeed not even a privilege of verse. In considering the question, 'What is the difference between poetry and prose?' Pound answers,

I believe that poetry is the more highly energized. But these things are relative. Just as we say that a certain temperature is hot and another cold. In the same way we say that a certain prose passage 'is poetry' meaning to praise it, and that a certain passage of verse is 'only prose' meaning dispraise. And at the same time 'Poetry!!!' is used as a synonym for 'Bosh! Rot!! Rubbish!!!!' The thing that counts is 'Good Writing'.[51]

The disjunctive and prejudicial dichotomy poetry/prose is resolved by the privileging of 'Good Writing' undertaken as an artisanal, scientific practice.

Since 'poetry' had come to be associated with the mystical and especially the rhetorical, the main values which needed to be incorporated into verse in order to generate this technical mastery and make it once more 'Good Writing' were the more public techniques of substantiality and clarity of 'the prose tradition':[52] objectivity, *le mot juste*, economy, 'presentation', the 'concrete' – a language, as Pound wrote in 'Credo', 'austere, direct, free from emotional slither'.[53]

These values are not invoked in order to sacrifice the traditional material of poetry, but to transform and further enhance it:

> The interpretative function is the highest honor of the arts, and because it is so we find that a sort of hyper-scientific precision is the touchstone and assay of the artist's power, of his honor, his authenticity. Constantly he must distinguish between the shades and the degrees of the ineffable.[54]

Pound's ambition is to synthesise the positivities of the best of 'poetry' and 'prose' in a model of 'Good Writing', a question of 'scientific' technique ('perfect control') which would thus restore to verse values it had lost to prose, but without prejudice to the spiritual bases of the art.

In summary, then, Pound is representatively modernist because, first, he suffers the fracture of the 'bifurcation' of subjective and objective realism, and dedicates his early writings to the expression of that dislocation, making us aware of how it reflects a problem of audience, of the poet's place in society, and of the language he may speak. Secondly, he is representative inasmuch as he responds to the division by attempting to synthesise the two 'tendencies', in a pursuit of an inclusive, rather than an exclusive audience, and without prejudice to his spiritual vocation.

III

Against the 'sublime selfishness' of the Symbolist movement, 'technique is thus the protection of the public, the sign manual by which it distinguishes between the serious artist and the disagreeable young person expressing his haedinus egotism'.[55] So, if the impetus for a tradition of 'Good Writing' is the quest for an audience of 'good faith', it should come as no surprise that the project is, from the beginning, fundamentally *political*. And this is the third major point of Pound's importance: not only does he representatively confront the modernist crisis and have a massive influence on its resolution, but his project brings poetry back into the political realm, from which it had seemingly felt itself forced to retreat.

In an advancing capitalist society, the poet cannot rest on his spiritual aristocracy; he has to discover a *productive* function. In 'The Serious Artist' (1913), Pound produces a defence of poetry in a technical, commercial, scientific and political context by means of an interweaving of aesthetic, ethical and epistemological claims.

He does this first by invoking the peculiar subject matter of art as specifically the immaterial field unattainable by natural science. Whereas art had previously staked this field out in reaction to advancing materialism in science and hence registered it in a basically mystical discourse, Pound returns to it in a new discourse as a complement to science and technology.

He is able to do this precisely because he is able to invoke and apply the 'prose' values that he seeks to integrate into poetry: values of 'objectivity', 'precision' and 'impersonality' which will produce 'good writing': 'By good art I mean art that is most precise.'[56]

As it is first presented, this is an *ethical* claim for art: 'good art can NOT be immoral'. But, since the ethical justification here is based on a positivity of the 'true', the claim easily becomes simultaneously epistemological. In this way

> The arts, literature, poesy, are a science, just as chemistry is a science. Their subject is man, mankind and the individual. The subject of chemistry is matter considered as to its composition.
>
> The arts give us a great percentage of the lasting and unassailable data regarding the nature of man, of immaterial man, of man considered as a thinking and sentient creature. They begin where the science of medicine leaves off or rather they overlap that science. The borders of the two arts overcross.[57]

The 'morality' and productivity of art is its 'scientific' presentation of psychic and ethical life, in the broadest sense, and expressed in non-mystical terms in such a way that the artist's 'work remains the permanent basis of psychology and metaphysics'.[58]

This is 'political' because of its ethical grounding. The data are not the generalities produced by moral dogma or positivist sociology, but the specificities of the ethico-psychological constitution of 'real' men. We might understand how this was a particularly live issue before the First World War – a period of the emergence of new psychologies and of new departures in political theory and practice.

On the one hand, psychology was seeking to establish conative faculties, such as 'purpose', within science – as we shall see in more detail in Chapter 3. The establishment of such new psychologies then allowed for their 'scientific' use in political economy. For example, Walter Lippman's important *Preface to Politics* (1909) welcomed the contribution of the 'new psychology' to political theory as a means of resituating 'man' at the centre of politics. Any new programme must 'recognize as the first test of all political systems and moral codes whether or not they are "against human nature" '.[59] This 'human nature' is not a religious or philosophical conception but borrows its terms from the new psychology, to be expressed, for Lippman, in terms of instinctual 'drives'.

It is in this line that we should view Pound's claim for the political productivity of art: in its precise rendering of human interests.

> If all men desired above everything else two acres and a cow, obviously the perfect state would be that state which gave to each man two acres and a cow.
>
> If any science save the arts were able more precisely to determine what the individual does not actually desire, then that science would be of more use in providing the data for ethics.[60]

In sum, by taking the traditional subject matter of 'poetry' demystified by, but not surrendered to, the discourse of 'prose', 'art' becomes the 'science' of 'immaterial' human nature – the source of data for the politics of human desire.

Hence Pound's further achievement was to take modernist poetry along a path it had, ultimately, to take. If he was to become the representative of dominant modernism, and its best practitioner, it was also because he put his vanguard techniques and values to the final test: to restore a political dimension to the art. This is a 'final test' inasmuch as the things which, as Pound quite rightly observes, 'interest' us – money, sex and tomorrow, and work – are definitively political. Such territory cannot be surrendered to the discourse of prose fiction. Politics becomes then the test of the social experience of a poet's art. It is peculiarly testing inasmuch as it is the most recalcitrant of fields in which the poet may reveal or celebrate his 'truths' – recalcitrant because 'imperfect': the most, as it were, 'prosaic', the most resistant to mystification and error.[61]

As we have seen, the basis for Pound's political poetry was 'desire', human nature in terms of its 'interests' in broad ethical and aesthetic terms, which were never for Pound separate from economic issues. Politics therefore were part of his modernism from the first. Whilst

Eliot hedged around two world wars,[62] Pound increasingly committed himself and his art to politics. His ikon for this became

```
R   O   M   A
O           M
M           O
A   M   O   R
```
[63]

His ideal: to build a 'Paradiso Terrestre', an ideal city on earth. Indeed, he answers Eliot's individualist religious pessimism:

> yet say this to the Possum: a bang, not a whimper,
>   with a bang not with a whimper,
> To build the city of Dioce whose terraces are the colour of stars.
> (74/425)

He sought a State constructed under the sign of Love. But he ended by putting his art to the service of a State under the sign of Death.

Something went drastically wrong. Pound's starting-point was the politics of human desire and equity which developed through his later Confucianism and his belief in the American Constitution as represented by Jefferson. He came to see Mussolini as a latter-day Jeffersonian, and so he broadcast for the fascists and, as he saw it, the Constitution, on Italian radio during the war. The broadcasts are rabid, offensive and pathetic – although his pamphlets and books are rather more coherent. Before the United States had entered the war, he had gone to Washington to try to avoid confrontation between his country and Italy; even at the end, he still believed that he could be of use. But he was arrested and thrown into a cage outside Pisa.

This is a picture we would do well to hold in our minds, without fear of melodrama: 'from the death cells in sight of Mt. Taishan @ Pisa' (74/427). The leading poet of America, sixty years old, hysterical under the sun, fevered by the night chill; an unrepentant fascist, in a cage next to a rapist and a looter, guarded by US troops. He had with him a copy of the Confucian Odes; in the latrine he found a copy of *Palgrave's Golden Treasury*, the popular anthology of English verse; he had access to *Time* magazine. The poet – the fascist, treated like a common criminal, if not an animal – clinging to his aesthetic philosophy and a standard compendium of English verse.

The mid-century drama continues. Although perhaps no one else had been listening seriously to the broadcasts, the FBI had been paying some sort of attention. Their stenographers had transcribed them with contemptuous inaccuracies. Pound was shipped back to the USA and arraigned for treason. His defence was that he was mentally unfit to plead: the apology of insanity. In a none-too-scientific exchange of opinions, the plea was accepted.[64] Pound was committed to a hospital for the criminally insane, St Elizabeth's in Washington, DC, for the next fifteen years, until a committee of poets, led by Robert Frost and e. e. cummings, obtained his release. In the meantime, the Pisan Cantos and the Bollingen Prize – and the row, which fed the self-righteous philistinism of the American Left, the paranoia of the emergent McCarthyite Right, and the perplexity of the liberals. Finally, as Davie has suggested for us, the effective political castration of the poet.

These scenes strike me as important because there seems to be very little to be said in anyone's favour, from any point of view. Art, Politics, the Law and the State all acquitted themselves deplorably. We might choose to focus here on the poet – Shelley's 'unacknow-ledged legislator of the world' – in the service of fascism; or on that same poet treated little better than an animal by the conquering army; or on the 'unacknowledged legislator' on trial before federal philis-tines; on the poet disowning his political responsibility with a plea of insanity; or on the poet (the political prisoner? the criminal? the mentally ill?) incarcerated in a mental prison.

We have seen it all since then in various forms – and we have perhaps been clear on where we stand. But we have not, I think, seen it in such a concentrated, unrelenting and irredeemably disgraceful form. The Gulag Archipelago is easier on the conscience than the Pound fiasco, in the sense that there is no way to take sides in this confrontation between an arrogant philistine State and a (possibly deranged) fascist poet. To argue for or against Pound means aligning oneself with arguments equally demeaning both to poetry and to political commit-ment.

So can any good come of the situation? Can the Pisan Cantos be regarded as the only good thing to be thrown up by a confrontation of lasting damage to the dignity of both State and artist? One is not going to question their poetic achievement: they are arguably the most impressive section of *The Cantos*. But they really cannot be considered outside their context any more than, for example, *Paradise Lost* can be considered without reference to the English Revolution. Not only do they, as I have already suggested, demand this textually,[65] but their contribution is vital precisely because of the putting into question which they, in their context, represent: that in reading and admiring them, we have to be prepared to discuss the issues raised by the gruesome circumstances out of which they emerge, but which they can never leave behind them; a confrontation, in short, between poetry and politics in which it is impossible to take sides.

George Steiner has been insisting for many years on the question of how we can listen to Mozart or Beethoven – not to mention Wagner and Richard Strauss – after their music had entertained the death-camp commandants. Here I feel we have an even more acute problem, which (perhaps unlike Steiner's) is by no means rhetorical. The problem puts itself in a sequence of questions which might begin as follows: if we grant – for the sake of argument, if you like – that Pound is at least *one* of the major poets of the century (and one hopes to affirm that he is more than that), we have to ask, how could 'one of the major poets of the century' turn out to be a fascist?

That is perhaps a question for literary and political/cultural history. But it is a question which necessarily prompts another. For it is not an issue of 'mere' history, which we can distance from *our own* literary and political history. Charles Olson indicates the problem for the writer:

> What is called for is a consideration . . . of how such a man came to the position he reached when he allowed himself to become the voice of Fascism. . . . If he were not first rate, it would be of little interest, mere sociology. If it were Auden and not Yeats, it would be the same. If it were his imitators and not D. H. Lawrence, so. But these three men, and James Joyce, constitute the major forces in the generation out of which we who are young now come.[66]

As Olson thinks the question as writer, we must likewise think it in our capacity as readers. Thus a rather more personally disturbing question presses on us. If – again for the sake of argument – we agree that Pound writes 'good' poetry, we must ask *how is that we enjoy and value the poetry of a fascist?*

We can, and should, generalise this question: is it possible to say – as many critics do – that this is 'good' poetry but 'bad' politics? In other words, as we drive deeper, Pound's experience leads us to this distressing question, a question which we should consider in discussing the literary history of our century, *our* literary history; and a question given new relevance by the policies of states such as the Soviet Union and the self-righteous reaction in the West: *what is the relation between*

*our (presumably spontaneous) aesthetic values and our political criteria
– between Pleasure and Sense?*

This is a problem once faced by poets – such as in Ben Jonson's cry,
'Still may Reason war with Rime' ('A Fit of Rime against Rime', 1611)
– until it was apparently temporarily quietened by the vulgar reading of
Keats's Beauty–Truth couplet.[67] Resurrected by the phenomenon of
Pound – in the fascist radio station, the poem, the cage, the courtroom,
the mental institution and the seminar room – it is now a particularly
modern problem, and lies at the heart of any discussion of Pound's
work. The problem puts itself acutely precisely because Pound's
poetry is so powerful and so influential (on us), and because his politics
are so repugnant.

Whatever else Pound may stand for, I feel that he stands for
questions such as these. Clearly this book does not seek to answer
them; but they are questions that have to be put; for the ultimate
productivity of Pound's honest and calamitous attempt to conjugate
the aesthetic and the political is precisely the demand it makes on the
reader not to evade, but to take a position in relation to these
questions. It is in these terms that I wish to conclude the chapter with
some reflections on these questions at large before turning to Pound's
poetic theory and practice in more detail; to try to clarify what I
perceive as the extent of Pound's importance in this context.

IV

Plato of course had an answer to the problem, in which theorists have
often, in one way or another, taken refuge: poets, except for
ideologues, have no useful place in the Republic.

> . . . we must remain firm in our conviction that hymns to the gods
> and praises of famous men are the only poetry which ought to be
> admitted into a State. For if you go beyond this and allow the
> honeyed muse to enter, either in epic or lyric verse, not law and the
> reason of mankind, which by common consent have ever been
> deemed best, but pleasure and pain will be rulers in our State.
>
> (*Republic*, Book x)

In his famous refutation, *A Defence of Poetry* (1821), Shelley was
neither able nor willing to refute Plato's basic premise (any more than
Sir Philip Sidney had been in his *Apology for Poetry*, 1595): that

poetry is primarily a function of pleasure. His refutation, like Sidney's, is based on interventions in the relation between pleasure, reason and truth.

For Shelley, law and reason had degenerated into a mechanical tyranny – the discourse of money. 'A poem', on the other hand, 'is the very image of life expressed in its eternal truth.' Inasmuch as such 'eternal truths' enter into conflict with political 'truths', it follows that the latter are partial – contingent upon a degraded 'reason', not the philosophical reason of Plato's wise Republic. Shelley effectively discredits Plato's political reason – truth equation by positing pleasure as an aesthetic reason 'truer' than the 'law and reason of mankind' as manifested in political thought. In the end he is able to achieve a similar inversion to Sidney's: what is true in Plato is his 'poetry'.

Does this help, then, Plato versus Shelley: a utopianism of politics versus a utopianism of aesthetics? Assuming, as both are bound to do, that poetry operates in the field of pleasure, it either is or is not commensurate with truth. According to Plato, it is not; according to Shelley, it is commensurate not with the partial truths of degraded law and reason, but with deeper truths. In other words, poetry will always produce 'bad' politics: either because, in the Plato model, poetry is necessarily deficient in relation to truth; or because politics are. In the latter case – the commonly held position outside Gulag – poetry will in fact produce 'truer' truths than the 'lesser' truths of politics. Plato's objection to poets is turned into a liberal irony: poets *are* dangerous to the State, as he says, but only because the State is not ruled by truth.

This is the implicit burden of George Orwell's famous liberal argument in 'Politics and the English Language' (1946), in the sense that it rests on the notion that 'ugly and inaccurate' language[68] facilitates 'indefensible' and mendacious politics, remediable only by certain stylistic improvements. The distinction between truth and untruth is an effect of the aesthetics of language in a subversion of dominant ideologies: 'In our time it is broadly true that political writing is bad writing. Where it is not true, it will generally be found that the writer is some kind of rebel, expressing his private opinions and not a "party line".'[69]

The same year, Orwell addressed the issue, in a manner quite relevant to the Pound question, in its most general form, under the title 'Politics versus Literature'. He confronts his distate for Swift's politics, along with his pleasure in reading him. The question of reason is liberally enlarged by being displaced to a question of relative 'sanity'. Orwell concludes that, so long as the ideology remains this side of sanity, 'enjoyment can overwhelm disapproval, even though one clearly recognises that one is enjoying something inimical'.[70] Aesthetic quality speaks to an economy of pleasure more reliable in terms of truth than ideological content, capable even of giving the latter the lie.

Clearly, if we are to 'believe in' poetry, we must reject Plato's ostensible project. But, if we are to reject him, do we have to do so along lines, such as Shelley's or Orwell's, which in their different ways make poetry commensurate with a notion of truth that transcends the so-called 'partiality' of politics? And where does such a line lead us? In my experience, it leads us into the tradition of liberal academic aestheticians, whose tendency to assert the transcendent truth of poetry leads them commonly to accuse anyone who seeks to call poetry to political account of bringing extraneous and partial political dogma to bear on the irresistible spontaneous truth of aesthetic experience. Such a tactic is obviously often used in Pound criticism. We are invited to treat the poem 'neutrally', in the faith that, where the ideas are 'ugly', the writing will betray itself; or we are invited to 'edit out' the aberrant political pieces, and recuperate the lyricism; or to distinguish between the pure contingency of the politics and the eternal aesthetic value of the verse. We are asked to 'save the text' by being true to the poetry whilst keeping the politics as 'another question', to be dealt with (or not) in a suitable place: the field of ideology.[71]

This position of the transcendent reliability of aesthetic values is very seductive, and quite dangerous. Generally speaking, it rests on the effective subordination of politics to art. When applied positively, it threatens to lead towards the principle which Walter Benjamin, in 'The Work of Art in an Age of Mechanical Reproduction', identified as determinate of fascist ideology: the subordination and construction of politics in terms of aesthetic criteria.[72] But, as Benjamin argues, the politics are not 'another question'. Indeed, where he analyses fascism in terms of an aestheticisation of political criteria, he proposes for us an alternative project: the politicisation of art. This is a (highly problematic) path which we might feel we require for our own general political and aesthetic reasons; it is however also necessary if one is to respond productively to Pound's own politicisation of poetry and to try to answer the particular questions he raises.

But how are we to conceive a 'politicisation of art'? How to do justice to the elements which give us pleasure? Subordinating art to politics is clearly no better than subordinating politics to art: it would return us to Plato's position, the assumption of a repressive proscription of the imagination. We cannot view the imagination and its pleasures as some sort of original sin or deviation from reason to be policed by the State.

I am being somewhat crude in my disposition of the alternatives as I see them, drawing the limiting implications of our positions in an attempt to clarify what is a basic but none the less sensitive point. With, on the one hand, the official postures of the Western liberal establishment (most of all its media) and, on the other, those of the Soviet regime, we are caught between a Scylla and a Charybdis of political aesthetics. Either we privilege politics, and take Plato's (or Stalin's) position; or we privilege art, joining a path that at best expels politics from poetry, and at worst too easily leads to the quasi-fascist ideology of hedonistic aestheticism. It appears to be a question, at this level, of a mutually exclusive aesthetic or political totalitarianism, founded in aesthetic or political utopianism. But Pound may provoke in us the desire still to pursue a politicisation of art that does justice to both politics and art.

Navigating in these dangerous waters requires a course plotted from both political and aesthetic co-ordinates. The first would benefit from developments in Marxism and feminist theory in the recuperation of psychoanalytic thought, enabling us to hold fast to Benjamin's project whilst adducing to it a perception of Plato's error: 'politics' is in no way exclusive of pleasure; 'law and reason' can no longer be constructed in an opposition to 'pleasure and pain' (the latter understood, in this context, in a more than utilitarian sense).

A second perspective is opened by a remark from Geoffrey Hartman: 'to attack art in the name of art is one thing; to attack it in the name of religion, social policy, or science, quite another'.[73] Let us suspend for the moment the meaning of 'art in the name of art'. We are at least bound to agree with the latter part of his statement. But we should note that Hartman here has not mentioned 'politics'. In this way he offers a useful – if apparently contingent – way out of the closures of the Shelley–Plato and Pound–FBI debates: those are quarrels between art and 'social policy'. If we find this distinction between 'politics' and 'policy' acceptable, we can at least say that aesthetic pleasure is not to be excluded from politics, but rather embraced by it, without being forced to assert the transcendence of that pleasure over politics. If we are to relate politics and art, we should then do so in such terms that pleasure is present as a *positivity*, while politics is not reducible to policy. The alternatives remain the shipwrecks of aesthetic or political dogmatism.

In a sense, however, this argument so far only de-defines 'politics': it does not yet redefine it for a 'politicisation'; nor does it explain Hartman's phrase 'art in the name of art', which, of itself, threatens to drag us back to the most aestheticist of positions. I would argue that we can best define both these terms – and avoid a collapse back into aestheticism – by coupling Hartman's phrase with Benjamin's: to make a critique of 'art in the name of art' consonant with a 'politicisation of art'. In this way art may be kept within a political field which takes due account of pleasure. Such a position would, I argue, be consistent with a Marxist critique of art which is not – *pace* its liberal opponents and Stalinist proponents – a repressive, proscriptive dogmatism; in these terms, the politicisation of art would not be a reduction, but a dialectical expansion of *both* terms.

Whereas in 'Politics versus Literature' (1946) Orwell saw a polarisation of the issue, the Catholic artist David Jones in his essay 'Art and Democracy', written the following year, saw things differently. He chose a pair of texts which he found inseparable: 'All men are created equal' and 'Manners maketh men.' He wrote of the first text:

> The well-known affirmation of the first clause of the Unanimous Declaration in Congress may not seem so 'self-evident' to us as it was to the fifty-six signatories in 1776, but there is at any rate one sense (without necessarily denying others) in which it is, if not 'self-evident', at all events 'true': all men are created equal in the sense that they are all creative beasts, whatever else they may or may not be.[74]

Whilst Jones would never have used such an expression as 'politicisation of art', this is none the less a political affirmation which comes 'in the name of art': 'all men are creative beasts' is an affirmation of the *democracy of art*.

A similar position, without the eventual implication of a religious base, is recognisable in Marcel Duchamp:

> But I shy away from the word 'creation'. In the ordinary, social meaning of the word – well, it's very nice, but, fundamentally, I don't believe in the creative function of the artist. He's a man like any other. It's his job to do certain things, but the businessman does certain things also, you understand? On the other hand, the word 'art' interests me very much. If it comes from Sanskrit, as I've heard, it signifies 'making'. Now everyone makes something, and those

who make things on canvas, with a frame, they're called artists. Formerly, they were called craftsmen, a term I prefer. We're all craftsmen, in civilian or military or artistic life.[75]

'Creation' is a function of 'making', with the professional artist merely a social category of maker under a division of labour which fetishises certain makings over others within a mystification of creation.

Despite his deeply religious framework, Jones redefines 'art' in a similar way when he quotes Joyce to the effect that 'Practical life or "art" . . . comprehends all our activities from boatbuilding to poetry.'[76] When Jones says that all men are 'creative beasts', he means that we are all *makers of signs*; and that this making of signs, this 'showing-forth' of self, constitutes our 'practical life' and our 'art'.

I would therefore venture, as a first postulate for a politicisation of art, that it has to base itself in a democratisation of art. A second postulate follows: for this to happen, our conception of what *constitutes* 'art' needs to expand towards a democratic horizon.

In order to understand this and to elaborate the model further, we need to integrate Jones's second text: 'Manners maketh men.' 'Manners' functions here in both its meanings: social relations or behaviour, and style or technique. If we think of the making of signs in terms of its manifestation as language, we can see how the ambiguity of 'manners' might operate: language is the vehicle of social relations, and these relations are manifested in the plurality of discourses ('manners') which make up language as a whole – tongues, dialects, codes, idioms, styles, idiolects. Our manner of speaking bespeaks our social relations.[77]

Jones's focus on sign-making has a religious intention: to relate this 'making' to his notion of 'sacrament', as part of a major affirmation of his Catholicism. But we need not be restricted to a theological reading of his argument: for Jones, the 'making' is a question of 'trying to make a shape out of the very things of which one is oneself made'[78] – in *his* case, his Catholicism. It is hence justifiable and most useful to secularise the theory. If this is legitimate, we can find in Jones a model in which manners make men, who in turn are makers (of what makes them). This is productively (if inelegantly) paraphrasable as 'social signification makes signifiers'.

Here then we have a dialectic in which the political and the aesthetic are mutually defining, like the interrelations of the orders of the Symbolic and the Imaginary. 'Politics' might then be seen as the *social relations of significant production* between 'artists'/producers/citizens.

Thus, far from poets' being a special class excluded from the State, democratic politics would be founded on a democracy of 'poets', understood as makers.

In thinking in this way, however, we must beware of reapproaching a fascistic model, in which 'politics' become subservient to aesthetic criteria.[79] What safeguards this model from such a collapse is crucially that such aesthetic criteria, far from being divorced from the social realities of production, would in fact be based in those realities, with corresponding consequences for notions of aesthetic value. In other words, there is no question of a hierarchy of 'great' poets, but rather a democratic definition of the poet himself and of the criteria of his evaluation. The social relations of politics pertain between people making signs; there is an aesthetic as much as a political difference from fascism.

This expanded sense of 'poets' or 'artists' within a politicisation/democratisation of art implies that our present aesthetic criteria – founded in their learnt notions of excellence and the privileged performance and personality of the artist – are not democratic. The criteria which we use to adjudge Pound as 'good' or 'great' are criteria that would reject the model we have extrapolated from Jones, which, holding that all men are variously creative, is not theoretically primarily concerned with a hierarchical conception of aesthetic or spiritual value.

Is this merely to state the obvious? I trust, not entirely; for myself, at any rate, I find the notion that my aesthetic criteria are undemocratic rather expensive and painful. But, if it is true, it raises a question mark over the defensive notion that their authenticity is guaranteed by the fact that they are spontaneous (in the personal sense) or objective (in the professional sense). They certainly feel spontaneous, and the critic endeavours to articulate them objectively. So, if we feel that they are spontaneous and potentially objective, does that mean that, in terms of aesthetic pleasure, we are 'spontaneously' or 'objectively' undemocratic? And, if we see such reactions not as spontaneous, but as determined, where does that leave us, with these none the less undeniable feelings of irresistible pleasure?

Perhaps we can say this much: that, inasmuch as we have an implicitly or explicitly hierarchical conception of art, we do not have a democratic model. This truism becomes problematic when, on the other hand, we (presumably) claim to have a democratic conception of politics. It is thus no wonder that the dilemma 'good poetry, bad politics' occurs. Its acuteness is precisely this: that, bringing us to the recognition that our aesthetic pleasure (spontaneous or determined) is not democratic, it forces us to ask, how truly democratic are our political values?

We can defend our political conceptions as democratic because political theory is seen as related to reason, law and practice – an enterprise essentially capable of justification or persuasion by reason. Aesthetic value, on the other hand, in being a function of pleasure, presents considerably more difficulties in the exercise of a comparable rationality. We defend ourselves against this contradiction by maintaining the discontinuity between the two realms of art and politics, raising either one or the other to the ultimate consequences of truth. But, without a critique of the politics of our pleasure, there is no genuine rationality in our general political position: we tend to find ourselves 'caught' in the contradictions of, for example, 'enjoying' the poetry of a 'fascist'. Thus either we can continue agonising over the contradictions generated by our incipiently undemocratic aesthetic values, or we can seek to theorise and transform them by undertaking the painful task of analysing pleasure.

And this is finally what Pound is most of all good for. Since his poetry is so pleasing, it offers us an opportunity for a critique of poetic pleasure at both an advanced and a representative level. For, from a historical point of view, as I have suggested, Pound can be seen as representative of the 'best' poetry and the 'worst' politics of our age. Such a collision seems to promise a useful point of insertion. A critique of pleasure of this sort has nothing to do with standards of taste (nor has it much to do with the new connoisseurship of popularism; indeed the critique of pleasure in 'high art' is only part of a project which is fulfilled by a critique of mass and popular culture). Within this model, rather than a playground of taste, 'art' is to be seen as the means of significant production, whilst 'politics' may thence be seen as the social relations of significant production.

An aesthetic critique – a political economy of pleasure – is related to an analysis of the means of significant production as in Stephen Heath's notion of 'specific signifying practices', or Pierre Macherey's 'means of production of literary effects' – or Pound's notion of technique. As such it expands towards the adjunct disciplines of linguistics, psychoanalysis, education and economics. In the present case, by analysing Pound's means of production of literary effects, we can do justice to the pleasure we can at the same time confess, whilst establishing grounds for its critique. In this way we can offer a critique of 'art in the name of art' which is a political analysis: an analysis of the politics of our literary pleasure.

In this there is no question of taking sides with Pound, with the US Government, with Pound's defenders or detractors; nor is an attack on any of these implied. Since the analysis proposes itself as an analysis of our pleasure, it is, if anything, an 'attack' on ourselves – on our fiction of spontaneous literary pleasure, our seduction by aesthetics, the contradictions of our aesthetic and political stances, and, finally, our determination by our literary history.

The phenomenon of Pound establishes a radical antithesis between terms from politics and those from art, which must be responded to by a radical synthesis of art and politics. Pound's calamity is the mature and courageous working-out of a concealed contradiction between art and politics at a particular moment in history, symptomatically expressed in the problem of the poet's productive place in modern society – a problem hardly resolved in our day. The radical nature of that contradiction has been subdued once more by a liberal reading of Pound's fate that would separate poetry and politics, the poet and the man, and, whilst preserving the autonomous authenticity of aesthetic response, render the poet as politician impotent. What it might provoke is rather another sort of conjuncture of the aesthetic and the political: a democratisation of art; what might in other terms be called 'cultural revolution'.

Such a revolution is clearly utopian without material trans-formations; but, within the limited scope we have as readers, critics, writers and teachers, we might contribute towards it by beginning with ourselves, in a critique of the politics of our literary pleasure. It is such a project which supplies the orientation of the partial study of Pound undertaken here, which seeks the political calamity precisely in the means of production of what is recognised as aesthetic achievement.

2 How to Write Well and Influence People: Pound and Imagisme

In discussing the discontinuity between our aesthetic and our political criteria, and how Pound takes us to a critical point in that disjuncture, I centred my comments somewhat polemically on the notion of aesthetic hierarchy. An important foundation of any such hierarchical conception of aesthetics is the assumption of what is necessary to 'good writing'.

We tend to assume, with little examination, a model of a reader and a cause-and-effect relation between certain techniques and their consequences for that reader. This is expressed at its most extreme in the notion of 'organic form': that there is a necessary and authentic form which is generated naturally from what is to be expressed, and hence productive of the desired effect. Orwell is not so extreme, but his criticism of excessive abstraction, decayed metaphors, pretentious jargon and long-windedness no doubt strike an approving note in the modern reader. It is curious how the six 'rules' he offers in 'Politics and the English Language' remind us of many strictures offered in Pound's critical writings, and how acceptable they both seem to us as requirements for 'good writing'. For, to a large extent, we too share their assumptions. We like our essays to be simple, clearly expressed, lucid and sequential; we believe it better to use short words than to employ polysyllabic verbalisations; we detest jargon where it is encountered in an on-going situation; we disapprove, if I may put it like this, of circumlocutions, digressions, non-sequiturs – and Latin-isms. All this points to a basic *normativism* of writing. It is such a normativism which enables us to conceive of 'composition classes' to teach scientists, lawyers and businessmen how to express themselves 'like a human being' (a similar attitude can even find its way into 'creative writing' courses).

We have in short a notion of 'good writing' which is beyond ideology, partiality or power, in terms of an autonomous literary model or model of communication, which plays a major role in traditional education.[1] This notion has much to do with our undemo-cratic criteria – seen more clearly in the social relations of significant production ('politics'): for example, in the correction of dialect in the schoolroom and in the structure and practice of teaching English as a foreign language. The critique of pleasure might then try to insert itself here, in the cause-and-effect relations of literary technique. Naturally, this is not an immediate recipe for political analysis; at this stage one seeks merely, in a limited way, to *historicise* the question of the modernist criteria of 'good writing' which we have inherited and assimilated to the extent that we effectively take them for granted, and to analyse their means of significant production.

As we have already seen, Pound confronts the decay of English poetry at the turn of the century in terms of 'bad writing': the way to regain an audience is to write poetry 'as well as prose'; 'technique', 'perfect control', 'good writing' are the requirements for claiming the attention of the reader. In his articles and letters from 1911 to 1913, we see Pound working out criteria under which poetry could once more be turned into 'good writing'. These considerations move towards Pound's first major and enormously influential contribution to mod-ernist poetics: the movement known as Imagisme.

Not only is Imagisme rightly regarded as the first major step towards poetic modernism in English, but the values it bears also inform our more general assumptions about good writing: economy, precision, concision, flexibility, concrete imagery; absence of pretension, ab-straction and didacticism; 'the right word in the right place' and a minimum of 'rhetoric'. If, then, our criteria of good writing have been influenced by the criteria expressed in Imagisme, it would be important to clarify exactly how these values appear in that movement.

Whilst critics and poets alike tend to agree that Imagism(e) represents a founding moment in the history of modernism, there is much disagreement over what it actually was. The debate over its history, constitution and spelling (with, or without, the 'e') can be seen as varying according to ideologies of modernism, in which there are basically two issues or confusions.

The first concerns the relation of Imagisme's general strictures on poetics to its theory of the Image; the second relates to the history of the movement and Pound's role within it – and hence to what extent the poetics of Imagisme (either at the level of general poetics, or as a theory of metaphor) can be identified with Pound. In this chapter I intend to deal with both issues – first with the relation of a general poetics to the Image, and subsequently with the history of the movement.

Hugh Kenner has helped us considerably with the first issue by showing that 'All the confusion about Imagisme stems from the fact that its specifications for technical hygiene are one thing, and Pound's Doctrine of the Image is another.'[2] Pound himself instigates the distinction, dividing the Imagisme of the Image from Imagisme 'As a "critical" movement', which, from '1912 to '14 set out "to bring poetry up to the level of prose" '.[3] But it is still necessary to specify the relation between the 'technical hygiene' and the 'Image'. I shall not concern myself here with the 'Doctrine' as literary theory, but will argue that the *practice* of the Image effectively emerges from the 'specifications for technical hygiene' as follows: the critical criteria – a crystallisation of the first, founding moment of Pound's poetics – outline a problematic to which the technique of the Image is a response.

The term 'Imagisme' has, as we shall see below, given rise to considerable confusion because of the debt apparently expressed to Pound's colleague the Bergsonian T. E. Hulme. What is the signifi-cance of Pound's references to Hulme? Is it, as the contemporary F. S. Flint, and the critics Samuel Hynes, Alun Jones and Peter Jones argue, that Imagisme was basically Hulme's philosophical principles put into practice? Straightforward literary rejections of this idea are plentiful.[4] Yet the references remain and can only, I think, be understood in terms of the literary politics of the 'movement', which are dealt with in the second part of this chapter. But out of the discussions of Hulme's place emerges an issue which is significant to the question now under consideration.

One alternative in solving the riddle of what I shall demonstrate to be Pound's calculated misrecognition of Hulme is Alun Jones's psychological sophism: 'It is a curious fact, attributable no doubt to some incident in his personal life rather than in his poetic career, that the militancy with which [Pound] institutionalised and publicised his views is offset by his reluctance to acknowledge their source.'[5] The speculation is actually ironic since, inasmuch as Pound had a 'source', he did acknowledge it repeatedly – although never directly in relation to the movement. Christophe de Nagy, for example, argues against the influence of Hulme on two counts. Flint claimed that Pound 'took' the Image from Hulme's 'table talk'.[6] De Nagy first observes that 'table talk in a restaurant, where many topics are discussed besides the image, would only appear to represent compelling evidence of a critical influence, if it were recognised by the presumed recipient'.[7] Pound, however, remembered Hulme's conversation as dealing in 'crap like Bergson'.[8] De Nagy's second point is more telling. He asks, if Pound's theories were formed in the conversations within Hulme's group in 1909 – as Flint *et al.* maintain – why did he wait until 1912–13 to articulate them? Furthermore, how did he come to publish his most archaic book, *Canzoni*, in the meantime? Whilst these are compelling arguments against Hulme, they are equally forceful arguments in favour of Ford Madox Ford.

There is no shortage of acknowledgements.[9] One can only intelligently employ the term 'influence' in this context in referring to the sort of demonstrably useful criticism proffered in the summer of 1911:

> [Ford] felt the errors of contemporary style to the point of rolling . . . on the floor of his temporary quarters in Giessen when my third volume displayed me trapped . . . in a jejeune provincial effort to learn, *mehercule*, the stilted language which then passed for 'good English' in the arthritic milieu that held control of the respected critical circles. . . . And that roll saved me at least two years, perhaps more.[10]

Given what we have said about the question of language and good writing, and of the advance represented by Imagisme, this moment is clearly of major significance. 'So it comes about,' as Pound wrote in 'The Prose Tradition in Verse' (1914), 'that Mr Hueffer [Ford] is the best critic in England, one might say the only critic of any importance.'[11] Hence, in short, one must go beyond Stanley Coffman when he says that 'Every one of the points made in paralleling Pound's Imagism with Hulme's might be made with equal validity in a comparison with Hueffer's theory'[12] and assert that Pound has a direct debt to Ford which far outweighs any long-term speculative debt to Hulme. Ford made a major difference between 1911 and 1912, and his values of 'the prose tradition' – as I have already suggested – lie behind much of Pound's critical modernist 'hygiene'.

Pound saw Ford as pre-eminently 'modern'. He called his poem 'On Heaven', for example, 'the best poem yet written in the "twentieth century fashion" '.[13] Ford's critical writings bear out this 'modernist' effort. He postulated as his audience the modern democratic reader, the man of the age; and Pound praised him for finding rhythms and a diction responsive to 'the actual talk of the people'.[14] In sum, Pound wrote, 'I find him significant and revolutionary because of his insistence upon clarity and precision, upon the prose tradition; in brief, upon efficient writing – even in verse.'[15] Ford's example was then very useful in terms of the problematic outlined in Chapter 1; for this reason, the values of the 'prose tradition' are all forcefully present in the values of the technical hygiene of Imagisme as a poetic designed to offer a 'language' which would reach a 'modern' audience.

Given all this, one is inclined to ask why Imagisme did not refer to Ford instead of Hulme. There appear to be two reasons. The first is again to do with literary politics: the fact that, by 1912, Ford had lost his entrepreneurial power and was the object of public scandal. But there is also a clear literary reason. Seeing the close similarity between the Imagiste hygiene and Ford's poetics, the literary reason why that similarity was not acknowledged in the movement's title, for example,[16] must have considerable significance for the location of Imagisme.

Ford's literary attitudes were collected under the title of 'Impressionism', and 'Imagisme is not Impressionism, though one borrows, or could borrow much from the impressionist method of presentation.'[17] This distinction provides an important reference point for Pound's poetics; the reason why Imagisme is not Impressionism is fundamental to Pound's theory as a whole.

The distinction between the two is based on

> two opposed ways of thinking of a man: firstly you may think of him as that toward which perception moves, as the toy of circumstance, as the plastic substance *receiving* impressions; secondly, you may think of him as directing a certain fluid force against circumstance, as *conceiving* instead of merely reflecting and observing.[18]

By the time of writing (1914), this crucial distinction had become the basis for Vorticism; later it was to develop into Pound's emphasis on voluntarist values, as expressed in the heroic qualities of a Malatesta, or a Mussolini. But the value was similarly operative at the beginning of Imagisme, as witness Pound's review of Ford's poems *High Germany* in March 1912:

> The *conception* of poetry is a process more intense than the *reception*

of an impression. Poetry is in some odd way concerned with the specific gravity of things, with their nature . . . and no impression . . . can, recorded, convey that feeling of sudden light which works of art can and must convey.[19]

The distinction here offered in fact engages many of the specifics of Pound's Imagiste and Vorticist poetics. It indicates once more the importance of the poet's having a *productive* place in society. 'Reception' cannot embrace his positive contribution as 'scientist' of 'immaterial man', for it condemns the poet to competition with more adequate, purely descriptive discourses (as Pound notices in 'Vorticism', the painter cannot compete with the camera as a register of mere data).[20] The poet's productivity still lies with his privileged subjectivity, which has to find a language for the modern world.

The basic opposition of receptor and conceiver is thus reflected also at the technical level. Pound's critique of Ford bears directly on this:

> Mr Hueffer (Ford) believes in the exact rendering of things. He would strip words of all 'association' for the sake of getting a precise meaning. He professes to prefer prose to verse. You would find his origins in Gautier or in Flaubert. He is objective. . . . This school tends to lapse into description. . . .[21]

'Association' is a technique for extending the 'precise' or 'objective' beyond the merely 'descriptive' – using 'exact . . . things' to generate subjective meanings through those areas of signification (connotation, suggestion, evocation, figuration) in which the term acts beyond its literal reference, but which blur, as it were, the concrete presence of the object. The lapse, the locus of the receptive attitude of the Impressionist, according to Pound, is a direct consequence of his technique of stripping words of 'association'. By barring the source of extension, 'interpretation' and 'conception' are lost; the objective is reduced to the level of description.

In seeking a language for a modern audience, Pound needs the sort of technical values represented by Ford, and these form the base of Imagisme's hygiene as the positive stylistic possibilities of Ford's Impressionism. But Impressionism does not sustain the active subjective values which Pound refuses to sacrifice to a modern language. He therefore dissociates the movement from Impressionism inasmuch as the latter tends to lapse into description as a function of its receptive attitude and its technique.

The full notion of Imagisme, while drawing strength from Ford's Impressionism, has to go beyond this, and safeguard the subjective realism dislocated in the nineteenth century and threatened here with its reduction to a modest empiricism. This subjective component is seen in terms of an active interpretation, an imaginative productivity of the artist, which Pound refers to as 'conception'. Whilst seeking the strengths of precision and objectivity, the poet must avoid their reduction; for this 'association', *or a substitute for it*, has to be retained.

In dissociating Imagisme from Impressionism, Pound was careful to establish a second reference point, counterbalancing his relation with Ford by supplying the second term of the actual dialectic of his day in London: Ford in the morning, Yeats in the evening. Pound put the two together in 1913: 'I find Mr Yeats the only poet worthy of serious study',[22] however, 'I would rather talk about poetry with Ford Madox Hueffer than with any man in London. Mr Hueffer's beliefs about art . . . are in diametric opposition to those of Mr Yeats.' Specifically, 'Mr Yeats has been subjective; believes in the glamour and associations which hang near the words. . . . He has much in common with the French Symbolists. . . . [he] tends to lapse into sentiment'.[23] Yeats is not, then, an alternative to Ford's tendency to description. One does not avoid the descriptive tendency of Impressionism by maintaining 'association', since this technique leads to an imbalance of the subjective: 'sentiment'. 'Conception' must come from some other technique. Yeats and Symbolism thus form a limit to Imagisme's literary field at the opposite pole of subjectivity – objectivity to Ford and Impressionism.

The topography is confirmed in the 1914 article 'Vorticism'. Pound again balances his dissociation from Ford with a symmetrical reference to the Symbolists: 'Imagisme is not symbolism. The symbolists dealt in "association", that is in a sort of allusion, almost of allegory. They degraded the symbol to the status of a word.'[24] This misunderstanding of Symbolism is testimony to the fact that Pound is not so much discussing the historical literary movement as producing a category of recent 'subjective' verse in order to situate Imagisme in relation to subjectivity and his sense of the symbolist inheritance. At the opposite extreme to Ford's Impressionism, this is a poetic in which the word loses its objective reference ('a hawk is a hawk') in favour of its figurative or abstract extension ('allusion'/'allegory').

In producing these poles, acknowledging their contributions, and defining Imagisme against both of them, Pound outlines the problematic of his theory: *the reconciliation of a desire for objectivity with a desire for conception.*

We have already sought to historicise this inherited disjuncture in terms of the tendencies of Symbolism and Naturalism, and I have sought to underline the importance of Pound's attempts to resynthesise subjective and objective realism. The importance of Imagisme, in this sense, resides in its attempt to place itself directly in the position of synthesis, articulating, in 1912–14, a dialectic which determines the main lines of Pound's poetics and practice throughout his career: a language of objects conveying the truth of conception.

The dialectic may be schematised as follows:

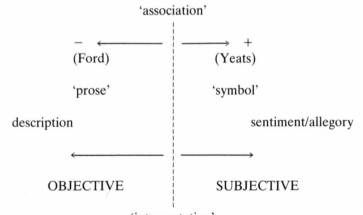

In its intended synthesis of objectivity and conception, Imagisme seeks the strengths of both the objective and the subjective, whilst avoiding their weaknesses. The stylistic techniques of Impressionism are a corrective to, but not a substitute for, the excessive, mystified and imprecise subjectivity inherited from the Symbolists; they hence form the basis of the hygienic function of a 'critical movement'. But a productive subjectivity has to be retained.

The poet's productivity cannot rely on a simple registration of phenomena, but is linked to an 'interpretative function' which had become unproductive by turning its back on audience and becoming sentimental. It is this recognition – the incorporation of 'prose' techniques into a poetics of 'conception' – which leads Imagisme as a technical hygiene into the need for a further component. The common denominator of the two poles is the question of 'association'; in this way, the problem of Imagisme is focused on a question of metaphor. It is thus, I would argue, that the second element, the 'Doctrine of the Image', arises to resolve the desired synthesis between objectivity and subjectivity in terms of a theory and practice of metaphor.[25]

A set of oppositions is engaged which may appear in terms of, for example, the literal and the figurative, the concrete and the abstract, or the denotative and the connotative. They pose the question to which, I argue, the Image seeks to present itself as an answer. A formulaic synthesis is presented in the article 'A Few Don'ts by an Imagiste' (1913), which echoes Pound's 'Credo' on symbols. Pound instructs the poet not to use such weak combinations as 'dim lands of peace' (concrete/abstract), since it 'dulls the image'; but a similar extension of the concrete is, he implies, none the less possible, so long as one realises that 'the natural object is always the *adequate* symbol'.[26] In terms of the discourse of poetics, as distinct from the practice of poetry, this formula represents Imagisme's answer to the problematic in which it is situated. It is to its practice that we now turn.

II

Inasmuch as the critical hygiene had involved metaphor, it had been concerned with its quality. Pound had called for a metaphorical language which was 'harder and saner . . . "nearer the bone" '.[27] Hence the synthetic formula of the 'natural object' as 'adequate symbol'. But, critically useful as this dictum is, it fails by itself to resolve the opposition of which it is born. In short, were the 'natural object' always the 'adequate symbol', the 'diametric opposition' between the schools of objectivity and subjectivity would not arise. The synthesis of the poles cannot simply *be* achieved at the level of qualitative (paradigmatic) *selection*, as the hygienic project may suggest. The Image, at least as a practice, involves the recognition that the 'object' can only be *made into* the 'adequate symbol' at the level of *combination*.

It has to do with the copula: 'the natural object *is* the adequate symbol'. As Wallace Stevens tells us, 'Things as they are / Are changed upon the blue guitar' ('The Man on the Blue Guitar'). How can an objective reality *be* at the same time a subjective symbol, something else? Yeats might write, 'I declare this tower is my symbol'

('Blood and the Moon'), making the symbolic 'being' of the object dependent on his subjective assertion. But then Ernest Fenollosa, endorsed by Pound, argues, 'There is in reality no such verb as a pure copula.'[28] Furthermore, 'The moment we use the copula, the moment we express subjective inclusions, poetry evaporates.'[29] The Image seeks to resolve this problem, and does so by rejecting the subjective weakness of 'being' ('is') in favour of an *enactment*: the vitalisation of the subject–object relation (the act of transformation of 'things as they are') in metaphor in terms of combination.

The first line in *Personae*, from 'The Tree', precipitates, as we have seen, the action: 'I stood still and was a tree amid the wood'. The metamorphosis, the most radical transformation of natural objects 'as they are', is accomplished by the mere assertive use of the copula. As such this is, in Pound's terms, provokingly inadequate; and it is this which characterises the tone of the poem, as a sort of challenge to the reader. The closing statement of this short poem underlines the challenge by repeating the assertion and adding the word 'Natheless' defiantly addressed to our incredulity. The poem, then, provokes a question about the copula which, at this stage (1908), can merely establish a problematic.

When we turn to the Imagiste years, we see a very similar theme treated in a quite different manner in the poem 'A Girl' (1912):

> The tree has entered my hands,
> The sap has ascended my arms,
> The tree has grown in my breast –
> Downward,
> The branches grow out of me, like arms.
>
> Tree you are,
> Moss you are,
> You are violets with wind above them.
> A child – *so* high – you are,
> And all this is folly to the world.[30]

The marvel of the first five lines is experienced in the effort of the mind – which always just fails – to grasp the movement of the syntax. In a sense, it is straightforward. The subject is always the tree and its metonymic portions ('tree', 'sap', 'tree', 'branches'); the verbs describe a progressive process ('has entered', 'has ascended', 'has grown', 'grow'); and the main predicate is also regularly a metonymic object ('hands', 'arms', 'breasts', 'me'). In this sense there is a metaphorical progression of identity between the tree and the girl via the verbs. But the movement is entirely *up*ward and *in*ward. Yet the last two lines of the first stanza direct us, as clearly as possible, *down*ward and *out*ward. This reversal of direction in the verb sets up a reversal of subject and object terms in the metaphor: 'The branches grow out of me, like arms.'

The arms that were (like) branches have become branches that are like arms. In other words, a metonymic portion of the subject 'girl' becomes a metaphoric term for a portion of the related totality 'tree'. Conversely, 'branches', a metaphorical term for the subject 'girl', becomes a metonym for a new subject. The appearance of the last simile is a magical coup which actualises the metamorphosis in the reader's mind as he becomes aware of the switch of subject and predicate.

This leads us into the second stanza, which begins with a summary response to what has just happened, addressed to the girl/tree: 'Tree you are'. Here both terms govern the copula equally (reversibility not being a common characteristic of the verb 'to be'). The acceptability of this line is testimony to the achievement of the previous stanza and contrasts readily with the deliberately inadequate use of the copula in 'The Tree'. Following the response of a more or less sympathetic observer, we begin a journey down and out of the tree, and down and out of the metamorphosis, via a sequence of metaphorical levels.

The eye is directed down the tree to the moss on its bark or base, and out from there to the violets in the field in which we presume the tree/girl to stand. At the same time, we move first from full metamorphosis to a subversion in 'Moss you are', with its possibly indulgent, deliberately figurative tone. Then comes the suggestive or evocative metaphor of impression: 'You are violets with wind above them.' We follow the movement until we come to the girl herself: 'A child – *so* high – you are', in which the reference is so literal, so actual, that we stretch out our hand to measure her height.

We should note then that the poem's dynamic is built from a *hierarchy of metaphors*, ranked in a process of construction and deconstruction. The totality 'Tree you are' is constructed from the double metonymic sets (hands, arms, etc.; tree, sap, etc.). This is then deconstructed through lyric figuration, evocation and finally literal reference. Within this hierarchy, it is clear that the 'metamorphic metaphor' ('Tree you are') is set at the opposite pole to the 'descriptive' ('a child . . . you are'). We can then establish a sequence of 'powers' of metaphor: reference, figuration, comparison and transformation. The latter is, I would argue, what Pound called a 'language beyond metaphor', the language of the Image at its strongest.[31]

The transformative technique need not, however, be limited to a metamorphic content. For example, in the poem 'Doria' (the first of Pound's contributions to the anthology *Des Imagistes*, 1914) we find a shift from orthodox comparison ('Be in me as the eternal moods / of the bleak winds') to a more radical form of metaphor in which the 'natural world', which begins as a metaphorical distance, becomes the actual scene of the poem:

> Have me in the strong loneliness
> of sunless cliffs
> And of grey waters.[32]

The subjects of the poem are injected into a world hitherto signified as metaphorical. 'Be in me as' is a metaphorical injunction; 'Have me in' is a metonymic injunction – yet the scene remains the same.

Another poem from the anthology, 'Liu Ch'e', exemplifies another aspect of the technique: instead of 'literalising' a metaphor, a metonymic detail is transformed, as in 'A Girl', into a metaphor.

> The rustling of the silk is discontinued,
> Dust drifts over the court-yard,
> There is no sound of foot-fall, and the leaves
> Scurry into heaps and lie still,
> And she the rejoicer of the heart is beneath them:
>
> A wet leaf that clings to the threshold.[33]

The first five lines present a scene both actual and emotional, according to the Imagiste hygiene, with the controlled presence of metonymic signifiers of 'natural objects' and sensual impressions, in their presence and absence, invoking a concrete scene of the courtyard and its drama. Then comes a gap and a last line. We are confronted with a syntactical discontinuity which is overridden (if the poem works for the reader) by an emotional coherence.

The discontinuity is worth considering. The dominant effect of the first stanza is dryness ('Scurry'), a lack of energy ('drifts') and absence. The signified of the last line is, on the contrary, a notion of presence, wetness and energy ('clings'). The point is that these contrasting 'tones' are both signified by the same 'object'. Every*thing* in the last line belongs metonymically in the scene as presented in the first stanza; yet its state and function have been changed. We can view the poem as a whole as a metaphor: a first term (the metonymically signified of dry leaves, and so on), a second, metaphorical term (the wet leaf, and so on), and a problematically silent relation between them. The relation cannot be strictly (literally) metonymically continuous (unless we invent an intervening story), because of the change of state; but, inasmuch as it is the same scene transformed, there is a more radical metonymic continuity.

The point can be illustrated by comparing William Carlos Williams's poem 'The Young Housewife'. She

> stands
> shy, uncorseted, tucking in
> stray ends of hair, and I compare her
> to a fallen leaf.
>
> The noiseless wheels of my car
> rush with a crackling sound over
> dried leaves as I bow and pass smiling.[34]

The leaf which appears first as an explicit metaphor is subsequently demystified when it reappears metonymically. The effect is disjunctive: an assertion of objective realities and differences over subjective relations. In 'Liu Ch'e', on the other hand, the leaf is first introduced as a metonymy, and then transformed into a metaphor – which continues, in a sense, as a metonymy.

The energy of Pound's poem is released in our participation in relating the shift at the level of emotional connotation. The effect is an elegiac resolution of discontinuity, the dominance of subjective transformations over the denotations of the actual, but which uses the material of the actual. This is thus achieved (and one might remark that in this case the achievement may not be as interesting qualitatively as it is technically) without recourse to didacticism, mysticism, allegory or abstract comment – without conspicuous subjectivism and without the loss of the concrete values of the signifiers. It is a question not merely of the presentation of 'natural objects', but of *making the object function at two levels*.

What we seem to have in Pound's Image and his hierarchy of

metaphors is a process in which the metaphorical or metonymic roles of signifiers are inverted. In 'Liu Ch'e' the metonymic scene was elegiacally transformed into a metaphorical scene; in 'Doria' the metaphorical scene was 'literalised'; and in 'A Girl' a metamorphic totality was generated by the inversion of the metaphorical relation of two sets of metonyms.

Thus we may say that the Image replaces the descriptive limitations of an 'objective' language and the subjective excess of a 'symbolic' language, with an activised transformation. Such an account concurs, I believe, with Pound's own explications of the 'Doctrine', such as the original definition:

> An 'Image' is that which presents an intellectual and emotional complex in an instant of time. . . . It is the presentation of such a 'complex' instantaneously which gives that sense of sudden liberation; that sense of freedom from time limits and space limits; that sense of sudden growth, which we experience in the presence of the greatest works of art.[35]

It is useful at this point to adduce a model of metaphor. Jonathan Culler has argued that there is only one basic trope, synecdoche.[36] Metaphor is the combination of two synecdoches, moving from a whole to a common part to another whole. Metonymy, on the other hand, moves from part to whole to part (*mutatis mutandi*, effect/cause, container/contained). Thus what characterises metonymy and produces its effect of the real is the congruence not of one part but of the unifying totality: an oak relates metonymically to the signifier 'tree' if all the parts agree; a 'tree' may be a metaphor for a man, say, if there is some point of partial similarity ('he is as tall as a tree'). In other words, we measure our sense of reality in terms of the totality of relation between two terms in an identity – as in science, in realism, the congruence of triangles or the equality of sets. Thus metonymy always implies a contiguous totality. In metaphor, on the other hand, there is a point of congruence or resemblance, but this does not usually extend to the totality: there is always a difference concealed in metaphor which is identifiable with the sum of the parts not included in the association. The residual 'dissimilarity in similars' is born by the conditional character of metaphor (most explicit in the weak copula and ellipse).

Thus we may say that the consequence of the transformative action of the Image in practice is not the fusing of parts but the production of totalities. If the copula retains the conditional, and hence partial, nature of metaphoric relation ('subjective inclusions'), then, by the same token, the use of transformation (from metonymy to metaphor) or injection or literalisation (from metaphor to metonymy) implies a non-conditional and hence total relation. This is a function of the totalising implication of metonymy itself.

Ernst Cassirer offers theoretical support in his book *Language and Myth*, in which he distinguishes between metaphor as such (the partial combination of two synecdoches in our model) and what he calls the 'radical metaphor' of mythic thought. Whereas the former is 'only the *conscious* denotation of our thought content by the name of another which resembles the former in some respect, or is somehow analogous to it',[37] the latter 'is not only a transition to another category, but actually the creation of the category itself'. He elaborates the latter process:

> we find in operation a law which might actually be called the law of the leveling and extinction of specific differences. Every part of a whole is the whole itself; every specimen is equivalent to the entire species. The part does not merely represent the whole, or the specimen its class; they are identical with the totality to which they belong.[38]

This is the process behind totemism, and is born out and summarised in Claude Lévi-Strauss's 'law of mythic thought that the transformation of a metaphor is achieved in a metonymy'.[39]

I am arguing that it is this sort of 'radical metaphor' that the Image, at its strongest, represents, in that it transforms a metaphorical relation into a metonymic relation or *vice versa*, and creates thereby a radical third totality. In that it is metaphorical, it remains 'creative' ('conception', as opposed to 'description' or 'reception'); and, in that it is metonymic, it has metonymy's valuable effect of the real. In this way, with the help of Cassirer and Lévi-Strauss, the Image may be related not only to metamorphosis, but also to *myth*.

One can illustrate this further with the help of the 1915 poem 'Ortus':

> How have I laboured?
> How have I not laboured
> To bring her soul to birth,
> To give these elements a name and a centre!

> She is beautiful as the sunlight, and as fluid.
> She has no name, and no place.
> How have I laboured to bring her soul into separation;
> To give her a name and her being!
>
> Surely you are bound and entwined,
> You are mingled with the elements unborn;
> I have loved a stream and a shadow.
>
> I beseech you enter your life.
> I beseech you learn to say 'I',
> When I question you;
> For you are no part, but a whole,
> No portion, but a being.[40]

This poem is concerned with the essence of significant production, creation: 'To bring her soul to birth / To give these elements a name and a centre!' There are two attempts at this primal naming: the first is a metaphor, the second an Image.

The former occurs in the fifth line, the latter in the eleventh. The first is a typical combination of two synecdoches: the totalities are 'she' and 'sun'; the partial qualities which relate them are qualities of beauty, fluidity and light. In the second case, two things happen. First, the interpretative quality is transferred to the verb (from beauty to 'love'); and, secondly, the partial qualities which mediated the metaphor are *totalised* into a new object or process: 'a stream and a shadow'.

The didactic last stanza refers not, then, to existential good faith, but to the metaphoric process: 'you are no part, but a whole, / No portion, but a being'. 'Being' is not a weak copula but a matter of substantial activity (process); in order to generate it, the metaphor of partial relation must be rejected in favour of a more active and total transformation. In this case, it is a question of raising the metaphorical part (light, beauty, fluidity) to the level of metonymic whole. 'She' is no longer signified by 'parts', but is 'the category itself'. Hence, as I have argued, the effect of the real. Congruence in its simple form functions in the tautologies of literal reference ('a hawk is a hawk'): this is the *reductio ad absurdum* of the realism of description; but in combination with metaphor it can generate another 'reality' at the other end of the scale: the literal/transformed reality of myth.

In conclusion, we can argue as follows. The critical tendency of

Imagisme locates itself in a dialectic of 'conception' and 'objectivity', seeking to maintain the concreteness of the natural object without sacrificing the subjective creative function, and *vice versa*. This dialectic focuses itself on the question of metaphor – escaping the subjective weaknesses of mystical Symbolism in a stronger technique which can convey *the same conviction* as realist prose.

Clearly, a simple realism would be too limiting; hence the 'radical metaphor' of the Image. The formula for synthesis had been formulated in a critical discourse as 'the natural object is always the *adequate* symbol'. But the copula is a weak and conditional form of articulating the object with subjective conception. The formula is more of a problematic than a policy. In looking at Pound's practice in his Imagiste poems, we discover a critique of the copula in relation to a substantial 'being' which will articulate in practice the process of interaction between the subject and the world in poetry. This articulation takes place at the level of subject–object transformations.

In the Image, then, we observe two, complementary operations: the raising of metaphoric part to the level of metonymy ('Doria', 'Ortus'); and the switching of a signifier from metonymy to metaphor ('Liu Ch'e'). 'A Girl', with its full metamorphosis, involves a complex of both operations. The former process literalises the metaphor by the metonymy's implication of a contiguous totality; the latter totalises a conditional relation into a transformation. In both cases, a third totality in the syntagm itself, striking in the similarity of its process to Image, different from either of the two metaphoric terms; a radical totality in the syntagma itself, striking in the similarity of its process to that which functions in myth. Hence the Image refuses to surrender creativity to mere description, but neither will it surrender objectivity or concreteness. It resolves the problem by using metonymy not as an agent of the literal, but, in interaction with metaphor, as an agent of the metamorphic or mythic.[41]

Thus we can analyse the signifying means of the Image and relate it to a literary category. We might say, for example, that the Image 'rediscovers the primal literary potency of myth'. And I think we should be right in a sense, even if we had expressed ourselves in a mystifying language. Imagisme is a response to a desire to 'write well'; writing well requires the satisfaction of criteria of realism, scientificity and objectivity, but, in order to avoid collapsing into merely passive, descriptive contingency, it must likewise still satisfy criteria of creativity, originality and interpretation. The devices of myth in a modern poetic context answer this desire – and (can we assume?) give us pleasure. As such, their analysis contributes to a base for the investigation of the sort of questions suggested in Chapter 1. I shall discuss them in the concluding chapter. For now, I wish to turn to some 'political' aspects of Imagisme: the history of Imagisme as a literary movement.

III

Handbooks of literary history are almost unanimous in viewing Imagisme as the first and most lastingly influential modern movement after Symbolism. It was Imagisme which cut out the fustian and rhetoric of the late nineteenth century and pointed the way for a modern poetic voice. It consolidated the modernity of free verse, of concise, compressed, 'impersonal' expression, and the use of images instead of imagery. To that extent it was a successful movement. It also served Pound's immediate and eventual reputations well. As leader of the Imagiste movement, his place in literary history is assured (however one feels about his subsequent achievements), as was his place in the contemporary literary scene. He gained major personal influence during these years – as foreign editor of the new *Poetry* (Chicago), regular contributor and reviewer for the *New Freewoman* (later, the *Egoist*), editor of the Imagiste Anthology and the *Catholic Anthology* (1915), and, with Wyndham Lewis, a leading light of the Vorticist movement – while Imagisme is seen as the modernist movement *par excellence*, a necessary step on the road to modern poetry.

As I have already indicated, however, criticism is far from unanimous over what Imagisme actually was. There exist basically two schools of thought concerning its history: one which claims that Imagisme was invented by Pound, and subsequently (in 1915) revised or purloined by Amy Lowell, the American millionaire poet; and one which argues that to claim as much is to misappropriate a movement to which Pound was merely an important contributor, and of which he remains a part, but which is really centred on T. E. Hulme. This line refers to an 'Imagism' moving from Hulme, Flint and Edward Storer in 1909 through to Amy Lowell in 1915, and on further. 'Imagisme' concentrates on Pound, Hilda Doolittle (H. D.) and Richard Aldington in the years 1912–14, seeing 1909 as a partial anticipation, and 1915 as a revisionist recuperation of Pound's modernist influence.

At the level at which the argument is often conducted, it seems to be little more than a row about the proprietary rights of literary innovation, bespeaking a peculiar concern with values of originality and ownership, and an authocentricity which ensures that literary history remains a history of kings, queens and generals. But an investigation into the case is valuable, for its resolution reveals much about the nature of literary history, and of Pound's in particular. Since the question of Pound's representativeness and influence is fundamental to the concerns of the present text, how he achieved it – at least in so far as Imagisme is concerned – is bound to be of interest.

The Hulme–Flint–Lowell line generates a considerably less radical, if possibly statistically more popular, modernism.[42] Here one is naturally more interested in Pound's more radical, and indeed more 'modern', line. None the less, both 'histories' share the assumption that there was such a thing as a literary movement called either 'Imagisme' or 'Imagism', which existed before Flint's 'History' in 1915. The ideological and proprietary battle comes to depend on the relations drawn between 1909, 1912 and 1915. This is an assumption I find both historically and logically rather doubtful. For me, the question is not whether Pound defaulted on a 'debt' to Hulme, or whether Lowell 'stole' something from Pound. What I wish to put in question is that something itself. I shall be arguing that we are not in the realm of a dispute over the history of an object, but indeed in a competition of *fictions presented as histories*, and consequently in the realm of ideologies.

The mystifications and contradictions surrounding Imagism(e) arise, I believe, in large part from retrospective readings of the 'movement' (retrospect being, as we shall see, one of its techniques of construction). But 'Imagism(e)' is not a retrospective (diachronic) classification – like, for example, Samuel Johnson's classification of 'the metaphysicals'. It is rather a peculiarly modern phenomenon, a self-defining, self-producing movement, and as such its history has to be a *synchronic* history.

The synchronic rehearsal I therefore offer here seeks to demystify the literary history of Imagism(e), seeing 'influence' not as the interpretation or transmission of necessary, impersonal or progressive forces, but rather as something which has to be *produced* within a market. In this sense, 'Imagism*e*' is undeniably something entirely of Pound's manufacture; but, by the same token, what he launched in inventing 'Imagisme' was not so much a movement as a *word*. This word, like any other trademark, stock or currency, develops a value according to a process of production, distribution and consumption. In terms of consumption – which comes, necessarily, after the event – it is clear that the value of this coinage is much debated, as the alternative literary histories and theories of Imagism(e) prove.

At the level of production, the word is evidently a compilation. Flint recollected, 'Like most inventors, Pound did not create out of the void. The "image" he took from T. E. Hulme's table talk. The "ism" was suggested to him by the notes on contemporary French Poetry which I wrote for Harold Munro's *Poetry Review*.'[43] Pound acknowledged the substance of this, with a subtle but significant alteration in the first part: 'I made the word – on a Hulme basis – and carefully made a name that was not and never had been used in France . . . to distinguish "us" from any of the French groups catalogued by Flint in the *P. R.*'[44] It is this reference to Hulme which has given rise to much of the debate and misunderstanding.

In terms of a reference of content, it is seriously misleading. Pound repeatedly denied – and the denials are born out by literary analysis – that he had been in any way influenced by Hulme; and it should by now be agreed that Imagisme was not Hulme's principles put into practice. This has been argued, as I have already indicated, but it has been quite adequately refuted.[45] The problem is, however, that those critics who disprove Hulme's influence do not explain satisfactorily why the reference exists and persists in being far from incidental. Not only is it there in the word 'Imagisme' for those in a position to perceive that reference (or, more likely – their curiosity aroused by the strange new word – to have it explained to them), but, what is more, in the first public announcement of Imagisme, in an appendix to Pound's *Ripostes*, published in October 1912, an explicit relation is drawn between Imagisme, Hulme's poems and his 1909 'Club'. It is my case that one can avoid being misled by this reference, and still explain it, only by maintaining a synchronic view; by tracing the actual history of the circulation or distribution of the *term*, rather than debating it diachronically or retrospectively at the level of comparative poetics.[46]

Although *Ripostes* appeared first, the ground for putting 'Imagisme' into circulation was begun a little earlier and led to its more thorough launching in the new Chicago journal *Poetry* in January 1913, through five poems by H. D., an accompanying note and an article by Pound ('Status Rerum').

At first sight, the event looks fairly innocent. According to *Poetry*'s editor, Harriet Monroe, Pound in fact said that Imagisme 'was started, not very seriously, chiefly to give H. D.'s five poems a hearing'. Stanley Coffman endorses this account: 'It began as a publicity stunt which circumstances soon proved to have a value beyond its immediate purpose.'[47] When we look carefully and contextually at this 'stunt', however, and put it next to the parallel 'stunt' in *Ripostes*, we find something considerably less fortuitous. As we shall see, the stunt is, from the beginning, elaborate enough to give the distinct impression of a scheme.

The story itself is well-enough known: probably in the autumn of 1912, Pound's ex-fiancée H. D. showed him five poems, including 'Hermes of the Ways'. Pound 'corrected' or revised the poem, and *signed it for her* 'H. D. Imagiste', promising to send the poems to *Poetry*. H. D.'s future husband, Richard Aldington, testifies to their reluctance to accept the puzzling appellation and their annoyance at Pound's condescension, but also to their more powerful gratitude for his efforts to get the poems published.[48]

Pound hence first created 'Imagisme' by making H. D. a member of a group of which there were – as yet – no other members (unless Pound himself is to be counted); Aldington by implication was also simultaneously enrolled. Thus the reality of the 'Imagistes' at this moment was very simple: it amounted to virtually a sort of family group, enlisted by Pound, with him very much in the dominant position.[49] From this somewhat reluctant base, Pound produced a 'movement' and/or a 'theory' *at the level of the signifier*: the word 'Imagiste' necessarily implies other 'Imagistes' and a notion of 'Imagisme'. It operates by means of the implied totalisation of a synecdoche: a partial quality of a poem is named ('imagist(ic)'), and this is inscribed in such a way ('Imagiste') as to imply another totality of an undefined plurality of writers with a common aesthetic.

One can hardly overemphasise the fact that this totality did not yet exist – merely the word. The 'movement' sprang into being with the stroke of a pen. Rather than *avant la lettre*, Imagisme is fundamentally – and I shall argue, definitively – *avant la chose*. And, although Pound cautiously covered himself when discussing Imagisme in 'Status Rerum' (January 1913) – 'A School exists when two or three young men agree, more or less, to call certain things good' – nowhere else in the text is there any suggestion that this is other than a full and coherent group. He even adopts tactics to promote the conviction: 'Space forbids me to set forth the programme of the *Imagistes* at length . . .', 'Among the many very young men . . .' (one could quite easily misread that 'very'); or, in a letter to Monroe, the generality of 'the laconic speech of the Imagistes'.[50]

Hence the pertinence of Aldington's remark: 'the Imagist

movement was H. D., and H. D. was the Imagist movement'.[51] But in what sense is H. D. specifically an 'Imagiste'? Only and entirely by Pound's 'say-so'. And what is he naming with this newly minted term? At this point the precise meaning of the word is a secret held privately by Pound (if Aldington is to be believed, not even he or H. D. understood what Pound meant by it). The term first shifts from the privacy of his own mind into a public arena (which is puzzled by it) by this process of *authoritative appropriation*. It is one man's made-up word for a quality in another person's poem (a poem he himself had 'corrected'), signified by a term which implies an already constituted movement and/or poetic theory. 'Imagisme' *first* comes into existence at the level of the signifier, based in a particular structure of authoritative appropriation.

Pound sent the poems to Monroe with a covering note in October 1912. But, in that the Imagiste movement and H. D.'s poems can be identified at this point, the latter cannot be read unconditionally: they become 'Imagiste', and 'Imagisme' comes to exist not through any collective notion, but through Pound's making it so. H. D.'s poems become the anchor of Imagisme by virtue of having their conditions of acceptance strictly denoted by Pound. This gives the poems the status of an exemplification of specific properties of the as-yet fictional movement.

The covering note read,

I've had luck again, and am sending you some *modern* stuff by an American. I say modern, for it is in the laconic speech of the Imagistes, even if the subject is classic. . . . Objective – no slither; direct – no excessive use of adjectives, no metaphors that won't permit examination. It's straight talk, straight as the Greek! And it was only by persistence that I got to see it at all.[52]

The framing expressions of spurious rarity and reluctance alert us to the pragmatic nature of this note. If its function is to give the young H. D. the dignity of modesty, it is at the same time to build the image of the new 'Imagistes': not only good, but reluctant, as if a guarantee of the integrity of their 'laconic' writing.

The body of the note is, however, more important. If we abstract the main critical points (modernity, objectivity, directness, economy, living but inventive prosody), we find that there is nothing new in these key specifically denoted properties. One has seen them before as central values in Pound's independent and personal poetic standards as expressed in all his critical writings of the period, and which, as I have argued, express his representative attempt to reattain an audience for serious poetry: his modernism. We can in fact trace a sequence from a 1908 letter to William Carlos Williams, through 'I Gather the Limbs of Osiris', to the acknowledgedly personal 'Credo' of 'Prologomena' (February 1912). We should furthermore note that it is by and large from these texts that the 'three principles' of Imagisme, as expressed in the March 1913 article 'Imagisme', arise.[53]

In a sense this is unremarkable enough: that Pound's Imagiste principles should emerge from his own developing poetics. But something more noteworthy begins to happen with the letter to Monroe and follows its course to the article 'Imagisme' (signed by Flint): those principles which had hitherto appeared under the personal authorship of Ezra Pound ('I Gather . . .', 'Credo'), have now been transposed to the authorship of 'Imagisme'/'the Imagistes' – a group which, I must emphasise, at this point *does not exist*. The movement of the 'movement' begins to come clear: from Pound's personal poetics to the 'objective', 'impersonal' principles of a school. If Pound's attempts to resolve the inherited disjuncture and to regain an audience and a position for the poet through an appropriately modern and efficient language (to 'write well') is representative, it is also at the same time designed to 'influence people'.

A look at Pound's relations with *Poetry* at this time, and indeed his entire involvement with Imagisme, alongside a series of articles he published in 1912, 'Patria Mia', shows that this 'movement' may have had an even larger ambition. 'Patria Mia' was begun in America in 1910–11, published in the *New Age* in 1912 and then supplemented by 'America: Chances and Remedies', essays for the same journal in 1913. The series begins by emphasising the function of literary magazines in the American cultural life. Pound argues that the enormous power they wield is employed without discrimination: it is imperative that suitable literary standards should be rigorously enforced by courageous editors (giving an example of advice to a 'neophyte' which is strikingly similar to what comes to be expressed under the heading of 'Imagisme'). This would provide the possibility of generating the propaganda and enthusiasm that would tap the unrivalled vitality of America. Once again, then, a potential mass audience exists, but will only be reached by means of 'good writing', which has to be mediated by the commercial structures of literary production with due 'seriousness' (good editing). Pound then proceeds to concentrate on the wealth of America and to argue for subsidies and endowments to be obtained from America's millionaires in order to liberate its poets from their financial dependencies and the demands of the market. And lastly he argues for the need for a 'Super-College' of the arts, as a corrective to the sterile universities, in which artists might learn from each other.[54]

I do not believe that it is coincidence that Imagisme and the major American literary project *Poetry* magazine are 'born' at effectively the same moment: *Poetry* had first appeared in October 1912, Monroe having contacted Pound in August, just before the 'H. D. Imagiste' episode, and at the likely time for the latest proof corrections for *Ripostes*. From Pound's correspondence with Monroe, it is clear that he was seeking to make this new and influential magazine into a force for the sort of 'Awakening' that he firmly believed in (and expressed in 'Patria Mia'), and he used 'Imagisme' in order to do this. There is a concerted effort on his part to raise his personal critical standards (often expressed, as I have said, in terms of impersonal *Weltliteratur* standards) to the level of the policy of *Poetry*. He took exception to Monroe's 'democratic' masthead – 'To have great poets there must be great audiences too' (Whitman) – in favour of 'my scale of criticism'. When Monroe resisted this attempt to impose his standards, Pound resigned (November 1913), agreeing to reconsider only if there were a 'general improvement of the magazine'.[55]

When he saw that this was unlikely on his terms, Pound switched his promotion of Imagisme to Amy Lowell (like John Quinn, who became an important financier for the Vorticists, one of Pound's American millionaires), to whom he had been introduced in the summer of 1913. First he tried to persuade her to buy the recently founded *New Freewoman*, without success. None the less, Pound persisted in trying to persuade Lowell to obtain a magazine for him, having been by now frustrated in his influence with *Poetry*. In the summer of 1914, he suggested to her that they start an international review. She would put up the money and have the right to publish her own poetry, whilst Pound would be salaried editor. Lowell claimed to be unable to afford this, and counterproposed an annual Imagiste anthology (the first, edited by Pound, having appeared the previous February as a special number of the *Globe*) for five years. Pound disagreed with her insistence on a 'democratic' method of selection for the anthology, and finally tried to 'sell' her the trademark in return for the sort of subsidy he demands in 'Patria Mia', $200 per annum from an 'indigent' poet of Pound's choosing. By this time, of course, Lowell did not have to pay for the use of the Imagiste label, and refused the deal. Finally, Pound gave up on Lowell as a source of funds for a magazine or a subsidy (both to be administered by himself), and shifted his attention to Wyndham Lewis's circle, using this rather more rigorous group, the Vorticists, as the base for, amongst other things, a College of Arts.[56]

Thus so much of Pound's activity of this period, especially in relation to Imagisme, particularly as a magazine phenomenon, can be viewed in terms of strategies specifically outlined in 'Patria Mia' for the American Awakening. Thus, inasmuch as Imagisme is a cipher for Pound's personal technical values, it is by the same token the vehicle around which he in large part aims to promote the new *Risorgimento*.

I have argued so far that Pound cannot be seen as the spokesman for a 'school' or 'movement', but was, rather, in the process of generating the *fiction* of such a group. But in March 1913 *Poetry* responded to the 'many requests for information regarding *Imagism* and *Imagistes*' by publishing a short article by F. S. Flint entitled 'Imagisme', accompanied by 'A Few Don'ts by an Imagiste', signed by Pound. These articles represent the first public normative statement of the movement, moderately and reluctantly breaking their silence. They certainly seem to represent a collective position, almost a manifesto, and indeed this is also the first time that Pound put his name to the movement, as himself merely 'an Imagiste'. The fact that the leading article is signed by the author of the 1912 *Poetry Review* survey of contemporary movements is important: the authoritative and unpartisan source of the 'manifesto' gives Imagisme considerable status as a genuine movement or school.

But the history of the article is illuminating, and again reveals that Pound was still effectively the sole author of 'Imagisme'. According to Patricia Hutchins's conversations with Flint, the latter

> thought Imagism a young people's joke, not all that serious. He described how Pound arrived one day with an 'interview with himself' already written but Flint would not sign, so when Pound left he rearranged this and sent it back. Pound made further improvements.[57]

Pound's original 'interview' is not available, but Flint's draft and Pound's corrections are.[58]

There are, first, a number of purely stylistic corrections, as when Pound crosses out Flint's opening phrase: 'The first shoot of green announcing . . .', with the marginal comment 'decoration'. He also censors Flint's sententious personal comments, as for example,

> I was delighted that such a thing as the founding of a poetic school in London was possible. The French device on the pennons of its lances at first shocked my English ear; but a school is a criticism; the language of criticism is, incontestably, French; and French criticism is my special pleasure, so that I was soon reconciled.

Similarly, when Flint responds to Pound's rejection of most contemporary verse – 'With this judgment I was inclined to agree' – this too is cut.

Thus far the stylistic criticism is simply in accordance with Imagiste criteria of 'good writing' – against ornamental flourish and didactic or sententious subjectivism. But the line between the purely stylistic and the tactical becomes rapidly blurred. Pound cuts all direct speech, and at the end advises, 'simple statement of facts without the conversation will get the thing much more compact'. But this desire for Imagiste compression and 'direct treatment of the "thing" '[59] demands both a change from the first person plural to the third, and the excision of any reference to Pound himself as the explicit subject of the discourse. Flint's comments such as 'went to Mr Pound' and 'Mr Pound became unprintably voluble for a few minutes' are all cut with a clear definite line. Thus we see an ostensible effort for concision and impersonality ('Good Writing') producing the effect of *concealing* the continuing subjective and personal source of these poetic values at the same time as the *illusion* of a public, collective discourse is generated.

Another set of excisions has even less to do with style. Reference to *Ripostes* is cut, along with the following: 'he told me later that the school consisted of three poets, one or two affiliated writers, and a . . . penumbra!' Furthermore, Flint's questions: 'What is Imagisme?' and 'But why *Imagistes*?' (sensible enough in themselves) are censored. Likewise the suggestion on the unpublished 'Doctrine of the Image': 'Is it that the poem should itself be an image, and that you reject *imagery* as merely ornamental?' Any account of the composition or central doctrine is deliberately, not to say methodically, excised – with the exception of the 'hygienic' three principles.

Three main consequences are produced, none of them strange to the literary effects of Imagiste techniques. The first is the metonymic perspective of depth conferred on the movement by its intriguing silences (as in Imagiste juxtaposition, or indeed the importance of its use of metonymy's totalising implication). Secondly, the lack of elaboration, highlights what is present – the three principles – as impersonal, secure and definitive; free from the subjective emotional 'slither' of rhetoric. And the third consequence is the inversion achieved between the impersonal movement and Pound's personal values. The trick is that many of the repressed points reappear in the longer accompanying article, 'A Few Don'ts by an Imagiste', signed by Pound. In this way, his personal values now appear as a supplement to or exemplification of[60] a public movement, which is in fact effectively made up of his personal values. By March 1913, then, although the enlisted 'Imagistes' – H. D., Aldington, and, as bemused critic, Flint – may have overcome their reluctance and entered at least into the spirit of the 'school', Pound is still the absent author of its doctrines, the *occluded source* of what is signified by 'Imagisme'.

Having established the essentially fictive or, at the very least, contingent composition of the Imagistes, we must now return to the text which has probably contributed most to the debate over Imagisme at the level of consumption (what we think it means), and indeed to Pound's eventual loss of his own trademark: the *Ripostes* appendix.

Here, in October 1912 (before the publication, but around the preparation of H. D.'s poems), Pound published the admirably brief 'Complete Poetical Works of T. E. Hulme' ('out of good fellowship' – although they had already appeared in the *New Age* earlier that year): five short poems, accompanied by an introduction in which Pound referred to 'the "School of Images", which may or may not have existed'.[61] He concluded that 'As for the future, *Les Imagistes*, the descendants of the forgotten school of 1909, have that in their keeping.' A history is hence generated, relating 1912 to 1909.

As we have already seen, Flint's reference to this text in his 'Imagisme' article – despite being merely a passing reference to the volume's title – was cut. Indeed, this connection between 1912 and 1909 remained entirely dormant for another three years, until Flint's 'History of Imagism' in the *Egoist* Imagist special number of 1 May 1915 sought to consecrate the notion that the Imagisme of 1912–14 was 'descended' from Hulme's 1909 group. Pound took enormous exception to this 'History', from which the critical debate has in large part followed.

As I have suggested, the notion of influence at the level of the theory of practice of the Image has already been disproved; our concern here is that of a synchronic account which bases itself on the documents which are responsible for generating the original idea that such a relationship may have existed and that Imagisme originated in the 1909 Club: Pound's note in *Ripostes* and Flint's 1915 article. Pound's response to the latter was 'BULLSHIT'. Flint's rejoinder: 'it is a matter of doubt whether you are an Imagist poet at all'.[62] This accusation is clearly absurd, unless and *only unless* the 'Imagism' of which Flint is writing the 'History' is something different from the 'Imagisme' which Pound not only invented but effectively constituted, and which furthermore, by virtue of the latter fact, can only be a revisionary deviation from Pound's 'movement'.

What is the warrant for 'another' Imagism prior to Pound's which the latter can be accused of, as it were, betraying? Where might one get the idea that Pound's 'school' had defaulted on an original debt? I would argue that it is fundamentally Pound's double reference to 'the "School of Images" ' and '*Les Imagistes*', produced in 1912 when the latter was a pure fiction, and left silent until revived by Flint as late as 1915. But there is an interesting irony here. Although there is an association between Pound and Hulme which dates from 1908–9, no one, as far as I have been able to discover, ever referred to the 1909 Club as anything like a 'School of Images' before Pound did so for the first time in 1912. Hulme himself apparently named it 'the Secession Club' (to emphasise its relation to 'The Poets' Club' of 1908–9).[63] Edward Marsh makes no mention of 'Images' when, as late as June 1913, he talks about the project for what he styles 'a "Post-Georgian" Anthology, of the Pound–Flint–Hulme school'.[64] Hence indeed Pound's rider, 'which may or may not have existed'. The Club certainly did exist, and Pound's personal and professional friendship with Hulme is not in doubt; but the 'School of Images' appears to be Pound's own *renaming* of the group. He calls the 'forgotten' 1909 Club back into existence as a 'School of *Images*' in a similar way to that in which he turned H. D. and Aldington into '*Les Imagistes*': by an act of authoritative appropriation, a fictive, synecdochic naming.

Despite the fact that the Club styled itself neither as a school nor in terms of the Image, the evidence for its 'Imagism' arises from Flint's statement in the 'History' that there was 'a lot of talk and practice among us, [Edward] Storer leading chiefly, of what we called the Image'. But, as Flint's accusation against Pound might suggest, the 'Image' they did (or did not) discuss – as far as one can judge from the poetry and/or theory of Storer, Hulme and Flint himself – has very little to do with the 'Image' in H. D.'s or Pound's theory and practice. Pound's reaction to Flint's remarkable accusation was, 'You seem to see no difference between imagisme and impressionism.'[65] This is both pertinent and true. In the 'History', Flint quotes his own praise of Edward Storer's 1909 *Mirrors of Illusion*, in which 'an image is the resonant heart of an exquisite moment', and his comments in the 1912 review of French poetry do not persuade one that he ever progressed beyond this post-Symbolist impressionism (the word is used here more in the painterly sense, rather than with reference to Ford's rather different literary theory and practice). Hulme is more explicit, as when he announces (probably in 1909) that 'What has found expression in painting as Impressionism will soon find expression in poetry as free verse.'[66]

But the 'School of Images' is a misnomer – or rather, perhaps, a 're-nomer' – not only in the specific, but also in the general sense, for the Club was by no means limited to the activity of Hulme, Storer and Flint. Any such impression is a consequence of the retrospective style of its re-creation in 1912 and 1915. Indeed, when we look at the 'forgotten school' as it was in 1909, our impression may be quite different. True, Flint and Hulme were the group's founders. But Hulme had completed his laconic poetic career before 1912; Storer, according to Flint himself, 'has recanted much since'; and Flint himself had shown little development either in theory or practice. On the other hand, the other members of the group – Florence Farr, Padraic Colum, Joseph Campbell, F. W. Tancred – had pursued their independent paths, were not published in the 1914 Imagiste Anthology, or indeed were never accused of being 'Imagist(e)s'.

In short, as Wallace Martin has shown, whilst some impressionistic idea of the 'Image (and that mostly in terms of an emphasis on the visual – emphatically not the central issue in Pound's Imagisme)[67] played *some* part in the aesthetics of Hulme, Flint and Storer, and whilst in turn they played *some* part in the Club, however important, 'Imagism' was far from central to or definitive of the group as a whole (any more so than it was of H. D.'s 'Hermes of the Ways', for that matter). If there is a genuine technical or aesthetic connection between Pound's 'Imagisme' and the 1909 group, it would appear to exist again at the 'hygienic' level of experiments in verse form, diction and concision, and *not* at the level of the 'Image'.[68] In this sense, 'Imagisme' would owe no more to this group than it does, say, to Ford – or even to Yeats.

Hence both Pound and Flint are in a sense right: Pound never was an 'Imagist' in Flint's impressionistic sense – and *vice versa*. Flint could have accused Pound of not being a disciple of Hulme, and there would have been no doubt about the question. But he is only enabled to express this idea in terms of Pound's not being an 'Imagist' by virtue of the retrospect produced by Pound himself. This retrospective relation between 1912 and 1909 is produced principally once more at the level of the signifier. 'Imagism' could not exist were it not for Pound's invention of 'Imagisme' and his *re*invention of the 1909 Club as a 'School of Images' – which, I maintain, it could only be called in the most partial (synecdochic) sense.

Thus, in the 1912 appendix, Pound draws a relation between two *signifiers* which each *appropriate* an approximate reality: the Imagistes of 1912 and the 1909 Club signified as a 'School of Images'. The relation thus generated is not entirely false, but it is so inscribed at the level of the signifier so as to transform the historical object and relation: to totalise, once more, a partial object and relationship into an effectively metonymic – and hence mythic – relationship between realities. The reason for so doing would appear to be the same as we have been observing throughout: to generate the illusion of a movement. Viewed in this way, the *Ripostes* appendix was in sum a masterful coup which created breadth and depth for Pound's fiction of a movement by means of the retrospective endowment of a patrimony.

There is a remark in Flint's 'Verse Chronicle' which seems to have been largely disregarded; but it may prove to be the most significant thing he had to say on the subject: 'The collocation of "image" with "ism" came to Pound after I had told him about Fernand Divoire's essays on "stratégie littéraire". Pound devised a "stratégie littéraire".'[69] Perhaps the greatest virtue of the 1909 Club in these terms (for both Pound and Flint) was that it had been 'forgotten', and hence was open to a carefully manipulated revival.

Imagisme then – this inaugural movement of poetic modernism – exists, basically, only on paper. It is an operation in language produced by Pound principally through three texts: 'H. D. Imagiste', the *Ripostes* appendix, and the articles 'Imagisme' and 'A Few Don'ts by an Imagiste'. A fourth text, the anthology of 1914, bears out the notion of an opportunistic creation of fictive collectivity: few of its assorted modernist writers would have claimed to be an 'Imagiste' (apart from Pound, Aldington, H. D., Lowell and Flint, we find Skipwith Cannell, William Carlos Williams, Ford, Joyce, Allen Upward and John Cournos).[70] The operation as a whole seems designed to represent Pound's personal poetic criteria worked out in his personal pursuit of a 'language' under the collective and authoritative authorship of a 'school', itself aimed at generating a social reality (a Poundian school) as part of an attempted Awakening.

As Pound wrote in another context in 1935, 'There is opportunism and opportunism. . . . There is also the opportunism of the artist, who has a definite aim, and creates out of the material present. The greater the artist, the more permanent his creation.'[71] Through this set of discursive practices, Pound shifted the authorship of his values away from their concealed subjective and partial source to the impersonal and collective authorship – public authority – of a school; and thus, finally, inaugurated modernism in poetry. 'Imagisme' was, however, such a powerful fiction (and so much a fiction) that it generated a further ironic reality: 'Imagism' without the 'e', the diluted form which Pound 'surrendered' to Amy Lowell and Flint as he went off to convert his poetics into Vorticism ('including such and such painting and sculpture and "Imagisme" in verse'[72]). The fact that the same sort of confusion or revision tends not to happen with the latter movement points to the major difference between a fictive and a relatively real 'school'. Vorticism had something of a genuine collective base and public discourse (albeit within a fairly closed circle), denotative and exclusive. Historically the Vorticists were thus able to resist, for example, both F. R. Nevinson's Futurist ambitions and Wyndham Lewis's 'literary history': 'Vorticism, in fact, was what I, personally, did, and said, at a certain period.'[73]

In 'Imagisme', however, Pound employed 'the opportunism of the artist' to create a literary movement, in which the relation of 'opportunism' to 'permanence' is conditional on the controversial degree of adhesion of its 'members' and the ensuing critical debate. But it is my contention that, more than a problematic 'movement', what Pound produced in Imagisme was a *literary history* – or rather, a fiction of a literary history, and hence a history of a quasi-mythic character.

We might regard this event as further evidence of Pound's importance as a *modernist*. Whereas the Symbolists, according to Valéry, sought to create their own 'aristocratic' public by renouncing the market Pound showed himself to be 'modern' in seeking to create his public in a more material sense. The emergence at this time of self-defining literary movements or schools, which is characteristic of twentieth-century literary politics, was yet another symptom of the poet's problematic position in society. Throughout history, the poet has been inserted into society in different ways, in relation to various class dispositions: from the private courtly coterie or the systems of political patronage and subscriptions, for example, to the contemporary 'writer in residence' and the PEN lobby. The fact that the writer will recognise himself as a professional, as a member of a particular class, but has yet to produce anything comparable to a trades union, is evidence that this activity has not yet achieved mass socialisation. Such modern literary movements as we witness in Imagism(e) are hence transitional. The group is still basically exclusive; yet, deprived of a closed circle of social support, it has to direct itself to a larger public, to which it refuses to pander. Simply to produce or supply is insufficient in the modern market economy into which the poet is forced; as with any other commodity, the conditions of consumption in the modern market have to be determined by the producer in order to intervene profitably in the dynamics of what is increasingly a constructed demand. In other words, confronted with the modern economy, the poet has to 'market' his commodity.

In this sense, Pound's fiction was relatively successful. 'Imagisme' is nowadays enough of a commodity to be traded at different values. But, more importantly, it has produced an influence – an intervention in demand. In this way, it has influenced *us* inasmuch as we are modernists. The criteria Pound introduced or publicised for criticism and which he exemplified under the name of Imagisme have helped in no small way to mould us. As I have already pointed out, many of the criteria which we use to criticise and evaluate modern poetry can be traced back to him. It is then no wonder that we see his writing as 'good poetry': he wrote well and influenced us.

Our ideological safeguard within this Whiggish circularity is a notion of the progressive continuity and literary history underwritten by a sense of necessity and adequation: Pound was a figurehead of a collective and, in the literary sense, historically necessary movement of artists who, through their art, reflect the changing conditions of existence in their language. As soon, however, as we perceive this literary history not in terms of the operation of impersonal or collective forces of adequation but as an act of intervention within specific structures of the production of history, that safeguard disappears. Hence it is that we need to historicise Imagisme in order to begin to analyse how our criteria have been determined by the object which we are judging, and to free ourselves from the tautology.

In this sense we become aware that the distinction between the language of lyric and the language of power may not be as clear as we may like to assume. Pound's way of influencing people is to 'write well'; his way of writing well is to employ 'mythic' techniques; and his way of influencing people is thus finally to create a historical myth.

The history of Imagisme offers a demonstration of the political consequences of certain effectively literary tactics. Both the poems and the movement itself are examples of creative 'good writing': from a hygiene of compression, impersonality, laconic style to the expansive implication of synecdoche and the totalising use of metonymy towards mythic effects. In one field, these tactics produce 'good poetry'; in the other they produce opportunist politics or a mythologised literary history. I am not putting into question the political probity of Ezra Pound, whose strictly personal motivations are not my concern, but this does have significance in relation to Pound's practical and poetic attitude to history and its production in the more strictly political sphere – as his own remark on opportunism may suggest.[74]

The history produced in Imagisme was, I have argued, based in a double fiction: the ideological resurrection of a forgotten 'origin', and the homogenisation of 'allies' enlisted under his occult banner. But the test of a produced history is History itself; and here, in a manner less drastic than, but none the less relevant to, Pound's later politics, History did, as it were, take its revenge by generating an irony. It was precisely Pound's creation of a myth of origin which gave rise to Flint's revisionism; his opportunist (synecdochic) appropriation of H. D. and Aldington gave rise to a Hellenicist revision or confusion;[75] and it was his expedient alliance with Lowell's capital which lost him the movement. The ambiguities of History – which extended to the point of putting in question Pound's authorship of his own 'movement', his own creation – are consequences of the very tactics employed in its fictive production.

The 'permanence' of Pound's creation belongs to the level of the signifier; and, as in all such attempts to produce history 'on paper', the concretisation of the conditionalities of fiction ultimately subverts that permanence: the materiality of the object and of the population of History prove themselves ultimately resistant to ideology – most of all ironically. As far as we are concerned, with our ideological burden of 'influence', we can only generate a position in which this irony can operate if we undertake an analysis of both our lyric pleasure and our debt of historical influence in relation to the signifier: the means and the social relations – the history – of the significant production of, in this case, Imagisme.

3　'The Drama is Wholly Subjective': Pound and Science

I

I have argued that Pound is richly symptomatic in his confrontation of the crisis of modernism's inherited dislocation, as represented by the parallel tendencies of Symbolism and Naturalism. This literary crisis can itself be read as a reflection of a larger dislocation, registered at different levels in various discourses, and associated with a particular stage of crisis in the development of industrial capitalism, on the eve of the First World War, the Bolshevik Revolution, and the birth of the mixed economy and Welfare State. One should not forget the radical state of political, social and economic confrontation existing in Britain during Pound's early years there.[1] For an author, the crisis expresses itself as a rupture in his relation with his audience; the problem is located as a search for a productive role for the artist, and hence for a suitable language. It is thus technically located, for such a poet as Pound, in the application to his poetic vision of a practical 'hygiene' of 'prose' values, and, most especially, in a revision of the technique of metaphor as the locus of the disjuncture of the subjective and objective. We have also observed how Pound is influential in proposing a modernist resolution: an attempt to regain an audience by a posture and a technique which would offer a new synthesis of the poet's specialised subjectivism with the 'objectivity' or 'concreteness' of 'prose'. The project is contained initially in the literary values of Imagisme as a critical movement, its public existence as a historical movement, in Pound's particular technique of the Image, and the theorisation of the 'Serious Artist' – subsequently to be extended fairly continuously through Vorticism and the theory of the Chinese script, towards its practical fulfilment in *The Cantos*.

Throughout, Pound characteristically seeks to preserve the mythic and mystical territories which had been dislocated, and to represent them in a modern form. This is the fundamental poetic stance, as Walter Baumann summarises it when he refers to 'Old World Tricks in a New World Poem'.[2] In its commitment to modern reality, this is simultaneously a political stance: to *real*ise the poetic truth in concrete modern forms, the mythic in history and in actuality. *The Cantos* is thus constituted – leastways, as Pound drew the thematic 'fugal' scheme for his father in 1927:

A.A. Live man goes down into world of Dead
C.B. The 'repeat in history'
B.C. The 'magic moment' or moment of metamorphosis, bust thru from quotidien [*sic*] into 'divine or permanent world'. Gods, etc.[3]

The modern condition – 'Live man', in the quotidian and in history – interacting with the magic world of the past, of recurring patterns, metamorphosis and the gods.

Pound's problem is, then, to evolve poetic techniques and a poetic form in which the 'Old World' can be made readable in the 'New' and in which modern reality can be sustained as matter for poetry. Pound's innovations in this direction are many, and I do not intend to analyse them all here. But it is true that, whatever innovation or device one takes, they all share a common metadiscourse in which they are presented and explained: one of Pound's principal and most important tactics for the modernisation of the vision and technique and for reaching the modern audience is the intervention of a scientific vocabulary. One can hardly exaggerate the importance of this consistent use of science. Ian Bell has recently demonstrated how a 'poetics informed by the disciplines of science' supplies 'the characteristic gestures of [Pound's] modernity' and is precisely a means of healing the rupture between poet and audience.[4]

Science is, obviously, the most 'prosaic' of the discourses generated by industrial capitalism, and none more so than the mechanicist materialism and technology of Victorian science. Whilst Zola, for example, had sought to use positivist science as a dominating model for his Naturalism, the Symbolists had reacted by affecting a contempt for materialism and by adopting a pose of religiosity. The continual presence of a scientific reference in Pound's critical writings is, then, a further testimony to the pressure issuing from the ascendent 'prose' discourses of industrialism, and to his commitment to positive response – not to an exclusive reactionary stance, nor to an aesthetic subservience, but to an attempted modernist synthesis which would incorporate contemporary conditions of 'universality'. Similarly, the successful incorporation of such a discourse is central to the modernist claims of Pound's poetics: the realist and totalising effect of this apparently most metonymic of discourses.

We have already seen how the 'Serious Artist' is defined as a scientist of immaterial man and as a professional technician in the control he exercises over his specialised materials. The key to the scientific reference at this stage is the representation of these specialised 'substances' of the immaterial in terms of a scientific reality comparable to that employed by other technicians.

Thus we find Pound in his first major series of articles ('I Gather the Limbs of Osiris'), offering a scientific 'New Method of Scholarship' which challenges both the quantitative and the qualitative dispersals generated by materialist and idealist epistemologies (the methods of 'multitudinous detail' and of 'sentiment and generalisation'[5]) through a compacting intensivity of presentation based on the 'method of Luminous Detail' – the means by which the scientific poet presents his privileged facts:

> Any fact is, in a sense, 'significant'. Any fact may be 'symptomatic', but certain facts give one a sudden insight into circumjacent conditions, into their causes, their effects, into sequence, and law. . . . In the history of the development of civilisation or of literature, we come upon such interpreting detail. A few dozen facts of this nature give us intelligence of a period – a kind of intelligence not to be gathered from a great array of facts of the other sort. These facts are hard to find. They are swift and easy of transmission. They govern knowledge as the switchboard governs an electric circuit.[6]

The means through which the poet controls and operates these facts is, naturally enough, words. So Pound illustrates this power through a 'cumbersome simile' in which he describes words as 'like great hollow cones of steel of different dullness and acuteness . . . charged with a force like electricity, or, rather, radiating a force from their apexes – some radiating, some sucking in'.[7] Poetic power comes from their technical control in arrangement: 'This particular energy which fills the cones is the power of tradition, of centuries of race consciousness, of agreement, of association; and the control of it is the "Technique of Content", which nothing short of genius understands.'[8]

The 'Osiris' articles are somewhat confused in their analogies, but Pound rapidly comes to dominate more coherently a discourse in which specialised *literary* energies are offered in *scientific* terms. Hence, in the 1912 article 'The Wisdom of Poetry',

> The Art of Poetry consists in combining these 'essentials to thought', these dynamic particles, *si licet*, this radium, with that melody of words which shall most draw the emotions of the hearer toward accord with their import, and with that 'form' which shall most delight the intellect.[9]

Control or technique involves the arrangement of words in such a way as to release or maximise their energy. Similarly, in 'The Serious Artist',

> We might come to believe that the thing that matters in art is a sort of energy, something more or less like electricity or radioactivity, a force transfusing, welding, and unifying. A force rather like water when it spurts up through very bright sand and sets it in swift motion. You may make what image you like.[10]

But Pound undoubtedly likes these images: the representation of poetic/literary energies in terms of the scientific energies of electricity, electromagnetism and radioactivity – synthetic, invisible and *modern* forces. This discourse makes a major difference to Pound's poetics: it gives his ideas an appearance of modernity and of substance, presenting them not in terms of an idealist or antique mysticism of the potency of the Word (as in the case of the Symbolists), but in terms of a real, albeit invisible, force.

As the Image represents a founding stage in the technical innovations of Pound's poetics, it too is defined in relation to a new concept of mental energy in psychology (the recent and most modern science of immaterial man):

> An 'Image' is that which presents an intellectual and emotional complex in an instant of time. I use the term 'complex' rather in the technical sense employed by the newer psychologists, such as Hart, though we might not agree absolutely in our application.[11]

It follows that 'The image is not an idea. It is a radiant node or cluster; it is what I can, and must perforce, call a VORTEX, from which, and through which, and into which, ideas are constantly rushing.'[12] This 'complex' is endowed with energy and hence productive of *form*: 'energy creates pattern . . . emotional force gives the image . . . the Image is more than an idea. It is a vortex or cluster of fused ideas and is endowed with energy . . . emotion is an organiser of form. . . .'[13]

The serious artist's responsibility is to express this energy in a scientific manner: that is to say, according to the values of precision and concision, objectivity and impersonality and 'true witness' – the values insisted on by Imagisme's critical hygiene. 'The touchstone of an art is its precision.'[14] At the same time, 'Good writing is writing that is perfectly controlled, the writer says just what he means. He says it with complete clarity and simplicity. He uses the smallest possible number of words.'[15] This precision, clarity and concision in respect of his specialised material guarantees the ethical and human data on which the serious artist's productivity depends.

Not only do this scientific metadiscourse of energy and the values of precision and concision characterise Pound's presentation of his technique and of the poet's function, they also work in large measure to define and transform his content.

In this way, for example, Pound uses electromagnetic analogies and the wireless model to demonstrate and substantiate the energy of chivalric love in 'Psychology and Troubadours'.[16] This sort of reference marks a major difference from Yeats, at the same time as it testifies once more to Pound's synthesis of the mystical vision and modern 'prose' values. As Herbert Schneidau has observed,

> The important point to be made is that Pound did not think of mysticism, such as he finds it in the Troubadours, as bodiless transmissions of vague visions. . . . Even of mystic visions Pound predicated exactness, precision, definition as the life-giving component.[17]

The formulation is important since it proposes that, for Pound, the antique vagueness in mysticism is moribund and that the *vital* element comes precisely from the area of prose values – science.

Thus Cavalcanti, for example, is not only a major technical resource for Pound (balancing Arnaut Daniel as a resource for musical experimentation with a language capable of handling thought),[18] he is also valuable because 'no psychologist of the emotions is more keen in his understanding, more precise in his expression'.[19] A key ideological value rediscovered in Cavalcanti is the notion of the *virtù*. The *virtù*, on which the 'Luminous Detail' depends, is the intrinsic source of extrinsic significance in the identities of the items of the world. Here Pound is again careful to distinguish his theory from religious and mystical dogmas of essence and from contemporary relativist Idealism: 'This virtue is not a "point of view", nor an "attitude toward life"; nor is it the mental calibre or "a way of thinking", but something more substantial which influences all these.'[20] This substantial source of illuminating meaning, which owes much to Walter Pater but which also has confessed mystical (Swedenborgian) connotations, is none the less offered in scientific terms of energetic intensivity and vitality:

> The equations of alchemy were apt to be written as women's names and the women so named endowed with the magical powers of the compounds. *La virtù* is the potency, the efficient property of a substance or person. Thus modern science shows us radium with a noble virtue of energy. Each thing or person was held to send forth magnetisms of certain effect; in Sonnet xxxv, the image of his lady has these powers.
>
> It is a spiritual chemistry, and modern science and modern mysticism are both set to confirm it.[21]

This quotation, if not the others, might give us an idea of the importance of this scientific discourse. Not only does it provide, on a local level, a way of presenting poetic energies in realistic terms, but it also appears to lend itself, on a wider level, to a particular and global synthesis of the mystical and the scientific.

This manner of presenting the mediaeval vision not only gives scientific substantiality to the energies of that vision and of language; it also comes, on that basis, to provide the terms for a major notion of form: scientific technique applied to scientific content – the form of a modernised 'radiant world'.

> We appear to have lost the radiant world where one thought cut through another with clean edge, a world of moving energies, *'mezzo oscuro rade'*, *'risplende in se perpetuale effecto'*, magnetisms that take form, that are seen, or that border the visible, the matter of Dante's paradiso, the glass under water, the form that seems a form seen in a mirror, these realities perceptible to the sense, interacting. . . .
>
> For the modern scientist energy has no borders, it is a shapeless 'mass' of force; even his capacity to differentiate it to a degree never

dreamed by the ancients has not led him to think its shape or even of its loci. The rose that his magnet makes in the iron filings, does not lead him to think of the force in botanic terms, or wish to visualise that force as floral and extant (*ex stare*).

A medieval 'natural philosopher' would find this modern world full of enchantments, not only the light in the electric bulb, but the thought of the current hidden in the air and in wire would give him a mind full of forms, '*fuor di color*' or having their hyper-colours. The medieval philosopher would probably have been unable to think the electric world, and *not* think of it as a world of forms.[22]

The precise control of the energies of language applied interpretatively to discriminate truly scientifically the energies of the world (against the imprecisions of the 'modern scientist', represented here in terms reminiscent of the blurred vision of the Symbolist) produces objective forms which reveal the 'enchantments' of the modern technological world.

Making it new out of the mediaeval. Subtract the scientific terminology and one is left with a more or less undistinguished piece of aesthetic mysticism, a fantastic revival of an archaic natural philosophy. Precisely what restores the 'lost . . . radiant world', what makes the vision new, and what grants vision to the new, is the scientific vocabulary. And thus it is that 'the rose in the steel dust' becomes a model for the 'organisation of form',[23] at once true to the 'Old World' and the 'new poem'.

II

This sort of image has been much used by Poundian critics to explain his formal practice. The fact is that Pound's purely technical and formal innovations are not only difficult (because innovative), but have often been the object of major attacks by critics of more classical schools. We find that defenders of Pound often reply to such critiques by invoking Poundian form in precisely these 'scientific' terms. This has had an important effect on Pound's acceptance, on our understanding of his formal innovations and his reputation as a modernist: on the way we read him and are influenced by him.

Thus, for example, Yvor Winters launched a powerful attack on Pound's practice in 1957. Writing from within a classical discourse, which opposed a rationalist category of ideas to an empiricist category of sensation, he claimed that in Pound 'what we get is sensory impression alone, and have no way of knowing whether we have had any ideas or not'.[24] Donald Davie's refutation has become a classic of Pound criticism and a springboard for a persuasive reading of his technique, from the Image–Vortex to the later Cantos. For Davie, Pound's practice is not a question of an associationism of ideas or of sensations, but of a third term – the *forma*:

> the point to be made is that Pound in the *Cantos* characteristically aims at re-creating not the concept, any or all of them, but rather the *forma*, the thing behind them and common to them all. By arranging sensory impressions he aims to state, not ideas, but the form behind and in ideas, the moment before that 'fine thing held in the mind' has precipitated out now this idea, now that.[25]

Davie arrives at this structural principle by linking and synthesising the quotation from 'Cavalcanti: Medievalism' cited above ('the radiant world') with the following passage from *Guide to Kulchur*:

> 'I made it out of a mouthful of air', wrote Bill Yeats in his heyday. The *forma*, the immortal *concetto*, the concept, the dynamic form which is like the rose pattern driven into the dead iron filings by the magnet, not by material contact with the magnet itself, but separate from the magnet. Cut off by the layer of glass, the dust and filings rise and spring into order. Thus the *forma*, the concept rises from death. . . .[26]

In other words, Davie is using Pound's own term, and its scientific terminology, to offer a notion of objective energetic form, which he then uses to explain what he demonstrates to be at work in *The Cantos*.

Davie extends his defence in a later work by relating these Poundian terms to other confirmations. Returning to the same issue ('Ideas in the Cantos'), he adduces Pound's 'vortex' and a contemporary analogue from Allen Upward – the 'ontwerp' (or 'throw-out') – to elaborate and make more precise the notion of *forma*. He thereby arrives at the basic formal principle of the double vortex or waterspout/ fountain.[27] It is to be noted that this complex of images is used not only as a clarifying explanatory device to account for poetic practice; it is also used to *validate* that practice in the face of objections such as Winters's – and to validate it as a specifically *modernist* practice.

The validation follows from the fact that the *forma* is, once more, not an 'idea' in the pejoratively idealist sense of insubstantial subjectivity, but is related to an objective structure in the world, as guaranteed specifically by modern science:

> Upward has too much respect for the honest materialist – in particular, for the physicist of his day – to forget, when he turns to look at the *im*materialist (or as he must call him, following Alfred Nobel, the *idealist*), how the materialist conceives of matter as knotted and equally opposed strengths, as in the wrestlers who tremble as they lock. This *is* the nature of matter. . . .[28]

Davie emphatically endorses the Pound–Upward model of material and immaterial energetic form. Lest Upward's metaphor for the conception of matter proposed by his contemporary physicists collapse back into its historical and metaphorical moment, he immediately supports it with a more up-to-date scientific reference: 'Upward of course did not live to see this inspired guess "at the first beat" astonishingly confirmed experimentally, when the bio-physicists Crick and Watson broke the genetic code to reveal "the double-helix" (that's to say, double-vortex).'[29]

In this way, Winters's objection is answered by means of a description of Pound's practice which, in using his own scientific metadiscourse, expanded, elaborated and updated, is also inevitably an endorsement. Pound works not with Winters's traditional philosophical categories, but with a modern third category: the *forma*. The *forma* is 'a process by which locked energies narrow into a cone, reverse themselves at its apex and thereafter flower as it were upside-down and inside-out'.[30] It is the poetic equivalent to the formal process which modern science has revealed to be objective and fundamental – not mystical or even philosophical 'ideas', but the formal structure of genetic creation itself. Or, as Pound would put it, 'Poetry agrees with science and not with logic.'[31] This argument, which may begin as a principle of explanation for Pound's actual poetic practice, precisely because it uses a scientific reference, becomes an aggressive validation of that practice in terms of *modern scientific reality*.

The argument is compulsive inasmuch as it is the characteristic of scientific discourse to grant affirmation a particular rhetorical authority in its effects of factuality, foundation, evidentiality, precision, reality, objectivity and universality. We call Pound's structural principle or process the *forma*, and we explicate it not only in terms of myth and mysticism, but also in terms of 'the rose in the steel dust' or the 'double-vortex', which we in turn explain in terms of the contemporary scientific 'facts' which themselves gave rise to the metaphor in the first place. What is lost in the argument which concludes that the *forma* has a scientific base is the originally *metaphorical* status of the scientific reference.

Far from being the most transparent and self-evident of discourses, science is in fact the most specialised and hence, for non-specialists, the most *mediated*. The 'fact' is always transformed by its mediation. Science thus provides metadiscursive validation not by bases of evidence, but by metaphors which mediate the 'fact'.

The 'rose in the steel dust' has connotations of a precise invisible structure of real existence which generates patterns, and is usable in a context of communication. It is a useful image, since it refers to a dramatic series of scientific events in the latter half of the nineteenth century, from James Clerk Maxwell's experiments and hypotheses concerning the electromagnetic nature of light and the existence of the ether to the development of wireless technology at the turn of the century – of significance to the history of science and to many key formulations and values in Pound. Gaston Bachelard makes an important point about Maxwell's hypotheses: 'Une telle soudure de deux phénoménologies aussi diverses que l'électricité et l'optique suggère des significations nouvelles. Autrement dit, les phénomènes immédiats, soit optiques, soit électriques, prennent de nouveaux sens.'[32] In other words, an equation puts into theoretical relation two orders of phenomena in which the individual phenomenal events potentially embraced by that relation are transformed by it. New phenomenal, conceptual and discursive conjunctures are made available, altering the meanings of their elements.

But the process by which this occurs is far from immediate: such new conjunctures and meanings have to be produced and recuperated by means of material processes of mediation. Within science, these involve progressive theoretical, experimental and technical refinement and development, in which new meanings are determined by the material necessities of scientific invention – the laws of the laboratory. But before this can affect the meanings of immediate phenomena – material and conceptual – in the public world, it has to undergo processes of socialisation.

The technical invention of science has to be transformed into a *technological product* (for example, the transformation of the iron-filing experiment and its chain into the wireless). Here the new meanings are determined by technological and economic values. We then experience these products in our everyday lives. Here the new meanings are governed by a *phenomenology of commodities*. But this process of social production is incomplete without the equally important process of mediation in terms of ideas and of language. New meanings have also to be mediated through a process of the *popularisation of science* in discourse, at the level of both terminology and epistemology. In this case, not only learned philosophical papers and professional 'Introductions to Science', but also pseudo-science and science fiction, are involved.

As the theory moves along the chains of mediation, it is naturally restricted, displaced, expanded and altered in terms of the new meanings produced. It is a question of register, or context: at each level, the iron-filing experiment, or the theory of electromagnetism, has different significances, different fascinations, different pre-dications and different functions. The process of production of new meanings is governed, and those meanings transformed, by scientific values, technological and economic values, and phenomenological, linguistic and ideological values. Our understanding of what is meant by 'nuclear power' should offer an example which does not require elaboration.

What then is the relation between these different series of mediation? They are clearly not autonomous. But, inasmuch as they obey different modes of production, different material imperatives, we can say that they are not identical. Inasmuch as it *is* scientific – inasmuch, that is, as the scientist is subject to rational laws of theory and the material laws of the laboratory rather than his ideological investment in his profession – there is a major transformation between the scientific product and the social product, be it commodity or discourse. It is for this reason that the invoking of 'science' does not guarantee the *truth* of a derived affirmation. But it does, on the other hand, because of the particular rhetorical authority of scientific terminology and syntax, affect its *acceptability*.

There are two dimensions to this question, the first relating directly to Pound, the second to his critics and hence his reputation. With respect to the first, as I have stated elsewhere,[33] an analysis of Pound's fascism is not satisfied by elucidating his 'beliefs' in order to show that his fascism was a consequence of his proto-fascist beliefs. It is rather a question of seeing how those beliefs come to be inscribed, and particularly how the inscribing *masks* their contradictions and absences. That is the question of acceptability: the means by which the ideological masquerades as knowledge, or partiality as 'truth'. If Pound's ideology determines and is determined by his poetic practice, we have to be able to account for how specific ideas and techniques are rendered acceptable to each other, and how the process by which that happens affects the extension of the value, particularly into the sphere of politics. Thus, for example, we might seek to analyse how the 'Old World' mystical values are successfully mediated into a 'New World Poem', how a mythic technique offers itself as appropriate to a modern world, or how, more generally, one can generate a synthesis of conception and objectivity.

Clearly the intervention of a scientific discourse does much to achieve this. But, in being a scientific discourse, it also has political consequences: the 'truth' that science makes acceptable is not, for example, the limited, exclusive truth of nineteenth-century religious mysticism or of contemporary relativist idealism. It is an 'objective', 'universal' and, perhaps most importantly of all, an 'impersonal' truth, and hence politically predicatable. In short, the successful intervention of a scientific discourse renders subjective truths acceptable as it simultaneously makes them 'objective'. This is, one might add, not a merely personal matter. The poet (or politician) can only employ a scientific discourse successfully if the contemporary public scientific language permits it. In this way, the ideological product may be analysed in terms of its relation to its surrounding historical context. It is not reducible to a personal vision, but expresses an adaptation of a public discourse.

The second aspect of the question of acceptability concerns Pound's critics, and hence his reputation and influence. The resistance or indifference of major schools of criticism in respect of Pound has given an important role to his explicators, commentators and defenders. The extent to which they have used not only his own vocabulary but also his scientific metadiscourse is significant, and has had a considerable effect on his influence. We have already seen this at work in Donald Davie – and the same case can be made in respect of Hugh Kenner. In this sense, Pound's poetics and their scientific framework as reproduced in the critics operate less as a simple elaboration of his practice and more as a complex mediation of it. Once again, because this is 'science', it makes a claim for the practice of a powerful sort. In making Pound's practice acceptable, such critics have made an implicit or explicit claim for that practice, in terms of its consonance with modern scientific reality, as in Max Nänny's symptomatical title for his study of Pound: *Ezra Pound: Poetics for an Electric Age*.[34]

We can, however, theoretically disarm this rhetorical authority by asserting that science is produced for social consumption by a highly mediated, ideologically fraught, historical process. The point of the assertion is not to accuse either Pound or his critics of being in error over the 'nature of things'. That would merely be to offer an alternative scientific metaphor to their own, and to seek acceptance through a similar process ('this is *not* the nature of matter'). What it does enable us to say is that Pound's poetics are informed by a *scientific discourse* without necessarily being a reflection of an *objective reality*, and hence without that being a guarantee of his achievement in those terms. In this way I shall argue that Pound's poetics and practice are most certainly modernist, not because they reflect an objective modern scientific reality, but because they reflect a specific 'modernist' historical ideology of science. In this way we might explain also how Pound's poetics become in their own way a victim of ideological contradictions already contained but masked in the discourse which he employs, and which helps transform his own.

III

One needs, therefore, to put Pound's 'science' into its historical context: to see what values it invokes, what model of science underwrites it, under what conditions it became acceptable to employ the sort of metadiscourse that characterises Pound's poetics. We have already observed some of the fields of science most commonly invoked – for our purposes, hitherto, electricity, electromagnetism, electrostatics, wireless technology, force and radiation. They all refer to a notion of *energy*, which is used to confirm and substantiate material, invisible forces and structures, generally of a synthetic nature, and to give concreteness, a sort of materiality – or at least substantiality – to ideas, communication and relations. Such energies have been invoked according to a principle of *analogy*, pertaining to the energies themselves, and extending to the energies of thought, emotion and poetic communication. Thus, whilst specialised literary energies are linked to modern electromagnetic or radiant energies, their control, according to principles of precision and economy and objectivity and conception, has placed the artist in the position of a scientist of the immaterial. At the same time, the constructive network of analogies has been set to confirm the mystical perceptions of the Old World in more precise and objective modern forms.

The 'rose in the steel dust' was an image of objective energetic form. But the poet as scientist cannot be satisfied with the passivity of the iron filings; these energies must be controlled, as Pound made clear in 1915:

> The vorticist is expressing his complex consciousness. He is not like the iron filings, expressing electrical magnetism; not like the automatist, expressing a state of cell-memory, a vegetable or visceral energy. Not, however, that one despises vegetable energy. . . . One, as a human being, cannot pretend fully to express oneself unless one express instinct and intellect together. The softness and the ultimate failure of interest in automatic painting are caused by a complete lack of conscious intellect. Where does this bring us? It brings us to this: Vorticism is a legitimate expression of life.[35]

Once again, Pound distinguishes himself from regressive mysticism and passivity in offering a modern synthesis: the expression of objective forces, synthesised with intellectual creativity, produces 'a legitimate expression of life'. In this way, the creative, conceptual element of Vorticism is brought to bear on the objective energies of the 'rose in the steel dust'.

How then does this application of 'conception' to the structures of energy remain 'scientific'? The principal formulations that Pound uses for his synthetic model come from mathematics, which is privileged in epistemological terms as a complement to the privilege accorded to physics in phenomenological terms. In 'Vorticism' (1914), Pound distinguishes four levels of mathematics, in a hierarchy from description to conception:

> *Fourthly*, we come to Descartian or 'analytical geometry'. Space is conceived as separated by two or three axes. . . . One refers points to these axes by a series of co-ordinates. Given the idiom, one is able *actually to create*.
>
> Thus, we learn that the equation $(x-a)^2 + (y-b)^2 = r^2$ governs the circle. It is the circle. It is not a particular circle, it is any circle and all circles. It is nothing that is not a circle. It is the circle free of space and time limits. It is the universal, existing in perfection, in freedom from space and time. Mathematics is dull ditchwater until one reaches analytics. But in analytics we come upon a new way of dealing with form. It is in this way that art handles

life. The difference between art and analytic geometry is the difference of subject-matter only. Art is more interesting in proportion as life and the human consciousness are more complex and more interesting than forms and numbers.[36]

This might remind us of the critique of Ford's limiting receptivity: 'no impression . . . can, recorded, convey that feeling of sudden light which works of art can and must convey'; or of the definition of the Image: 'that sense of freedom from time limits and space limits; that sense of sudden growth, which we experience in the presence of the greatest works of art'.[37] Here the mathematical analogy transforms the subjective act of conception and the Longinian sublime with which it is associated in this poetics of liberation into absolute and impersonal form.

But the analogy is not a simple equation between the poet and the mathematician; it is qualified by their different subject matters. This is more explicit in 'The Wisdom of Poetry' (1912):

What the analytical geometer does for space and form, the poet does for the states of consciousness. . . . By the signs $a^2 + b^2 = c^2$, I imply the circle. By $(a-r)^2 + (b-r)^2 = (c-r)^2$, I imply the circle and its mode of birth. I am led from the consideration of the particular circles formed by my ink-well and my table-rim, to the contemplation of the circle absolute, its law; the circle free in all space, unbounded, loosed from the accidents of time and place. Is the formula nothing, or is it cabala and the sign of unintelligible magic? The engineer, understanding and translating for the many, builds for the uninitiated bridges and devices. He speaks their language. For the initiated the signs are a door into eternity and into the boundless ether.

As the abstract mathematician is to science so is the poet to the world's consciousness. Neither has direct contact with the many, neither of them is superhuman or arrives at his utility through occult and inexplicable ways. Both are scientifically demonstrable.[38]

The 'serious artist' becomes the scientist of immaterial man by adopting a mathematical practice of conception in relation to man's consciousness.

The scientificity of the artist – his provision of the data of psychology and metaphysics – rests then on a *coupling* of the 'mathematician' and 'psychologist':

Now that mechanical science has realised his ancient dreams of flight and sejunct communication, [the poet] is the advance guard of the psychologist on the watch for new emotions, new vibrations sensible to faculties as yet ill defined. . . . the poet's true and lasting relation to literature and life is that of the abstract mathematician to science and life.[39]

This curious double term of the mathematician–psychologist is constructed from a number of localised metaphoric conjunctions, and serves to justify the assessment of the scientific psychology of, for example, Cavalcanti, and the *psychological scientificity of myth*. Thus we find in *The Spirit of Romance* that 'Poetry is a sort of inspired mathematics, which gives us equations, not for abstract figures, triangles, spheres, and the like, but equations for the human emotions.'[40] We have already seen how this produces a theory of myth – 'a work of art that is – an impersonal and objective story woven out of his own emotions, as the nearest equation that he was capable of putting into words'.[41] Finally, again in the article 'Vorticism' (1914), Pound invokes the coupling in almost direct reference to the first poem by him in the Imagiste anthology, 'Doria':

> Great works of art contain this fourth sort of equation. They cause form to come into being. By the 'image' I mean such an equation; not an equation of mathematics, not something about *a*, *b*, and *c*, having something to do with form, but about *sea*, *cliffs*, *night*, having something to do with mood.[42]

We can see from these brief but significant examples how this conjunction not only registers the synthesis of conception and objectivity, but also plays a part in the scientific validation of mythological and mystical practice, of form and the theory of the Image.

We need then to ask how it is that this mathematician–psychologist can be produced, and how such a discourse can validate a 'science' of 'immaterial man' and a principle of form. How does the creative equation become associated with objectivity and impersonality? How may it be conjoined with psychological material? In other words, we have to consider the status and function of mathematics and of psychology and of their conjuncture within science. In identifying the epistemology which underwrites these associations, we shall also find, in due course, to what extent it accords with much of Pound's poetics;

how, more precisely, the 'object' is, as it were, dematerialised, and 'objectivity' hence relocated as a mathematical *relation* extrapolated from concrete sensation as a reflection of the structures of energy; and how analogy becomes an epistemological principle – all of which has important consequences for Pound's poetic theory and practice.

IV

Towards the end of the nineteenth century a major crisis in science took place, in which Clerk Maxwell and Heinrich Hertz made a major contribution. Up to this point, a mechanicist Newtonian world view had dominated scientific, and hence general, thought. This world view was based on the solid material atom existing in a neutral space. Clerk Maxwell had proposed, and Hertz had demonstrated, that 'all electrical and magnetic phenomena could be interpreted in terms of the stresses and motions of a material medium'.[43] 'Space' was not a neutral area in which 'action-at-a-distance' was, as in the Newtonian model, instantaneous, but an invisible material medium in which electrical and magnetic phenomena were shown to move with a finite and measurable speed:

> The advent of Maxwell's theory is of the greatest significance in providing a firmly experimentally-based theory of electromagnetism, of complete internal consistency, but which is incompatible with Newtonian mechanics and Galilean relativity. This incompatibility becomes the more apparent the more the experimental implications are explored.[44]

In short, traditional materialist discourses were *gradually* being revealed as inadequate to the new facts. Elsewhere, physicists were advancing through the discovery of the electron (Lorentz, 1892), X-rays (Röntgen, 1895), radium (1898), cathode rays and intra-atomic energy. As these discoveries were made, each of them gradually and further undermined the dominant scientific model. In 1908, Henri Poincaré, the French mathematician and epistemologist, was forced to recognise that six basic principles of physics had been endangered by the discoveries that physics had itself made: Carnot's principle of the degradation of energy, the principle of Galilean relativity, Newton's principle of the equality of action and reaction, Lavoisier's law of the conservation of mass, Mayer's law of the conservation of energy, and the principle of least action.[45]

We find ourselves, then, in a period of *transition*: from the gradual breakdown of the mechanicist universe to the gradual emergence of a science based in energetics. We should not at this point forget the profoundly negative weight that this mechanicist universe bore for the 'life of the spirit' in the latter half of the nineteenth century, effectively an index of the alienation caused by the technological advance of industrial capitalism. On the other hand, we should also bear in mind that the problems raised by its gradual collapse did not begin to be recuperated until the establishment and acceptance of Einstein's theories and their later elaboration (and it is to be noted that the 1905 and 1915 theories were hardly known until after the First World War – in 1908, for example, Poincaré does not mention Einstein in his review of the crisis in physics).

Hence what we find in this interim is a range of reactions: there are idealists and vitalists who rejoice in the collapse of Science, as they see it, and materialists who attempt elaborate holding-actions on its behalf.[46] A third area, as I have observed elsewhere,[47] saw the threat to mechanicism not as reason for consternation, nor as an opportunity for aggressive anti-scientism, but, on the contrary, as a new promise for science. This promise was characteristically not restricted to the problems of the ether (the invisible material medium of space), but extended beyond what was newly constituting science, in order to claim the new area in advance for science, rather than using the revolution to claim science for mystical agnosticism. Gustave LeBon, the discoverer of intra-atomic energy, for example, sets the tone:

> It is hardly to be imagined that the forces of nature are limited to those with which we are acquainted. . . . During the last twenty years, science has annexed the Hertzian waves, the X-rays, the cathode rays, the radioactive rays, and intra-atomic energy to the small kingdom of forces known of old. It is difficult to believe that the end of these discoveries is reached; and mighty forces surround us without our knowing it.[48]

There thus arose a positive scientific language of energetics before there existed a recuperating theory to secure it. The discourse was, however, very popular, since, being based in a physics of invisible energies into which the old solid matter was dissolving, it offered the possibility of escaping the materialism/vitalism debate through a third term which could be used to unify a wider totality of experience for science.

At the same time, it made available a discourse for revalidating antique perceptions hitherto threatened by mechanicism. Thus, for example, J. Arthur Thomson, in his popular book for the Home University Library series, launched in 1911 – *An Introduction to Science* – was able to assert that 'Science never destroys wonder, but only shifts it, higher and deeper.'[49] He saw the new science and its promise as a potential resynthesis of scientific and poetic experience: 'Looking at radium-containing rock and the like with modern spectacles, we get a glimpse of the powers – like charmed genii – that may be imprisoned in the apparently inert dust.'[50] The promise extends in two directions: first towards a restoration of poetry as knowledge: 'what we sometimes call Fairy Tales, many of which are *artistic expressions of very sound science*';[51] and secondly towards a reinvestment of wonder in the material world – as he writes of the ancient personal relation of man to nature:

> the modern forester may lose this with the change in the world's pace, but there comes to him instead, in proportion as he knows his business, a vision of the tree translucent, with its intricate architecture and its intense life. 'The Dryad, living and breathing, moving and sensitive, is again within the tree.'[52]

The extension of this promise of energetics can, as I have likewise argued, be seen to constitute a body of discourse, a paradigm, in the collective practice of the Society for Psychical Research (founded 1882), which used such a synthetic discourse of energetics to produce a coherent paradigm of a scientific and not a metaphysical or mystical account of non-material phenomena. Generally speaking, it achieved this largely through a similar use of analogical links between modern energetic phenomena and other immaterial energies – for example:

> the theory of 'ectenic' or 'psychic force' . . . attributes the phenomena to some extension in space of the nervous force of the medium, just as the power of a magnet, or of an electric current, extends beyond itself and can influence and move certain distant bodies which lie within the field of the magnetic or electric force.[53]

Radium and the ether substantiated the proposition that there were forces and objects in nature which defy Newtonian explanation but which may none the less be deemed scientific by the progressive new science. Hertz's discoveries in the field of electromagnetism, in producing a field of energy and a spectrum of waves, enact the logical principle of an extensive gradation of these forces. The guarantee of scientificity for the Society is its commitment to scientific method – precision, economy and objectivity; or, as William James wrote in an affirmation important to Pound's strategy: 'The spirit and principles of science are mere affairs of method; there is nothing in them that need hinder science from dealing successfully with a world in which personal forces are the starting-point of new effects.'[54]

In this way, we may take the Society as providing a public discursive model which underwrites Pound's use of 'energy' in pursuit of scientific synthesis and a scientific discourse of the mystical. We can thus demonstrate how Pound's practice corresponds not to a direct scientific reality, but to a *discursive use of science* permitted and practised within a specific stage of scientific crisis. This crisis and the terminologies it threw up were popularised in such a way as to open a possibility (amongst others) for such a synthetic discourse as we have seen in Pound. But the crisis is also constituted by a radical shift in epistemology which also informs Pound's model of science – especially in terms of the synthesis of conception and objectivity.

The revolution in physics was leading to a point where science seemed to be negating its own laws, and hence a reconsideration of the epistemological status of scientific law was called for. It is generally agreed that it was Ernst Mach who was the first to respond to the discoveries of physics and to initiate the necessary critique which, in the face of the proven inaccuracy of what had been taken for unshakably truthful laws, sought to recuperate the scientificity of scientific law in modern terms. As Thomas Szasz writes,

Until the turn of the century . . . it was thought that the proper aim of 'Science' was to produce 'objective descriptions' of nature and to formulate these economically by theories which are 'true'. Mach challenged this illusory security of 'science' and 'truth' which was associated with Newtonian physics.[55]

The confidence of Newtonian science rested on the notion that science was a direct ('true') reflection of nature. Mach's recognition was that science was a *mediated* vision in which the subject (the scientist) was not directly confronting a transparent and absolute nature but rather knew that world only through the sensations in which it was experienced and the categories in which these sensations were organised. 'Things-in-themselves' were unknowable, and the scientific discourse which had claimed to be reflecting and recording this reality in direct objective description in the Newtonian mode was in fact producing only *fictions* of such 'things-in-themselves' – like the solid atom. These fictions were revealed as such by their recent collapse. Mach argued that, far from science being a transparent view of a true nature, the current upheaval proved that it was operated by the *metaphysical assumptions* which intervene in and *organise our perceptions* of the world. In opposition to this, 'Mach sought to reformulate Newtonian mechanics from a phenomenalist standpoint.'[56]

Within this perspective, the job of the scientist therefore becomes the critique of these assumptions – now revealed as the unconscious object of the old science – so that they cease to dominate the genuine concrete experience and its rational formulation which constitute true science. Attention is thus focused on the notion of *science as a language*. Science is no longer to be defined by a self-evident material ('things-in-themselves' – which, in any case, were dissolving into invisible energy), but as *a* reflection of the universe dependent, like any other reflection, on its principles of organisation. Hence follows a proposal of importance to Pound's epistemological model; the English Machist Karl Pearson argues

> The law of gravitation is not so much the discovery by Newton of a rule guiding the motion of the planets as his invention of a method of briefly describing the sequences of sense-impressions, which we term planetary motion. . . . The statement of this formula was not so much the discovery as the *creation* of the law of gravitation. A natural law is thus seen to be a *résumé* in mental shorthand, which replaces for us a lengthy description of the sequences among our sense impressions. Law in the scientific sense is thus essentially a product of the human mind and has no meaning apart from man. It owes its existence to the creative power of his intellect.[57]

The key values, then, are the primacy of sense impressions, and their creative construction, on a principle of economy, by language.

Since science is no longer a set of objective laws, an accumulated body of knowledge, guaranteed by the absolute reality of its material object, but only a particular form of creative language, its objectivity must come to be guaranteed by the properties of that language. That is to say that, as science becomes defined not by its content but by its method (an important step as much for Pound as for the Psychical Researchers), and since there is no science without a notion of necessity, this language, though mediated by a subject, must remain objective and universal. Its principles of organisation have to guarantee the special properties of scientific language. Mach's path therefore aimed first at expelling metaphysical assumptions by developing a *critical* language, held for its self-conscious non-metaphysical precision and 'objectivity' in treating sense experience. Only thereby may one achieve the language of true knowledge as opposed to that of metaphysical fictions.

Mach was seeking to produce a science which responded to the new energetic reality. The contradiction between the nature that was revealing itself and the mechanistic laws that were unsuccessfully trying to contain it led to the conclusion that the mechanical regularities and categories of scientific law were not natural facts, but actually *subjective constructs*: 'Nature exists once only. Our schematic mental imitation alone produces like events. Only in the mind, therefore, does the mutual dependence of certain features exist.'[58] Further, if the failure of materialist, mechanicist science revealed the metaphysical assumptions on which it had unconsciously and erroneously rested – the concept of Matter, of the solid atom, of Absolute Time and Space – then critical attention must first direct itself to the basic constituent of this language, the 'heart of the matter' of materialism: *substance*. Mach writes, 'All our efforts to mirror the world in thought would be futile if we found nothing permanent in the varied changes of things. It is this that impels us to form the notion of substance.'[59] In a world of emerging energies, the materiality of materialism is revealed as a subjective, metaphysical, constructed fiction.

It is, however, important to note that this switch of subject and object (from substance to mental category) is not posited as entailing the assumption of a position of idealism. For the illusory category of substance and the metaphysical category of objective nature ('things-in-themselves') are substituted by a new complementary emphasis on empirical experience as the basis of reality: Mach's central category of 'elements of sensation'. As Karl Pearson explains, 'Of what is beyond . . . "things-in-themselves", as the metaphysicians term them, we can know but one characteristic, and this we can only describe as a capacity for producing sense-impressions, for sending messages along the sensory nerves to the brain.'[60] The object, as solid, substantial element of matter, is thus replaced by the notion of the *phenomenon*: 'Any group of sense-impressions we project outside ourselves and hold to be part of the external world. As such we call it a *phenomenon*, and in practical life term it *real*.'[61]

The phenomenon is a constructed fiction of the real based not in metaphysics but in the concrete reality of sensation, and is mediated by processes of association. This redefinition of scientific reality and the scientific object (phenomenon and elements of sensation) produces a central and radical correction to the revealed pseudo-objectivity of Newtonian science:

> It thus comes to pass that we form the notion of a substance distinct from its attributes, of a thing-in-itself, whilst our sensations are regarded merely as symbols or indications of the properties of this thing-in-itself. But it would be better to say that *bodies or things are compendious mental symbols for groups of sensations* – symbols that do not exist outside of thought.   (Emphasis added)[62]

A crucial inversion in the language of science thus takes place. Instead of 'real things' being signified by sensations (materialism), sensations are represented by constructed 'things' or 'substances' which are merely signifiers of groups of sensations. In short we can say that in the Machist school *the 'object' is shifted from the level of the signified to that of the signifier*.

This shift is, as we shall see later, of major importance to Pound's poetics and his practice. But we also find in the Machists a basis for his characteristic synthesis of conception and objectivity – a conjunction which in fact follows from this shift. Mach's 'empirio-criticism', as it is known, is not a simple empiricism, despite its basic emphasis on sensational experience, since it concerns itself as much with the constructivism of 'the creative imagination'[63] as with the empiricism of sensation. As we have already seen, pure sensation would be merely an undifferentiated mass of unique events. In order to turn this into knowledge, it has to be organised according to processes of association. In this, the scientific method 'proceeds from the direct – what might perhaps be termed the physical – association of memory, to the indirect or mental association; it passes from *perceiving* to *conceiving*'.[64] The accurate recording of real experience, the concrete base of science, is of course crucial and leads to the privileging of values of economy and precision as guarantees of scientificity; but this is only the first necessary step towards a fully scientific discourse for the Machists:

> When the aim of Science is spoken of as 'description' the word is
> used in a slightly technical sense. There is a preliminary description
> which is not more than a faithful record of observations. . . . But
> this is only intellectual photography, good, but only as a means to an
> end – to a higher kind of description which is characteristically
> scientific.[65]

This 'higher kind of description' is the language of *formula* and *law*. In
this passage from recorded impressions and observations to
constructive law, scientific discourse appears in short to model the very
route from Impressionism (of which it might also be said, 'good, but
only as a means to an end') to Imagisme.

Records of sense impressions have, then, to be subjected to a
conceptual language which is simultaneously a *convenience* of
expression (in resuming that experience) and a *critical safeguard*
against misrecognised metaphysics: 'All laws', as Poincaré observes,
'are . . . deduced from experiment; but to enunciate them, a special
language is needful.'[66] Science is a language, but a language of a
special sort. Not only does it need to be precise and economical, but it
also has to be amenable to constructive generalisation in law. This
special language, especially for the physicist, is hence basically
mathematical, and specifically analytical. That is to say that laws
cannot be derived immediately from experiment because initial
measurement, however precise, is already, by virtue of its economy
and the inevitably constructive element, none the less only
approximate to a reality which is defined as resistant to mechanical
regularity. Thus specific operations are required to determine the
permanent tendency beneath the approximative scatter of figures.
Two basic mathematical operations achieve this: the first is algebraic
(the substitution of letters of variable value in a conventional system
for quantities); and the second is geometric (plotting a graph through a
mean of a range of values). The two operations come together in
analytic geometry, and thus we find Mach installing such a
mathematics at the *centre* of scientific language:

> The aim of research is the discovery of the equations which subsist
> between the elements of phenomena. The equation of an ellipse
> expresses the universal *conceivable* relation between its co-
> ordinates, of which only the real values have *geometrical*
> significance. Similarly, the equations between the elements of

phenomena express a universal, mathematically conceivable relation.[67]

We must remember that this privileged mathematical model or language is based on an extrapolation from real sensational experience, whose accurate record continues to be the anchor of scientific truth. It is, moreover, scientifically productive in a further related sense. The concrete experience/experiment is by nature pluralistic: 'Every particular truth may evidently be extended in an infinity of ways . . . it is necessary to make a choice, at least provisional.'[68] In the context of continuous energies, where the entire universe is constantly in play in any particular event, the scientist needs a means by which he can select the significant relations involved in phenomena. Poincaré asks, 'In this choice, what shall guide us?'; and he answers, 'It can only be analogy. But how vague is this word! Primitive man knew only crude analogies, those which strike the sense, those of colours and sounds. He never would have dreamt of likening light to radiant heat.'[69]

But it is precisely this *higher form of analogy* which mathematics can provide: it extrapolates from potentially infinite series of individual concrete events a variable *signifier of relations* which can then be displaced and applied analogically. On this basis, Mach constructs his theory of the special language of science in terms of *relational analogy*: 'That relationship between systems of ideas in which the dissimilarity of every two homologous concepts as well as the agreement in logical relations of every two homologous pairs of concepts, is clearly brought to light, is called an *analogy*.'[70] If science is a method and a language, and that language is mathematical, then the privileged conceptual instrument of science is this principle of relational analogy. It is, moreover, for Mach, 'an effective means of mastering heterogeneous fields of facts in unitary comprehension' and offers itself finally as a pathway to a totalisation of experience and truth, '*a universal physical phenomenology* embracing all domains'.[71]

Empirio-criticism thus proposes a global system of formal conceived relations, drawn from the experience of phenomena, which may be signified by objects but does not in any case cease really to signify concrete experience. The problem it faces is to avoid the theory collapsing back into subjectivism on the basis of the constructive and empirical components. This science, which in fact does remain fundamentally subjectivist, has to guarantee necessity and objectivity for itself. It does so basically by asserting four things.

In the first place, it posits a necessity in the perceptions on which the scientific law is based, inasmuch as perception reflects the energetic structures which determine sensation, in being relational: 'The order in which we arrange conscious phenomena does not admit of any arbitrariness. It is imposed upon us.'[72] This assertion relies on the possibility of a scientific account of the very processes of perception – which leads us, in due course, to the central position to be held in this epistemology by psychology. In the meantime, since the 'objectivity' of this necessity cannot be drawn from the materiality of the 'object' (which is after all, merely a classification of sensation), it equally well cannot be drawn from the pure subjectivity of the *quality* of sensation. Thus the second major assertion posits the *objectivity of relation*:

> Sensations are . . . intransmissible, or rather all that is pure quality in them is intransmissable and forever impenetrable. But it is not the same with relations between these sensations. From this point of view, all that is objective is devoid of all quality and is only pure relation.[73]

Necessary sensational experience is then freed from its subjective limitations of quality by being expressed in objective relations of scientific law, according to principles of relational analogy. Such laws are the result of an act of conception based on discursive conventions and forms which have a value of convenience in rendering experience comprehensible. But this act of conception – which is used by the empirio-critics to attack the subjective and metaphysical bases of the materialist convention – is saved from collapsing into the idealism of which they accuse the mechanicists by a third assertion which raises the *intersubjectivity* of conception and convention to the level of *universality*:

> It will be said that science is only a classification and that a classification can not be true, but convenient. But it is true that it is convenient, it is true that it is so not only for me, but for all men; it is true that it will remain convenient for our descendants; it is true finally that this cannot be by chance.
>
> In sum, the sole objective reality consists in the relation of things whence results the universal harmony. . . . [such classifications of relations] are . . . objective because they are, will become, will remain, common to all thinking beings.[74]

This assertion thus depends on a humanisation of the subject, by which his constructive laws and their analogic structure gain universal status.

The universality, objectivity and necessity of scientific law is, however, further guaranteed by a fourth and crucial assertion: that there is a determining interaction between the world of nature and the subject who experiences that world in terms of his conceptions of phenomena and their relations (the 'continua', in Poincaré's terms, within which we classify experience), and hence that universal conventions do in fact, through the necessity of the sequences of experience, the objectivity of pure relation and the universality of the human subject, reflect natural relations. As Poincaré writes, 'It is the external world which has imposed the continuum upon us, which we doubtless have invented, but which it has forced us to invent.'[75] This is the characteristic empirio-critical sentence in which the complex movement of the theory is expressed: we construct the world in thought, but that construction is determined by the necessary relations experienced and conceptualised in our sensational experience of the world, translated, through a language of conceptual convention, into law.

In sum, the negative part of the empirio-critical critique raises the subjectivity of science as it was then conceived. It takes 'objective descriptions' of 'things-in-themselves' and reveals them to be fictions whose truth is not objective reality, but their own subjective categorisations which operated the description and were registered in their language. Thus the material of the former science was unwittingly its own language and metaphysical assumptions. The solid atom, for example, did not signify an object in nature, but a hypothetical category in thought. The positive polemic replaces the fiction of 'things' and 'substance' with 'elements of sensation', the experience of phenomena. The subjective element is theoretically returned to its proper place, and 'objective description' is replaced with the critical language of conception and convention. This creative subject in science produces laws and formulae which are the scientific reflection of relations between phenomena in the conventional language of mathematics, governed by a global principle of analogy. Under the control of experience, these formulae reveal the perceptual and conceptual necessities that nature imposes on us, which once confirmed by experiment, thus become 'objective, universal, impersonal' and 'scientifically valid'.

The particularity of the Machists lies in the conjunction of their label: 'empirio-criticism' – a coupling of experiential, concrete reality through sensation with the recognition of the constructive instrumentality of concepts. The one without the other would present a very different picture: straightforward empiricist sensationalism on the one hand; simple idealism on the other. This group, however, manages to synthesise the two tendencies in their complex discourse. The combination is certainly problematic, but discursively successful. In the first part of their critique, against mechanism, the Machists are aggressively subjectivist; in the second part, where they seek to recuperate criteria of scientificity, they have to claim that their critical subjective approach is not mere subjectivism. Thanks to what are ultimately ambiguous models of sensation, subjectivity and language, they are able to recover objectivity and universality at another level. In order to do this they have to assert necessity in perception and raise relational sensation and analogical conception to a level of human universality which can then be affirmed as objective. This is where a science of psychology becomes vital to the model.

V

The Machists' central proposition – that they brought critical attention to bear on the modes of experience and the metaphysical assumptions used to organise them – led them necessarily towards the establishment of a centralised science of psychology. Where, for example, Berkeley had posited sensation as a primary but metaphysical category – with reference to the philosophical nature of reality – the Machists made it a scientific problem in terms of the study of psycho-physiology. This is the shift behind, for example, Mach's *Analysis of Sensations* (1885), where the Newtonian 'metaphysical' categories of Absolute Space and Time are subjected to a psycho-physiological critique founded on recent work in the field (in the tradition, as Mach makes clear, of Fechner's work in optics, for example). In this way we can see the Machists' entire science tending towards such a reflexive discourse; or, as Pearson writes, 'The progress of science is thus reduced to a more and more complete analysis of the perceptive faculty.'[76]

The centralisation of psychology and its conjunction with an objective language of mathematical law is not so much permitted by the new science as *predicated* by it: the Machist epistemology depends on a science of perception. The central term – 'elements of sensation' – is basically and deliberately ambiguous, looking simultaneously outward to objects (phenomena) and inward to the psycho–physics of perception: 'In this way, accordingly, we do not find the gap between bodies and sensations . . . between what is without and what is within, between the material world and the spiritual world.'[77] The division of phenomena and sensation is a merely arbitrary classification of what remains essentially a *continuous* universe of energies. This synthetic quality of 'elements of sensation' thus permits a most important assertion for this modernist epistemology: given the double reference of the ambiguous central term and the continuity to which it refers, 'From our standpoint, the antithesis of subject and object . . . does not exist.'[78]

Mach thus argues that,

> the great gulf between physical and psychological research persists only when we acquiesce in our habitual stereotyped conceptions. A color is a physical object as soon as we consider its dependence, for instance, upon its luminous source, upon other colors, upon temperatures, upon spaces, and so forth. When we consider, however, its dependence on the retina . . . it is a psychological object, a sensation. Not the subject-matter, but the direction of our investigation, is different in the two domains.[79]

One must then study both 'objects' (phenomena) and the sensations on which our perception of them depends – especially if one is to avoid being a victim of metaphysical assumptions which creep into our perceptual constructs. Looking out is physics; looking in, psychology: 'If we look at the matter in this unbiassed light it will appear indubitable that the method of physiological psychology is none other than that of physics; what is more, that this science is a part of physics.'[80] They are complementary methods of viewing the same 'object', and thus, 'The science of psychology is auxiliary to physics. The two mutually support one another, and it is only when they are united that a complete science is formed.'[81] Mach's position can thus be represented by the following model:

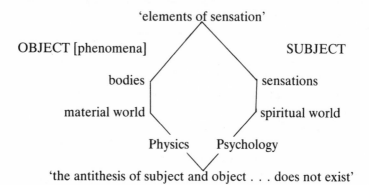

'elements of sensation'

OBJECT [phenomena]   SUBJECT

bodies   sensations

material world   spiritual world

Physics   Psychology

'the antithesis of subject and object . . . does not exist'

A scientific psychology of perception is therefore a necessary complement to the basic epistemological position of the Machists, and effectively the only grounds for the objectivity of their conceptual and perceptual critique. Since such a psychology must be defined as a science within the same epistemology, explicitly auxiliary to physics, it would likewise have to be formulated by laws along mathematical lines. Even so, we must note that this scientific psychology is restricted, for Mach, to the science of perception; it is not by any means the same thing as a psychological science of 'mood', 'emotion', 'purpose' or 'desire'.

The difficulty of extending the scientificity to a study of non-physiological psychology, so as to include specifically affective or conative experience, remains. Attempts to render such a science acceptable encountered considerable hostility at this time. But the hostility can be overcome by the use of an empirio-critical argument, which we can illustrate in the work of the psychologist whom Pound invoked as a scientific support for his 'Doctrine of the Image', Bernard Hart. Hart, in his turn, explicitly and crucially bases his case for a science of 'immaterial man, man as a thinking and sentient creature' on Pearson's empirio-criticism. As he reflected, in a useful summary of the argument, in 1927,

> The problem at issue is essentially a part of the wider problem as to whether psychology and interpretations in psychological terms have a right and a place in science. This claim was for a long time disputed, the opposition reaching its culmination in the materialistic philosophy of the Nineteenth century scientists, who held that psychology dealt with non-material and non-spatial processes which were 'epiphenomenal' and 'unreal', and therefore incapable of scientific treatment. Their view arose from two bases, the first being the unsatisfactory condition of the psychology of those days, for it was then an armchair production achieved by methods radically distinct from those which were proving successful in the building of chemistry, physics, and other science; while the second base was a *total misapprehension of the real nature of science. This misapprehension was cleared away by the work of Karl Pearson and other investigators. . . .*[82]

The main problem for such a psychology was the introduction of subjective categories of motivation: centrally that of 'purpose', which had been placed by Kant in the area of metaphysics. A mechanical, causality-based psychology – which would be a psychology of reception – is scientifically acceptable; but it would have to be a purely physiological psychology of the brain. Conversely, a science of *mind* requires a category of internal motivation, hitherto unacceptable to dominant scientific paradigms. Thus Hart finds that he has to counter the argument 'that the introduction of purpose as a determining factor is incompatible with the notion of causality, and that, as causality is the foundation stone of scientific method, no conception involving purpose can have a place in science'.[83]

Using the Machist argument that the objectivity of mechanicist science was a pragmatic subjective construct, Hart is enabled to convert causality itself into a 'mechanistic limitation of science'. Then, by exploiting their attack on the fiction of substance and the conceptual nature of scientific elements, he can give his category the same scientific status as the concepts of physics, as he refers ironically to 'The naive notion that [psychology] deals with flimsy abstractions unworthy of being ranked with such solid realities as electrons and ether waves.'[84] In summary, Hart presents an important statement which demonstrates the epistemological possibilities opened up by the empirio-critical argument:

A body of knowledge which has traversed only the first two steps [collection and description] has attained to the level of a descriptive science, but it is imperfect and inadequate until it has succeeded in passing on to the third step. This third step involves a transition from phenomena to concepts. The 'laws' which it formulates are not phenomena which can be observed in nature, but are constructed by the human mind in order to account for those phenomena. They are, in other words, conceptual abstractions whose sole claim to validity is that they do explain the observed facts. It is to be noted, moreover, that these 'laws' are not only conceptual in character, but are frequently built out of imagined entities which cannot possibly be observed, and may even involve qualities contradicting our general experience. For example, the phenomena of light are explained by the assumption of a weightless and frictionless ether, which not only cannot be observed, but is imagined to possess qualities different from those shown by every substance which has been observed. This freedom from the trammels of phenomenal reality, which scientific conceptions claim to exercise, will be found to be a point of fundamental importance when we have to consider the justification of such psychopathological concepts as the 'unconscious'.[85]

Thus, using the empirio-critical assertion that science is defined not by concrete material but by intellectual method, Hart uses Pearson's criteria of scientific method in a point-by-point comparison of psychology and chemistry, and declares that the former satisfies these criteria just as well as the more accepted sciences. He can then conclude that 'The introduction of purpose, therefore, removes psychology from the mechanistic sciences, but this does not justify its removal from the whole field of science.'[86]

Hart thus makes the case for a science of immaterial man, an empirio-critical psychology, by extending the Machist argument, which had only gone so far as to centralise a psychology of perception regarded as an auxiliary to physics. What, then, is the relation of Hart's mental science to physics? This is a question that Hart himself felt bound to ask:

What then does he mean when he distinguishes the mental and the material? The answer is that he means two different modes of conceiving human experience. On the phenomenal plane the physicist and the psychologist are dealing with the same entities, sense impressions; the distinction between them lies in their different conceptual methods of resuming these sense impressions so as to express them in simple formulae. . . . Neither method is in itself better, or more perfect, or more real than the other, both have an equal right to be incorporated into the structure of science.[87]

But he proceeds, 'there must be no jumping from one mode of conception to the other. The physiologist must not introduce a psychological conception into his chain of cause and effect, nor must the psychologist fill up the gaps in his reasoning with cells and nerve current.'[88] On the other hand, Hart himself defines his psychological notion of the action of the complex, in a manner important for Pound and his Image, as 'the psychological analogue of the conception of force in physics'.[89]

For Mach's physiological psychology, psychology was subsumed under physics as different conceptual notions in a continuous order. They stood in metonymic relation, and the evidence of one science could be brought to bear on the other inasmuch as one was auxiliary to the other. On the other hand, since Hart's science is parallel to physics, and not auxiliary to it, its elements stand in a relation of *analogy* to those of the 'harder' science.

Hence we have in sum a new science of the immaterial, which gains its discursive acceptance through a transformation of 'science'. This transformation is based on and draws its rhetoric from the overthrow of mechanics as the dominant scientific paradigm. In consequence, the energies and elements of the new physics had established a new paradigm which might permit the consideration of other invisible forces and 'substances' as equally 'scientific'. It had further freed science from its definition in terms of its material object in such a way as to permit new definitions of objectivity and scientificity in the new epistemology. Mental psychology is thus presented according to an empirio-critical account of science, and again invokes the privileged principle of analogy.

In its dependence on antimechanicism and a discourse of energetics, on a synthetic continuum, the criterion of method, and the analogical relation to physics, the claims to acceptability of this science of 'immaterial man, of man considered as a thinking and sentient creature' parallel those of Pound's own discourse (and, indeed, to a large extent, that of the Society for Psychical Research). Empirio-criticism alone permits the conjunctions, analogies and assertions that Pound invokes as scientific. We can thus say that Pound's science reflects the modernist scientific *discourse* of empirio-criticism. We shall see in the concluding section of this chapter how Pound's mature poetics corresponds to this new scientific discourse, before turning, in the next chapter, to an analysis of elements of his technique in *The Cantos* – which we shall likewise be able to characterise as an 'empirio-critical' or 'phenomenalist' poetics.

VI

In 1913, Pound was given charge of Ernest Fenollosa's notebooks. Although he had already written Chinese-style poems (such as 'Liu Ch'e'), they had been based on contemporary English translations. With Fenollosa's notes and transcriptions, Pound was enabled to 'make it new' not only out of the mediaeval but also out of the Oriental. Thus we see, in 1915, the publication of a book of modernist translations, *Cathay*, and, in 1916, *Noh, or Accomplishment* (transla-tions of Noh plays). But the Fenollosa manuscripts not only made available new materials and techniques (and, indeed, a new cultural interest which was to lead Pound to Confucius and Chinese history); they also made available a theory of language in which Pound was able to crystallise most of what he had been arguing towards since Imagisme, which he published, in 1920, as *The Chinese Written Character as a Medium for Poetry*.

When I discussed the Image as a practice within a problematic of subject and object, I had occasion to refer forward to this text in order to illustrate an opposition between the weak, empty copula of subjective metaphor and an active, substantial or energetic notion of metaphoric transformation. In this text, the question of metaphor is inscribed in a context which brings together a number of the notions which we have so far raised: the notion of energy in language, the transformation of the terms of science, and the change in the subject–object relation of its epistemology. By virtue of the focus on the copula here, Pound draws together once more the local technical practice and the metatheory which surrounds it: the implicit relation between the practice of the Image and/or Vortex and the statement that 'poetry is a science'. Or, as Pound himself puts it: 'Poetry agrees with science and not with logic. The moment we use the copula, the moment we express subjective inclusions, poetry evaporates.'[90] In order to understand the relation of this formulation to its context and its Machist background, we have to reconstruct it from the surrounding argument.

Pound defines the merits of Chinese script by opposing it to what he calls 'the tyranny of mediaeval logic':

According to this European logic thought is a kind of brickyard. It is baked into little hard units or concepts. These are piled in rows according to size and then labeled with words for future use. This use consists in picking out a few bricks, each by its convenient label, and sticking them together into a sort of wall called a sentence by the use either of white mortar for the positive copula 'is', or of black mortar for the negative copula 'is not'.[91]

Like the Machists, Pound maintains that this abstract and uncritical procedure of concept and convenience represents a misrecognition and falsification of nature: the imposition of mechanical, schematic categories on reality – an offence which will grow in severity throughout Pound's career. His argument here relies on the proposition that the fixities of mechanicist laws of nature – which, we should remember, still dominated generalised scientific thought – were due to the abstract hypostasis of their mental, methodological and linguistic categories, which so dominated the discourse of mechanical materialists as to have taken the place of the real.

Pound's attack on each part of that mechanist sentence illustrates the scientific support behind his discourse. In the first place, science shows that isolated solid particles – rows of 'separate "particulars"'[92] – do not in fact exist in nature. All is now a question of the inseparability of matter and energy:

> A true noun, an isolated thing, does not exist in nature. Things are only the terminal points, or rather the meeting points of actions. . . . Neither can a pure verb, an abstract motion, be possible in nature. The eye sees noun and verb as one: things in motion, motion in things.[93]

Not only does Pound's critique bear on substantives as Mach's did on substance, but it also depends on the same correlative model of the primacy of phenomenal perception: 'The eye sees' – the eye that later in the text sees '*things move* under its microscope'.[94] In the second place, if the isolated substance does not exist, but all is a movement of energy, then it follows that the neutral space that separated the substance (atoms) does not exist in nature either: 'There is in reality no such verb as a pure copula, no such original conception.'[95] This attack on the copula in its function in a mechanistic model of logic returns us then to the key formulation, 'Poetry agrees with science and not with logic', by virtue of its rejection of the copula.

Thus, if 'science' is different from 'logic', and if the latter is defined with reference to a mechanistic model, then the 'science' with which poetry agrees has to be the contemporary alternative to mechanicism: the emerging science of energetics. By the same token, since the specific contribution of the Machists was that the error of mechanistic logic lay in its unacknowledged subjectivism, the copula, as the operator of that logic (and image of instantaneous 'action-at-a-distance' through neutral space), becomes the locus of that subjectivism. This is a radical reversal, if one considers that the copula, as an equals sign, as it were, of the mechanistic equation, functioned, in the Newtonian system, as an index of objectivity. But poetry, if it is to correspond to the new, more scientific science, must find a form that will respond to the discourse of energetics, which, in a certain model, may be said now to constitute science. Thus, as the concept of the active, material ether replaces the concept of space, poetry has to energise the copula in metaphor.

The subjectivism of the copula likewise applies to the linguistic instruments of this logic as a whole. In this too Pound uses a Machist vocabulary, criticising the signifiers of logic as 'abstractions', 'arbitrary symbols . . . sheer convention' and 'mental counters'.[96] But the Chinese script is different; and the way in which it differs is similar to that which transforms Mach's and Poincaré's scientific language from the unconscious subjectivism of their opponents into the universality and objectivity of their revised notion of formula and law.

Pound's alternative language is first introduced in relation to normal signifiers with phonetic values as 'symbols equally arbitrary', but differing in that these characters do not have their signifying basis in sound. The Chinese symbols, although necessarily conventional, are of a different order of convention:

> Chinese notation is something much more than arbitrary symbols. It is based upon a vivid shorthand of the operations of nature. In the algebraic figure and the spoken word there is no natural connection between thing and sign; all depends on sheer convention. But the Chinese method *follows natural suggestion.*   (Emphasis added)[97]

It is a question of orientation. Given that all symbol systems are conventions, the Chinese script, like the language of Machist science, has *a* necessity, *a* connection between 'thing' and sign – bearing, on its face, its recognition that language is a convention and attempting always to approximate that convention to the natural world. In giving a 'vivid shorthand of the operations of nature', like the scientific law, it fulfils the empirio-critical ideal of basing itself in the necessary sequences and relations of experience.[98] The Chinese script follows 'natural suggestion' away from the abstract mental categories which had masqueraded as natural laws and towards the experience 'imposed on us'.

We can understand the status of this language by considering the presentation of its claims to necessity and objectivity, which can be divided into two equally important parts: grammar and metaphor. The first takes up the question of the sentence:

> how many people have asked themselves why the sentence form exists at all, why it seems so universally necessary *in all languages*? Why *must* all possess it, and what is the normal type of it? If it be so universal, it ought to correspond to some primary law of nature.[99]

The question itself is a Machist question. The 'ought' of the final sentence operates only if one shares the empirio-critical model of intersubjectivity and objectivity (as opposed, for example, to the idealist conclusion that the sentence form is no more than a universal structure of the human mind). The universal law is 'doubtless', as Poincaré writes, invented by men, but, in the empirio-critical model, invented under the constraint of nature. It is hence a small step from Poincaré's 'It is the external world which has imposed the continuum upon us, which we doubtless have invented, but which it has forced us to invent' to Pound's account of the primitive and universal invention of the sentence: 'The sentence form was forced upon primitive man by nature. It was not we who made it; it was a reflection of the temporal order in causation.'[100]

The second question in the above quotation is also Machist: 'what is the normal type of it?' Given a range of empirical manifestations, one endeavours to discover the formal, structural law of relation behind them – like the analytic equation for diverse circles. Pound answers the question by adducing the evidence of modern science, once more according to an empirio-critical principle:

All truth has to be expressed in sentences because all truth is the *transference of power*. The type of sentence in nature is a flash of lightning. It passes between two terms, a cloud and the earth. No unit of natural process can be less than this. All natural processes are, in their units, as much as this. Light, heat, gravity, chemical affinity, human will, have this in common, that they redistribute force. Their unit of process can be represented as:

| *term from* | *transference* | *term to* |
| *which* | *of force* | *which*[101] |

Two things are to be noted about this construction of what becomes a general model of poetic syntax in its juxtapositional structure, an elaboration of what we have observed in the Image and the energising of the copula. The first is the status accorded to energy as the prime term of nature. The second is that the model works by using an underlying energetic conceptual structure to mediate by analogy between the diverse phenomenal manifestations from which it is abstracted – that is, first formal relations and then analogy as the relation of relations, which bridges the gap between the physical and the psychological world.

Compare, for example, the following passage from Poincaré:

we may perceive mathematical analogies between phenomena which have physically no relation either apparent or real, so that the laws of one of these phenomena aid us to divine those of the other.

The very same equation, that of Laplace, is met in the theory of Newtonian attraction, in that of the motion of liquids, in that of the electric potential, in that of magnetism, in that of the propagation of heat and in still many others. What is the result? These theories seem images copied one from the other; they are mutually illuminating, borrowing their language from each other; asking electricians if they do not felicitate themselves on having invented the phase flow of force, suggested by hydrodynamics and the theory of heat.

Thus mathematical analogies not only make us foresee physical analogies, but besides do not cease to be useful when these latter fail.

To sum up, the aim of mathematical physics is not only to facilitate for the physicist the numerical calculation of certain constants or the integration of certain differential equations. It is besides, it is above all, to reveal to him the hidden harmony of things in making him see them in a new way.[102]

It is by means, then, of a structural analogy implying empirical realities of energy that this form of sentence gains objective and natural status, in contrast to the fixities of the 'logical' sentence, which merely reflects the static abstractions of mechanistic thought. On the other hand, a sentence form which reflects the energetic relations of nature, in dynamised analogy, permits the perception and representation of the patterns and revelations of the natural and human worlds which *The Cantos* seek to embrace.

In *The Chinese Written Character*, Pound proceeds to pursue his 'natural' linguistic model into a full grammar. The parts of speech have to reflect the reality of energy as much as the sentence itself: 'The verb must be the primary fact of nature, since motion and change are all we can recognise in her.'[103] The noun, which can no longer represent isolated substance as a natural reality, now reflects a reality of sensation and motion; it is therefore to be 'a *verbal idea of action*'.[104] As Mach shifted substance into a signifier of sensation, Pound replaces the substantive noun with 'shorthand pictures of actions or processes'. A part of speech becomes 'all that it does',[105] and hence grammatically flexible – with important consequences for the poetic practice, as we shall see in the next chapter.

Adjectives are an interesting case, since they are a part of speech used to denote the quality of an object, and to represent the first step in the sequence of subject–object interpretation. It is also the operator which grounds the 'concrete' or sensational aspect of an object – as Pound had written in 1912: 'By epithets of primary apparition I mean those which describe what is actually presented to the sense or vision. . . . Epithets of primary apparition give vividness to description and stimulate conviction in the actual vision of the poet.'[106] Here Pound transforms the adjective so as to reflect quality in terms of active scientific energies:

> every verb is also an adjective. This brings us close to nature, because everywhere the quality is only a power of action regarded as having an abstract inherence. Green is only a certain rapidity of vibration, hardness a degree of tenseness in cohering. In Chinese the adjective always retains a substratum of verbal meaning.[107]

Pound similarly recasts prepositions and conjunctions, passive forms, intransitives and negatives, always invoking scientific support for his 'nature' in order to produce forms which reflect it, as in the Chinese.[108]

The strength of the Chinese is thus its concreteness, not in terms of materiality, but in terms of the dynamic energetic structures of natural phenomenal form. But this principle has to be extended beyond 'primary apparition', the physical realm of recording or describing:

> But Chinese would be a poor language, and Chinese poetry but a narrow art, could they not go on to represent also what is unseen. The best poetry deals not only with natural images but with lofty thoughts, spiritual suggestions and obscure relations. The greater part of natural truth is hidden in processes too minute for vision and in harmonies too large, in vibrations, cohesions and in affinities. . . .[109]

The merely phenomenal 'lapses into description' (as Pound says of Ford's otherwise admirably objective Impressionism); what is needed is some means of access, via conception, to the profound and occult: the deeper relations which, for example, Poincaré maintained that mathematical discourse provided.

It is here that Pound again puts his emphasis on the role of metaphor: 'the Chinese language with its peculiar materials has passed from the seen to the unseen by exactly the same process which all ancient races employed. This process is metaphor, the use of material images to suggest immaterial relations.'[110] But, in passing from a grounding in empirical description of phenomena to a language of conception and creativity, the Chinese language has, for Pound's purposes, once more to avoid collapsing into subjectivism. As in empirio-criticism (or, for that matter, in Imagisme), this conceptual, creative language has to retain its objectivity.

Pound achieves the transition by asserting, like the empirio-critics, the objectivity of relation and its analogic possibilities, thus claiming that the conceptions and insights of 'primitive metaphor' are objective:

> the primitive metaphors do not spring from arbitrary *subjective* processes. They are possible only because they follow objective lines of relations in nature herself. Relations are more real and more important than the things which they relate. The forces which produce the branch-angles of an oak lay potent in the acorn. Similar lines of resistance, half-curbing the out-pressing vitalities, govern the branching of rivers and of nations. Thus a nerve, a wire, a roadway, and a clearing-house are only varying channels which communication forces for itself. This is more than analogy, it is identity of structure.[111]

Needless to say, the empirio-critical definition of 'analogy' – in Mach as much as in Poincaré – is precisely this notion of identity of structure, rather than the weaker sense of one of the conditions for Aristotelian metaphor. And so here too we have relation established as the centre of nature, the universal physical phenomenology of energy invoked to link and extend individual manifestations analogically.

Whilst observing that this very analogical procedure has characterised Pound's *use* of science throughout, as an actual discursive tactic, one must also emphasise that here it is this model and valuation of relational analogy which performs the crucial shift from subjective interpretation (the conditionality of traditional metaphor) into the realm of the profound, objective and necessary truths of relations in nature. The steps of Pound's argument about poetry and knowledge are all supported by contemporary Machist arguments about reality, science and language. They are involved in a similar subject–object problematic, a similar dislocation of the objective and substantive, with a similar resolution. The whole argument culminates in the typical Machist reversal that relations, not 'things', are the source of objectivity. Since metaphor is a process of relation, it can thus be said that 'Metaphor, the revealer of nature . . . the very substance of poetry . . . is at once the substance of nature and of language.'[112] In short, poetry becomes the discourse of reality, it 'agrees with science', through metaphor: metaphor, that is, in terms of energetic relations.

We may now draw together the network of relations which constitute the crystallisation of Pound's poetics contained in *The Chinese Written Character*. It is merely a matter of drawing the parallels in the text itself. First, 'In diction and in grammatic form science is utterly opposed to logic. Primitive men who created language agreed with science and not with logic'; and 'Poetry agrees with science and not with logic.'[113] The relation between poetry and primitive language (the 'Old World' energies of poetry) is also explicitly drawn: 'Poetry only does consciously what the primitive races did unconsciously.'[114] Hence follows the scientificity not only of poetry and of primitive language but also of the poetry which employs primitive techniques. The Chinese script belongs amongst such techniques: 'The Chinese written character . . . retains the primitive sap. . . . It retains the creative impulse and process, visible and at work.'[115] Finally, the Chinese conforms grammatically with science. Since metaphor mediates between all four terms, every term is thus in relation with every other, with the prime association of the text contained in the title: *The Chinese Written Character as a Medium for Poetry*.

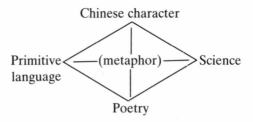

This text is important because it offers a coherent poetics and a bridge between the techniques of the Imagiste–Vorticist period and *The Cantos*, establishing a more detailed and extensive scientific framework for Pound's techniques – of grammar and metaphor – as opposed to more assertions concerning the general nature or function of poetry. It elaborates techniques we have seen at work or in theory, most especially the transformational action of the Image and the patterning of the Vortex. These develop continuously, through the Chinese material, into 'The Ideogrammic Method or the Method of Science', the larger-scale elaboration of Image and Vortex, which can be seen as a major organising principle for *The Cantos*.[116]

But *The Chinese Written Character* is also important because of its use as an explanatory device by the critics, and thus in its mediation of Pound's practice. Typically, the references to nature are generally endorsed by the critics, and, even where Kenner, in his chapter on 'The Persistent East' in *The Pound Era*, puts the Fenollosa material into a context of Western attitudes to Chinese script and universalist theories of language in science, going back to Leibnitz and Bacon, he fails to connect this with Mach's interest in relating his notion of universal scientific analogy to a universal language.[117] Pound's version of the Fenollosa manuscripts owes a considerable debt to the discourse of the Machists, in terms of the notions of reality and language offered.

In sum, Pound's discourse of science is an important and characteristic means of representing the productivity of the poet and plays a major part in his synthesis of poetic and prose values – of conception and objectivity, of subject and object in metaphor, of the 'Old World' and the 'New . . . Poem', of mythic and other primitive techniques and mystical vision in modern contexts.

It appears, in one sense, progressive: a courageous and apparently necessary attempt to confront the problem of poetry in the modern world without prejudice to its qualities. We have looked briefly at some important strains in this discourse – energetics and empirio-criticism. A more thorough study, with greater emphasis on the Vortex, on biology, tradition and 'race', can be found in Ian Bell's indispensable work *Critic as Scientist*, which also demonstrates much more thoroughly the degree of revalidation of primitive notions offered by the new science and exploited by Pound.

The fact that this is a discourse of science transforms the values it expresses, by presenting them in terms of 'objectivity', 'reality' and 'universality'. This transformation – which, as I shall argue in due course, has major consequences for the poem – is also mirrored in the Poundian critics. Pound's acceptance and reputation thus owes a good deal to the reproduction and revalidation of the scientific metadiscourse he used to explain and render acceptable his ideas and techniques for a modernist poetry. In this way, Pound is presented (and presents himself) as a modernist master, since his poetic practice and theory reflect modern scientific reality.

I have sought, on the other hand, to show that science is always a mediated discourse, produced in a given historical context. In this sense, Pound's science is metaphorical. A specific popularising discourse of science intervenes between the phenomena and theories and their significance and evidential values. Pound's poetics are modernist, then, not inasmuch as they reflect a real scientific world, but inasmuch as they reflect historically specific discourses about that world.

By the same token, however, they remain vulnerable to the potential contradictions concealed in those discourses, themselves in pursuit of a synthesis in a moment of crisis and transformation. At such a moment, only *partial* theories are available; but the demand, at the time, to guarantee the scientificity of science at a moment of its apparent failure ensures that the objective and universal signifiers of science dominate the partial theories that it is capable of offering in the crisis (this is, no doubt, always to some extent the case; but it is particularly acute at a moment of such radical epistemological crisis).

Machism, then, represents a theory of science whose specific property is to fill the gap between the collapse of one paradigm and the gradual recuperation of another. Thus, for example, in his obituary on Mach, Einstein acknowledged a great debt to the man 'who shook this dogmatic faith . . . [in] . . . mechanics as the final basis of all physical thinking'.[118] He also remarks that Mach 'was not very far from requiring a general theory of relativity'. Indeed, Poincaré came closer than anyone but Einstein himself to actually producing one. But then in his *Autobiographical Notes* Einstein writes, 'in my younger days, however, Mach's epistemological position also influenced me very greatly, a position which today appears to me to be essentially untenable'.[119]

The epistemological satisfaction of empirio-criticism belongs to the level of the signifier. It is valuable inasmuch as it defended science against an outmoded and restrictive mechanicism or a vengeful and regressive idealism, and inasmuch as it helped to open new fields for scientific discourse. But it is dangerous inasmuch as its epistemology is determined by the transitional crisis. It is, furthermore, problematic inasmuch as its discourse, which permits the extension of science into other fields, also permits extension into fields whose epistemology is in fact different from that of science, without clarifying its differential limits. In so doing, it permits the transformation, in a problematic and dangerous manner, of the constituents of those other fields. Before we can consider the consequences of this for modernism, we should first observe how the poetics which reflects this science operates in practice, with a relatively brief look at some of Pound's more important techniques in *The Cantos*.

4 'And . . .': Reading *The Cantos*

What do we know about *The Cantos*? For one thing, it is a very big work. There are 120 Cantos in all, ranging from only a few lines to more than twenty pages;[1] their composition is spread over more than half a century; they are concentrated and succinct, and discursive and sprawling. We might also know that they are difficult; the style is elliptical and allusive. But they are difficult in more than one sense. Not only is Pound perhaps at first sight irritatingly difficult in the arcana of his references, but he is also difficult in a more serious sense in his very technique: he does not render up his meanings easily. In both cases, the difficulty is a consequence of the poem's ambition and is hence deliberate: not in order to obfuscate, but to demand the reader's participation in decoding the message.

In fact, the difficulty of reference is not necessarily that great. Apart from the existence of ever-more-thorough guides to the allusions, which the reader may consult, most of the time the poetry does make considerable sense without pursuit of all its references, through the usual devices of poetry (albeit in Pound's modernist development). Again, although it is true that *The Cantos* covers a wide area of what appears to be eccentric material and arcane knowledge, we might consider whether it is the fact that Pound uses references that disturbs people, or rather the fact that he refers to areas which are not as well known as, for example, the Bible, Shakespeare, Milton and Words-worth. We have already seen the source of this dislocation: the sense of poetry in crisis, the unusability of the tradition which had brought it to that crisis, and the pursuit of an alternative tradition which might resolve it. It is not as if the modernists invented the device of literary allusion: poems have always referred to other poems. What makes the modernists difficult is not that their dependence on allusion is necessarily greater than, say, the Romantics', but that they tend to allude to material away from the developing mainstream culture. It is in this sense that the difficulty of the modernists in general and of Pound in particular is symptomatic of their modern condition: the more difficult the context of reference or the more eccentric the cultural resources, the more radical the distance marked from the inherited orthodox culture. Furthermore, Homer and Ovid, the Troubadours, Camões, Dante, Sigismundo Malatesta, the Medicis, the Bank of Siena, the American Constitution, Jefferson and Adams, Sir Edward Coke, Richard St Victor, the Chinese character, Chinese history and culture, mediaeval philosophy, and economic and literary history are perhaps people and things that we should be incited to know about.

The Cantos presents itself as a modern epic, assembling its own tradition. Producing a twentieth-century epic was a remarkably common ambition amongst the major modernists. James Joyce, for example, has his hero, Stephen Daedalus, in *A Portrait of the Artist as a Young Man* (1916) commit himself to a project (which issues in *Ulysses*) to 'forge in the smithy of his soul the conscience of his race'; T. S. Eliot sought 'To purify the dialect of the tribe' (*Little Gidding*); and David Jones's *The Anathemata* (1953) strives, as he writes in the Preface, 'to make a shape out of the very things from which one is oneself made'. Pound specified the epic as 'a poem including history':[2] not, like Jones's, a personal history; nor, like Joyce's, a national (or anti-national) history; but a history of global civilisation and culture, consonant with his lifelong ideology of the international 'better tradition' of good writing and, hence, of good government, and reflecting the modern inter- or multinational cultural and political context.

The Cantos in this sense recalls and fulfils the project announced in Pound's first series of articles, 'I Gather the Limbs of Osiris', in an attempted totalisation of the fragments of the 'better tradition' on an apparently global scale. Assembling the didactic and exemplary elements of this tradition, the poem presents itself as 'a portable substitute for the British Museum',[3] or, as Hugh Kenner has usefully characterised it, a 'curriculum'.[4] Like Homer, Pound sought to represent the maximum of human knowledge within his text – most of all to present the wisdom, as he saw it, of constitutionalism, economics and aesthetics within a demystified, poetic (objective) form, and thus to incite the reader into activating that wisdom. The poem becomes a cross-index to itself and to a mass of culture. Reading *The Cantos* is, in this sense, an education.

But *The Cantos* is not only epic in the sense of synthesising a cultural history; it is so also in a technical sense, in that it is modernist. That is to say that it puts to use the highest level and fullest range of modernist literary technique according to the ideology of modernism already observed in Pound: the culmination of the international *Weltliteratur* living tradition of good writing and the scientific privilege of the serious artist designed to recuperate poetry's cultural centrality. This is what, most of all, makes the poem historically important, as it manifests the dedicated maturity of Pound's central and influential poetic modernism, the highest point of technical achievement of his innovations. The poem's failure – if such it be – in no way detracts from its significance in this regard.

There are many ways of approaching *The Cantos* and, given the extensiveness and variety of the text, they are all necessarily partial. But, within the lines of my argument hitherto, we should look in the poem for some governing image of *form* which links the text with its distant technical origins in Pound's apprenticeship, and which would permit us, however partially, to investigate how the poetic techniques, theory and their scientific base translate themselves into the poem.

Usefully for us, if there is one image above all which organises the progress of *The Cantos*, it is that of the crystal/light. It is, in fact, much the same image–object as that which enabled Pound to refer to Dante's *Paradiso* (which elsewhere represented the 'radiant world' of 'the rose in the steel dust') as

> the most wonderful *image*. By that I do not mean that it is a perseveringly imagistic performance. The permanent part is Im-agisme. . . . The form of sphere above sphere, the varying reaches of light, the minutiae of pearls upon foreheads, all these are part of the Image.[5]

In *The Cantos*, this image is likewise built up of different objects, in many registers and with various elemental extensions – sun/moon, light, air, water, stone, gems – which are fused and unified along the poem into the crystal. As such, this image and its registers characterise the most seemingly innocent aspect of the poem, its lyricism. At the same time, they embody many of its central assertive values. Such values do not refer only to the area of technique or form – where the poem is talking about itself – but also to where it reaches out to 'nature' and politics.

The peculiar nature of the crystal/light image in the poem is indicated by our inability to decompose or limit it in terms of single elements: light, crystal, stone, air or water. It is constantly in a process of *mediation* between the elements in interactions of light and water, light and stone, light and air, light and fire. These mediations work together to construct, unify and operate the poem's central image of form, as in both 'and saw the waves taking form as crystal' (25/119) and 'that the body of light come forth / from the body of fire' (91/610). The force of this light imagery and its relations to heat and energy – 'in the light of the light is the virtù' (74/429) – may remind us of Hertz's proof that the same wave, at different frequencies, gives off light and heat. The generalisation of this experimental and mathematical demonstration into the electromagnetic theory of light was central to the new theories of energy and the ether on which Pound's scientific reference so depended.

This image, reflecting, then, the new physical basis of reality as it was emerging at the turn of the century, is far from incidental to the poem. Eva Hess tells us that 'the light imagery of the *Cantos*, the "light tensile" (Canto LXXIV), stands for the umbilical cord that links the individual with the universe'.[6] Not only is it a universal medium ('omnia, quae sunt, lumina sunt' – 83/528) and a mediating structure in action and thought ('the light of the doer, as it were / a form cleaving to it' – 41/251), but it is also the energy of mind: ' "Et omniformis": Air, fire, the pale soft light' (5/17) and 'Et omniformis, . . . omnis / Intellectus est' (23/107). In short, the basic relation between the objective world and the subjective vision – 'all things', 'form', 'Intellectus', the very material of the poem and the coherence of its universe – is constructed in the image of the crystal/light. Thus the ambiguity of a 'visionary' poem – seeing and seeing through – is made 'tensile', substantial, through the crystal/light.

The image as it appears through the poem connotes such a wide range of Poundian values – primal, civic, intellectual and aesthetic – that Boris de Rachewiltz, for example, sees a case for the crystal as a symbol of the 'philosophers' stone' in the poem.[7] For him, the fire relates to 'perceptions deriving from sensual experience' and the light to 'perceptions deriving from the intellect'. They are related through an image of interaction: 'from fire to crystal / via the body of light' (91/615).[8] Thus it is that Donald Davie links our discussion, in identifying his central value in the poem, its notion of form, with this object, the 'body of light': 'What is meant by "the crystal" we have seen from Canto XCI; it is the wooing into awareness, and the holding in awareness, of the *forma*.'[9] The climax, according to Davie, Kenner and others arrives in Canto 91 with the lines, 'in that clarity / Gods moving in crystal' (91/611).

It is indeed to Canto 91 that one should look to see the climactic realisation of the crystal/light image in terms of the key values of the poem which the image has connoted throughout. It is the high point of the poem's central 'symbol', in the sense, as Boris de Rachewiltz argues, that, 'if the *Cantos* are to be regarded as "a permanent metaphor" in the direction of "a belief in a permanent world", certain recurrent expressions and images which gradually grow increasingly "objective" necessarily assume the status of symbols'.[10] But, since such an objective symbol has to be constructed from 'natural objects', we should do better for our purposes to look to its original introduction, in Canto 2. In studying this, and pursuing some of the chains it engenders, we shall indeed see an elaboration of Imagiste techniques and their associated ideas, readable in terms of an empirio-critical model and/or the poetics of *The Chinese Written Character*. In focusing on the crystal/light image as the image of form which mediates and unites the objects and elements of the poem, we shall observe precisely the operation and ramifications of the empirio-critical 'object signifier' (phenomenon), the principle of analogy and the grammar of energetics.

II

Canto 2 is in many ways an important Canto. It introduces Sordello and the problem of history and fiction; as well as the Helen/Eleanor figure (a central female figure throughout the poem). It introduces the sea goddess (Tyro), who prefigures the goddesses forming in Canto 25, whose return is crucial to the 'gt / Healing' of Canto 91, as well as presenting the fertility god Dionysus. It is also in Canto 2 that the crystal/light image and a number of other elements recuperated in Cantos 90 and 91 are introduced, and it is here that the 'Gods moving in crystal', that image which is to punctuate the poem, building into the 'GREAT CRYSTAL' of Canto 91, is born. Finally, as befits a poem in which the gods make a first, dramatic appearance, Canto 2 is also a poem of metamorphosis, a value vital to *The Cantos* as a whole.

The Canto is also of interest because, whereas Cantos 1 and 3 are basically linear narrative in character, Canto 2, whilst retaining a long narrative section, is the first truly non-linear Canto. As Kenner writes, distinguishing it from the first Canto, it has 'an Imagist instead of a

Seafarer surface'.[11] By the same token, the Canto itself moves to an important value of the poem's own construction. As Canto 1 predicated the rest of the work on its final line – 'So that:' – this Canto ends, 'in the half-light. / And . . .' (2/10). The word 'and' has already been prepared for our attention in the narrative sequence of the Canto, where it recurs with remarkable frequency and under considerable tension. It is by no means an innocent conjunction here, but the very process of conjunction: not the logical, neutral 'and' of mechanics but an energetic transformation between terms.

The linking of the signifier of conjunction with the 'half-light' image plays a large part in the articulation of the work as a whole. 'Natural light' as a setting for actions and transitions in *The Cantos* is almost always in a condition of half-light.[12] The conjunction of light and darkness, dawns, dusks, mists, gold in the gloom, and so forth, establishes a world where, in Kenner's terms, 'everything . . . is unstable; what is named is not quite there'.[13] This is a principle bred from Imagisme: a process of metaphor which, according to Kenner, 'seized phenomena just on the point of mutating' and of which this Canto is, in his opinion, typical. It is also typical of the manner in which it is impossible to reduce the crystal/light to any one determinate medium: the image itself signifies transformation.

In short, *The Cantos* is not, obviously, based on a 'logical' form with copula conjunctions and innocent 'ands'. It is structured like an Imagiste or Vorticist poem, on a larger and more extensive scale embracing an extremely wide range of temporal and phenomenal materials and discursive registers. Natural (and, in due course, historical) phenomena are related in a process of energetic interpenetration and mutation, in a world of radiant energies – like that, as Pound has it, of Dante's *Paradiso*. Hence the importance of the half-light images and the notion of conjunction or articulation, which exist neither as light nor darkness, but as the margin of their transformation; and of the crystal, the achieved form of those transformations.

Before the half-light image appears, however, we find the beginning of the crystal/light value, presented first in the context of water and air. The introduction of this value is prepared and reinforced by a grammar which bases itself on the switching of syntactical functions between the parts of speech. This is a basic and important technical device for Pound, consistent with the theory of grammar enunciated in *The Chinese Written Character*. Technically, the very movement of the Canto is largely determined by *compounds* which produce *shifts*. For example, in line 6 – 'spray-whited circles of cliff-wash' – the adjectival phrase is a compound of a noun and a past-participle verb; 'circles' is a noun describing the hypostasis of a verb; and 'cliff-wash' is a noun phrase based on an action. Similarly, from 'the wave runs in the beach-groove' (line 10), we move to 'the beach-run' (line 23), where the verb becomes a noun.

The compounding of words in this way gives rise to a process of syntactical interchange or shifting. This process is characteristic of Pound and of the texture of *The Cantos*, most especially in the use of a class of positional nouns whose place in the utterance is taken by phrases based on what are conventionally adjectives or verbs. This results in positional shifts of semantically equivalent terms into different positional environments.[14] Pound's 'nouns' in this sense signify the momentary hypostasis of a quality or process, rather than discrete solid objects, corresponding to the idea of the noun as a 'verbal idea of action' in *The Chinese Written Character*.[15] In that this is most often a shift of a signifier of quality or action into the positional environment of a noun – inasmuch, that is, as the 'object position' is occupied by a signifier of process – it gives us a grammatical operation which corresponds to the shift of the object from the signified to the signifier, and its replacement, at the former level, by energies, in empirio-criticism.

We may observe an effect of this compounding and shifting at work in the metamorphosis itself, when the ship's crew who tried to kidnap the god are punished, and particularly in line 58: 'Ship stock fast in sea-swirl' (2/7). The term 'fast' not only signifies (semantically) both 'firmly' and 'rapidly', but also occupies an ambiguous position as adjective or adverb, dependent upon the syntactical function of 'stock'. This ambiguity gives rise to the tension between stasis and action in the line, and contributes to that tension in the metamorphosis of the sea, boat and crew. Similarly, by a simple compounding, 'the swirling sea' reverses its adjective–noun relation in an unequivocally hypostatic and substantive form, which continues the tension between action and stasis.

Thus we look to 'stock' in order to determine the predominant meaning of 'fast' and hence the dominant tone of the line. But what we find is that this word most of all maintains the ambiguity of the rest of the syntagm. It has the position of a verb, with its semantic overtones of 'stuck'. Although this would supply the most obvious meaning, 'stock' is not a past-participle form or variant of 'stuck', even in archaic forms. The term does have some rare verbal meanings, such as the obscure but appropriate scientific usage 'to stiffen'. But in this case the verbal position would be occupied either by 'stocks' (present indicative) or 'stocked' (past indicative/participle). By the same token, the form 'stock' has morphemic and positional indicators of a noun. Again there are some more or less obscure and more or less relevant meanings which could operate here, such as the 'stock' of a plant (preparing for the vegetative metamorphosis which follows). Similarly, in the plural, the term is used to describe the frame on which a ship under construction is supported (anticipating the less ambiguous lines 84–5). The point is that all these semantic contexts may be intended or operative, but no one of them is entirely and thus exclusively adequate in terms of syntactical form and position. In this way Pound is able to play on all the meanings and to produce a tension, a tone of ambiguity, in the syntagm as a whole, as verb turns into noun. The syntagm as a whole denotes stasis, yet the individual signifiers ('fast', 'swirl') carry connotations of violent action; this semantic ambiguity is supported by syntactical ambiguity and the resultant tension signifies the paradox of metamorphosis.

As we turn specifically to the first image of the crystal, we find that it brings with it the engendering of the gods and goddesses. Technically, we find a similar process of syntactical disruption involved in the presentation. The key moment occurs in lines 23–7:

> And by the beach-run, Tyro.
>   Twisted arms of the sea-god,
> *Lithe sinews of water*, gripping her, cross-hold,
> And *the blue-gray glass of the water* tents them.
> *Glare azure of water*, cold-welter, close cover.
>   (2/6; emphasis added)

There are, as I have emphasised them, three related moments to this presentation. The first gives the god and the goddess; the second initiates the crystal image; and the third permits the extension of that image out of its element, preparatory to the unification of the elements in the poem. All this takes place against a continuing background of compounding and positional shifts (for example, 'beach-run' and 'cross-hold', and the use of 'tents' as a verb and of 'cover' as a noun).

The key term in the first moment which *substantiates* the initial presentation of the goddess and simultaneously invests the elemental image with divinity is 'sinew'. The set of signifiers 'arms . . . god . . . gripping' determines the reference of 'sinews' as an *object* (its meaning as tendon or muscle). But the predicate 'of water', which denotes the immediate environment, determines the signification of another meaning of the word: an abstract *sensation of force*. Both references are given semantically in the word itself. Thus, where 'sinews' is an object (tendon), by metonymic implication, the water is anthropomorphised into a god. In that it is not just a god, but more locally denoted as being a property of water, the ultimate signified is neither the god nor the water, but the *energy* through which the natural phenomenon is invested with divine presence, both of which are simultaneously signified by the syntagm.

What we are observing therefore is that here 'sinews' is a signifier denoting at one level an object, but connoting in its totality a sensational energy of natural and supernatural dimensions. The process is clarified when the image is decomposed towards the end of the Canto, in lines 132–3: 'Lithe turning of water, / sinews of Poseidon' (2/9). The juxtaposition here, splitting the original syntagm, indicates how the 'sinews of Poseidon' (signifier of an object) had operated to signify 'turning of water' (sensation of energy). The projection of the divine presence into the natural phenomenon is thus *produced by and produces* the object signifier which *substantiates* the image. If we give Poseidon his other name (Ocean), we may schematise this even more simply:

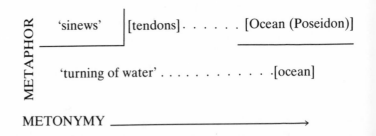

There is a correlative operation further on in the metamorphic episode (lines 88–9): 'void air taking pelt. / Lifeless air become sinewed' (2/8). Here the image of 'taking pelt' is substantiated retrospectively: lifeless air is imbued with energy ('become sinewed'); sinews as an object metonymically engenders 'pelt'; and thus the eruption of energy can be signified directly by the objective phrase 'taking pelt', which in its turn metonymically engenders the creatures and their master:

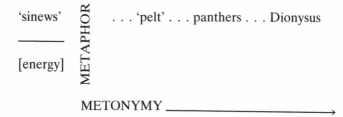

An important general point arises from this example. The process we have been observing involves essentially the shift of the object from signified to signifier, and its replacement by sensation/energy as the ultimate signified. This process, by which energetic sensations are signified by 'natural objects', rather than *vice versa*, is, as Pearson himself points out, essentially a process of *projection*. Sensation is the subjective (internal) experience of the objective (external) world. But, when sensation is projected into the place of objects as the signified reality, what was 'within' becomes 'without'. Thus there is in the poem a basic technique of physical projection: objects or positional nouns signifying sensations or energies. The point to be made is that this constitutive physical projection is linked to a *psychic projection*. This is clear when the object used to signify the sensation or energy is an animal or human metonymy (creatures have 'sinews', not water). When an object is used in this way, the relation it bears to the sensation or energy it signifies is metaphoric (were it metonymic, we would be back in a materialist paradigm). But, inasmuch as it is an object, it necessarily continues to engender a metonymic chain of its own ('arms . . . sinews . . . pelt', etc.), from which the god is implicitly constructed.

Thus, in a very Imagiste way – through the interaction of metaphor and metonymy – this technique predicates the gods inasmuch as it uses creaturely objects. Furthermore, the gods themselves, as objects, logically are also projections of subjective experiences and energies, signifiers of 'states of consciousness'.[16] And we have already seen in effect how this is in fact Pound's theory of myth: 'A god is an eternal state of mind';[17] myths are 'objective and impersonal stories'[18] signifying such 'states of consciousness'. We can thus propose a continuity between the use of objects to signify sensations of energies and the mythic construction of the poem, inasmuch as a myth is a psychological projection, and the use of object signifiers, as we have been analysing it, is a central technical device for accomplishing this.

Returning now to our wave/crystal image, we find that this technique of the object has important variations and extensions in terms of the *interpenetration of elements*, which is also a major characteristic of the poem's texture. The two moments of the originating image – 'blue-gray glass of the water' and 'Glare azure of water' – are related. The first works in a manner similar to the 'sinews' example, except that it deals with light instead of force. It is simply a matter of the injection of a seemingly neutral object ('glass') into the syntagm to signify another sensational quality shared by the immediate object, 'water' – this time, the clarity of its 'blue-gray' colour. It is, almost literally, an objective hypostasis of water. Through this simple device of the object signifier, the complex light–water–crystal, and its relation to the gods, so important to the poem as a whole, is engaged.

The range of this image is broadened significantly in the following image of 'Glare azure of water'. Both juxtaposed moments are related through the sensation they both ultimately signify by their objects or nouns. Here the object ('glass') gives place to a sensation of energy ('Glare'); and the quality ('blue-gray') gives way to an object ('azure' – the word denotes a colour, but is also used, particularly poetically, to signify the sky, heavens or sea). In both of these substitutions and with the loss of the verb, there is a shift in the syntax. This is important not only for the tone it gives to the unit, but also because it gives rise to a reciprocal chain in the following Canto through the grammar of relational analogy. An operative coupling, very characteristic of the poem's divine and mutative phenomena and the mediation of its elements, is thereby established: 'Glare azure of water' and 'Gods float in the azure air' (3/11).

'Glare' (apart from its phonetic association with 'air'), as a noun or as a verb/adjective stem, signifies the abstract sensation of an action of light through the medium of air. Though seemingly a noun, its precise positional status is here left undetermined, which has the effect of giving its adjectival or active quality the overtone of substance, and *vice versa*. 'Azure' has a double ambiguity: as noun or adjective, referring conventionally to either the sky or the sea. The unit as a whole, 'Glare azure', is then a noun phrase of sensational action with its conventional positions switched. The subjective impressionism of 'azure glare' is disarmed in favour of an attempted objectification.

Given this calculated shift of position in the syntax, the obverse is impressively simple in Canto 3. In place of the 'verbal idea of action' in air ('Glare'), we have a simple substantive, which is the energy's proper element ('air'). 'Azure' (noun) is normalised as an adjective and in turn attached to its medium. But, with these normalisations of action, quality and substance, a space is opened for a verbal idea of action in water to complete the syntagm. Where, in Canto 2, in the context 'of water', a noun invoked an action in air ('Glare'), here, in the context of air, we find action signified by the more normal 'float', also in its normal position as a verb. Since 'the cherry tree is all that it does'[19] and *vice versa*, a signifier is not dependent upon its part of speech for its contexture: 'It is not exclusive of parts of speech, but comprehensive; not something which is neither a noun, verb, nor adjective, but something which is all of them at once and at all times.'[20] This polyvalency makes positional disruptions acceptable. Thus the explicit verbal action concealed in Canto 2 by the position of 'Glare' is supplied reciprocally by the normalisations in Canto 3. The gods present in the water are then simply explicitly evoked in the air.

This process (more complicated to describe than it is in action) becomes clearer when we observe the general effect of the two syntagms. In their play of denotation and connotation, they produce *a new signified*, which is neither limited to the object 'water' nor to the object 'air', but situates itself in the relation between them. In each moment the syntagms are denoted in their element ('of . . .', 'in the . . .'). But the terms associated with each of these elements belong equally well to (indeed, they come from) the other, with 'azure', applicable to sky or sea, mediating. In other words, the elements are united in the light sensation, which is signified by terms taken from one medium and applied to the other; thus:

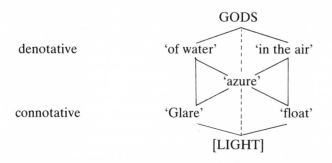

WATER/AIR

Thus we find a process of *analogy* operating between the media at the level of energetic relational structure. The objects signify sensations, which are then abstracted from the phenomena they construct at the level of energetic relations, which are given a privileged autonomy over the phenomena and thereby a role of *mediation* between the two realms. There is a sensational relation of energy which transcends the barriers of objects. If, then, objects do not signify real things but only signify our sensational experience, objects which are commonly constructed by this experience exist in a relation dependent on their unifying sensations and energies. The objects, their associated terms and their positional classes therefore become transposable themselves through the analogy which founds itself in that relation. There is in consequence a metaphoric interpenetration across the boundaries of the objective media: things can 'float' in air, or 'glare' in water. It is this sort of operation which produces the poem's half-worlds and transformations through which the natural world is conjured into a supernatural or divine environment.

There is one more important correlative operation to be noted before we leave this Canto to pursue some of the chains it engenders. The first section, setting the scene for metamorphosis with the compound words, the interpenetration of media, and the projection of the gods, ends as follows:

> There is a wine-red glow in the shallows,
>   a tin flash in the sun-dazzle.
>
>   (2/7)

There are two moments: the first is pure sensation of light on water ('glow', 'flash', 'dazzle'). But each of these is qualified by an object acting as an adjective: 'wine-red' (as classical as the 'azure'), 'tin' and 'sun-'. Once again, objects are adduced (with positional shift) to signify sensations. The point is that, whereas, when maintained in this register, the objects offer substantiality and the possibility of analogy, here the *literalisation* of a set of one of those metaphoric objects carries a metamorphosis at the level of 'objective story'.

At this first stage, 'wine-red' is an object word used figuratively, in the traditional manner. But, as the metamorphosis occurs, terms which belong to the literal set of metonymic associations of this term – ivy, grapes, vine, and so on – gradually take the place of the literal set of metonymic associates of the water, boat, crew, and so on. No longer is the sensation of one object being signified (metaphorically) by another, but, as in the radical metaphor of the Image, a third category of phenomena is produced: the metamorphosed scene. The relation becomes totalised as the change in the metaphor and the dramatic scene occurs. This is normalised and the process of literalisation drawn attention to towards the end of the sequence: 'wave, colour of grape's pulp' (line 147). Whilst 'colour' and 'glow' mediate the relation between the objects, the wine merely signifies towards the mediating sensation. But, when that mediation disappears, the relation becomes totally metamorphic: 'grapes with no seed but sea-foam' (line 60). By thus engineering the transformation of objects, Pound signifies a new and radical psychic state, witnessed by the change of figurative distance into literal location. Once more then, the use of objects to signify sensational energy permits the unification or transformation of objects at many levels, making them interpenetrate or metamorphose. This particular use of natural objects is hence a basic technique of the poem's movement and the production of its values.

III

The Canto which, in a sense, partners Canto 2 is Canto 17, where again Dionysus and a sea goddess (Nerea) appear. In addition, pursuing our water element, we find here an expansion of what Eva Hess calls the 'submarine world' of the poem: the place beneath the sea, in which creation originates.[21] In this case, the creation which rises out of the water is the stones of Venice taking form – the architecture which is, in its turn, another important image of form in *The Cantos*. This Canto further demonstrates the use of objects to represent sensations and their relations, and the process of formal analogy in *The Cantos*, this time with particular reference to stone and gems.

In the first place, the dawn 'half-light' again gives substantiality to the mutating world, making a noun out of a compound adjective: 'With the first pale-clear of the heaven' (17/73). This once more introduces an important transformation:

> Flat water before me,
>   and the trees growing in water,
> Marble trunks out of stillness,
> On past the palazzi,
>   in the stillness.

This is a significant moment in the whole complex of architecture and nature involved in the vision of Venice that follows, and in the use of stone as an image of form in the poem: 'stone knowing the form which the carver imparts it' (74/430).

The importance of stone, sculpture and architecture as embodiments of form and synthesis for Pound date from his pre-First World War enthusiasm for Gaudier-Brzeska and Jacob Epstein (whose Vorticist sculpture 'Rock Drill' lent its name to a book of *The Cantos* published forty years later) and his support for Brancusi through to the central idea of the Temple in *The Cantos*, which is in turn related to the political image of the new city to be constructed, as by Amphion, through the poem.[22] Thus, when Pound wrote of the 'Mediterranean sanity' of the radiant world in which mythic energies had not been perverted by dogmatism or asceticism ('Cavalcanti: Medievalism'), in those paragraphs which we have already cited, his examples came from architecture:

> the Mediterranean sanity. The '*section d'or*', if that is what it meant, that gave the churches like St Hilaire, San Zeno, the Duomo di Modena, the clear lines and proportions. Not the pagan worship of strength, nor the Greek perception of visual non-animate plastic, or plastic in which the being animate was not the main and principal quality, but this 'harmony in the sentience' or harmony *of* the sentient, where the thought has its demarcation, the substance its *virtù*, where stupid men have not reduced all 'energy' to unbounded undistinguished abstraction.[23]

Likewise, in a schema Pound wrote for *The Cantos*, he indicated this Canto as 'Par. Ter.', the earthly paradise.[24] The stone is, then, an image of form, sculpture a privileged Vorticist art, expressing the conceptual intelligence in synthesis with the materials of the natural world: the 'legitimate expression of life'. Similarly, its architecture, in churches and cities, becomes a public value, representing the precise energies of the Dantesque vision in a synthesis of thought and nature, intelligence and sensuality, artistic and vegetable creation.

Here the impossibility of determining the primacy of trees or of stone in 'Marble trunks' expresses that idealised synthesis and points to the fact that neither object is being exclusively signified by the syntagm. Maintaining the line in that synthetic register makes nature monumental and naturalises architecture. Where Donald Davie may again argue that this refers to an objective organic unity of the phenomena,[25] I would maintain that what is signified in this powerful lyricism is the analogic unity of the experience of the energies focused and embodied in the trees/columns for the observing subject.

The association of stone and wood leads in due course to a vision of the taking of form, in the 'song of the boatman':

> 'There, in the forest of marble,
> the stone trees – out of water –
> the arbours of stone –
> marble leaf, over leaf,
> silver, steel over steel,
> silver beaks rising and crossing,
> prow set against prow,
> stone, ply over ply,
> the gilt beams flare of an evening.'
>
> (17/78)

The first section exploits the metonymic chains engendered by 'marble trunks': stone for marble; forest, trees, arbours and leaf for trunks. If objects signify experience, that experience becomes transposable according to the principle of analogy – the structural (relational) unity of experience. The objects themselves are thus equally juxtaposable and transposable: constituted by energies, they all signify the same structure of energetic experience. In this way, paralleling 'marble leaf, over leaf' we have a new analogical set introduced: 'silver, steel over steel'. Immediately one recognises that the object signifies a sensation, since 'silver' refers to the colour, not the material ('steel'). It is also transposable to 'beaks', which is itself a figurative object ('prow'). The presentation focuses continually, then, on the *formal relation* of analogical objects as perceived by a viewing subject (the boatman). The focus extends, however, not only to the relation between, for example, gondolas and other gondolas, but also to that between gondolas and leaves. Thus it deals finally with the formal relation 'behind' their individual formal relations.

Leaves, beaks, prows, steel and stone become a set of objects in relations which may be substituted to signify the unity of the formal relation, which is finally stated in its more abstract register: 'ply over ply'. By means of this abstraction of formal relation from phenomena, those objects which, at the level of denotation, are hard and discrete, enter a context which makes them remarkably flexible. The resultant unity represents, in consequence, an aesthetic harmony between the different realms of nature and art within a phenomenal synthesis through a principle of relational analogy. The place is finally transformed into an ideal image of the harmonious striving of the poem itself through its elements.

This objectively signified ideal is offered here, as in Canto 91, as a result of a descent into the subaquatic world of Nerea–Thetis, where we find, in its turn, the unity of stone and light in the use of gems:

> in the stillness
> The light now, not of the sun,
>   Chrysophrase,
> And the water green clear, and blue clear;
>   On, to the great cliffs of amber.
>   Between them,
> Cave of Nerea.

> (17/76)

The supernatural vision here, fulfilling the project of 'The Flame' and ' "Blandula, Tenella, Vagula" ', is a vision of colour and light hypostasised in their object signifiers, presented through the displacement of the source of light sensation from sun to gem. The light thence becomes supernatural ('not of the sun'), paradoxically free from the darkness of night. Chrysophrase is a gem like beryl (associated, as we have seen, with *virtù*), golden green in colour, to which, in the Middle Ages, was attributed the quality of shining in the dark. Here then it is an object isolated in the text to signify that supernatural shining and its specific sensation (colour). This colour is decomposed into other objects which in turn generate the constituent colours of the central gem. Immediately, the water provides the green (and its own blue shade), and the cliffs (stone) take up the golden, through the object signifier 'amber'.

Finally, a sequence which recurs fairly frequently and always significantly in the poem – ' "In the gloom the gold / Gathers the light about it" ' – frames the song of the boatman. In this way, these objects – water, amber, gold – find their unity in the total given colour relation of the synthetic phenomenon chrysophrase. Once again, objects – in this case, stone and gems – are used to signify a unified image of form, here extending our complex central image of the water/air/crystal/ light, below and above the surface of the water in which it was first formed, towards the sources and the products of creation.

The image is further consolidated in a passage from Canto 25 which Eva Hess interestingly relates to this moment of subaquatic creation:

'As the sculptor sees the form in the air . . .
'As glass seen under water,
'King Otreus, my father . . .
And saw the waves taking form as crystal,
notes as facets of air,
and the mind there, before them, moving,
so that the notes needed not move.

(25/119)

These lines refer us back to Canto 2 and forward to the return of the gods from the sea in Canto 91, as well as to the Dantesque form of radiant energy in 'Cavalcanti: Medievalism'. I would further connect the passage with another significant moment in *The Cantos*:

cosi Elena vedi,
In the sunlight, gate cut by the shadow;
And then the faceted air:
Floating. Below, sea churning shingle.
Floating, each on an invisible raft,
On the high current, invisible fluid,
Borne over the plain. . . .

(20/92)

Here the primary element is not water, stone or gems, but the normally less substantial *air* (which we have already seen following on the aquatic in Cantos 2 and 3). Whilst the other media represent the natural and cultural products among which the poem operates, this medium has a particular importance in that it most of all signifies the poem's own element: ' "I made it out of a mouthful of air." ' As an image of form, it generates an analogy between the concrete images hitherto observed and the formal energy of music – clearly the vital formal medium of a poem.

By now the process is familiar: the sensations of energy (light/ shadow) 'cut' the medium into a form signified by an object ('gate'). At the same time, the verb 'cut' engenders its own more direct chain in terms of light. The prime term of the chain is the latent image of the crystal, signified metonymically through 'faceted'. Thus, through the use of objects which are operated by the sensational term 'cut' (light), the air is associated with the crystal and the stone, the two major images of substantial form:

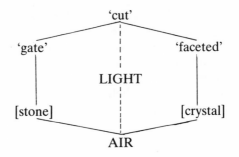

It follows then, by analogy, that, as a jeweller sees the facet in the crystal (a 'rose in the steel dust'), the sculptor sees the form in the air ('As glass seen under water', or the gems of the subaquatic world).

Thus the multiple interpenetration of water, air and stone is established through the unifying metaphorical intervention of the crystal, which is consistently an object functioning as an image of the formal relations of energies:

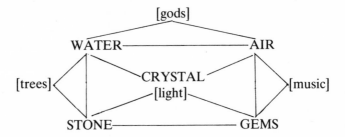

The elements and objects of the poem are thus harmonised through his image. Moreover, via this process of analogy, the vacancies of form and air as the medium of the poem itself are bodied forth through the other objects, and the medium of the poem is engaged with the harmony of the other elements, natural and cultural, in it.

Returning specifically to Canto 20, we find that the 'faceted air' is associated with 'Floating', as in Canto 3. Here, 'Floating' is explicitly juxtaposed with the water: 'Below, sea. . . .' As in Cantos 2 and 3 then, 'Floating' relates the two media. And thus the term which mediates between the poem's objects and the poem itself, between Odysseus's voyage on the surface of and the goddesses below the water, the gods in the subaquatic world who must emerge into the air, and the form in the air, is then made explicit: 'an invisible raft, / On the high current, invisible fluid'.[26]

An invisible fluid which pervades all things, including (if not especially) the air, and on which the invisible raft of the poem's voyage is borne, translates into the poem the radical notion of the ether – the invisible material medium through which all forms of energetic communication travel, and which collapsed the discrete barriers between objects as materialities. The term 'current' provides an anchor for such a reading. When the fluid is invoked in Canto 25 – 'and saw the waves taking form as crystal, / notes as facets of air' – it is transferred analogically from the communication of vision (light-waves) to that of sound. In *The Cantos*, the crystal image operating the water/air mediations serves the function of an 'ether' in providing a transcendent universal 'substance' by which to focus and unify all phenomena and all communication.

IV

It must be emphasised that this transferability between different elements via the unity of structure is not a case of simple synaesthesia. Indeed, Pound's critique of Yeatsian Symbolism attacked its use of suggestion, association *and* synaesthesia, a characteristic Symbolist technique. Pound specifically admonishes, 'Don't mess up the perception of one sense by trying to define it in terms of another.'[27] His technique differs in its use of a dynamic category of *objects* onto which sensation is *projected*. In other words, the notion of form generated in the poem and imaged in the crystal is not synaesthetic but *phenomenalist.*

Generally speaking, objects are used as signifiers of energies of sensational experience and are subjected to transformations, inter-penetrations and juxtapositions productive of and consequent on a profound unity of relational experience, which permits the use of structural analogy. Through this conceived unity, the objects shift from medium to medium, producing a third category, which is the poem itself: a complex energetic image of water, air, stone, light and jewels. These focus together, along with music, towards the crystal, which one may take in large part as the major lyrical constitution of the poem. The external signifier of these media is another phenomenon: the universal metaphoric principle of the ether and the transcendence of energy.

We have looked at only a few passages from a few Cantos, but even so we have observed many important elements of the poem as a whole.

At the level of technique, we have noted the compounding of words and their syntactical (positional) shifting, conjunction and transformation, metamorphosis by literalisation of object signifiers of sensation, as well as projection, analogy and transposition of objects and elements, and harmonic synthesis. At the level of texture, we have observed the production of the half-worlds (half-lights) of the poem, the interpenetration and mutation of elements, the natural and the supernatural, the lyrical imagery of gems, stone and crystal, images of harmony, and the loci of the gods. In terms of the poem's values, we have noted the production of internal symbols borne by the divine presence in the elements, and their contact with the human, which control abstract as well as natural values (which, since this is not an essay on the themes or ideas of *The Cantos*, I have not denoted; interpretations of such values may be found in the ample library of Poundian commentaries). We have concentrated on the building of the crystal image, the way in which analogy operates (with implicit consequences for the poem's relating of its various historical and cultural references), and finally how the poem situates itself within the harmonies and values with which it populates itself.

My analysis of these techniques does not, in general, greatly differ in substance from most orthodox Pound criticism in terms of such details as notions of form, analogy, impersonality, transformation, structure, metamorphosis, and the use of concrete 'particulars'. It does differ, however, in terms of reference. These techniques may be 'explained' with reference to the poetics of *The Chinese Written Character*, of 'Vorticism' or 'Cavalcanti: Medievalism'; and indeed they are consistent with, as they are the mature development of, Pound's project for a modernist poetics. But, for that reason, it is not sufficient to reduce Pound's practice to his own theory. We have already seen how it is likewise not sufficient to explicate those theories in terms of a reality that we elect as 'scientific'; in this sense, Davie's glossed 'forma' is no more clarifying than Pound's own term. This is not, however, to claim that Yvor Winters was right. As we have seen, this is not a technique of a naïve Lockeanism of 'association of sensations'. We have neither the presence of sensation as a purely empirical event (as pure quality), nor a process of subjective associations; rather we have the presentation of 'objects' deployed and related by conceived formal analogies.

By the same token, as we are not presented with Lockean sensations, no more are we presented with objects in a materialist sense. The *surface* of objects, inserted in a universe of formal relations which permits analogous shiftings and interpenetrations, conveys a phenomenalist, and not a materialist, universe. That is to say that the 'object' is not defined in terms of material limits and difference, but as a phenomenon – an external object which, as a signifier of process, is projected out from subjective sensations in terms of a network of unifying formal relations abstracted 'objectively' from experience according to an organising principle of 'conception'. A phenomenalist poetic is therefore not materialist in that it remains basically *subjective*.

However, this is a subjectivism of a special kind. It would be quite wrong to classify the poem as idealist; one cannot subtract Pound's 'belief' in the objectivity of his vision from the poem and turn it into an idealist work, since the objective value operates in the very *form* of the poem. Pound's objects are not abstract, static 'ideas of things' and their relations are not impressionist associations. There is a difference between a subjectivism which signifies itself in terms of ideas, impressions, abstractions and partialities, and one which is signified 'objectively'. Pound's poetics, as theory and practice, differs from an idealist poetics (for example, as in Yeats's 'I declare this tower is my symbol') in a similar way to that in which empirio-criticism differs from straightforward idealism: by retaining 'scientific' values of impersonality, objectivity and universality, most of all in its local means of signification.

An idealist work announces itself as such in its form by locating its elements, analogies, metaphors and fictions in the subject. The subject himself is foregrounded as a vital signifying *presence* in the poem. He defines his limits as a distance from a nature/reality which he can only partially appropriate; where he fails to do this, the poem threatens to take on the form of a hallucination.[28] Phenomenalism, on the other hand, as soon as it projects sensation out onto an apparently real object, generates immediately an *occlusion* of that subject and a collapse of that distance: reality becomes a projected and concealed subjectivity.

Pound's practice in a poetics of objectivity and impersonality depends on the displacement of the subject, which would otherwise 'dull the image' by using 'abstractions' or generate 'subjective inclusions'. The subject is absent as a signifying presence, concealed within the projected objects and implied objective relations which signify the universe of the poem. Consequently the world is signified and organised not within a paradigm of sensational impressions, nor within one of solipsistic ideas, but within a universal 'nature' which guarantees the poem's elemental symbols – that very 'Natura' which is violated by the social evil 'Usura', as in Cantos 45 and 51.[29]

In sum, we can observe that Pound's attempted resolution of the modernist problematic – his project for 'objectivity' and 'conception' – put into practice a technique which uses signifiers of objects with a formal flexibility which generates a vision that unifies an objective world in a harmonious universal 'natural' structure: the 'natural object', indeed, as 'adequate symbol'. These techniques – based, I maintain, in the Image, and elaborated along the lines indicated in our brief analysis of the mature practice – cannot be recuperated as materialist, sensationalist (in Winters's sense), or idealist. Its particular synthesis can only be accounted for in some other paradigm specific to its practice. It may only be posited as objective and impersonal if the absence of the subject as a signifying presence is not a simple evasion or hallucination, but the consequence of a paradigm which authorises such phenomenalist formalism as universal and objective. The scientific phenomenalism of the empirio-critics offers itself as a possible model which would permit the particular synthesis of object and form which we have observed in Pound, *and* would authorise its inscription as objective and impersonal not only in the metadiscourse but also in the very technique of its presentation. Through this scientific model, the necessary synthesis is not a metaphysical but a 'scientific' reality – as, indeed, it has often been read.

This model – which is at least as useful an explanatory device as those used by the more orthodox critics – has the advantage also of avoiding anachronism.[30] Empirio-criticism was an epistemological discourse which sought to respond to a crisis in science comparable to the literary crisis confronting Pound. Having inherited the antithetical tendencies of a materialism perceived as a negation of spirit and an idealism which sought in the achievements of science the destruction of materialism, they generated a synthetic discourse in a frequently popularising mode, which preserved the realism of science whilst permitting the extension of such 'prose values' to spiritual or non-materialist fields.

Empirio-criticism operated in the territory of 'third terms', mediating between matter and spirit in energy and between the subject and the object in 'elements of sensation'. It produced a model of science defined by method and language rather than by its material object. The object itself was replaced by the phenomenon, surviving only as the substantial representation of a sensational process within a universe of energies. Scientific generalisation was then only possible through the abstraction or conception of relations between phenomena according to the rigour of the scientific language and according to a principle of universal analogic relations. The process was saved from collapse back into idealism by the assertion of the primary necessity of experience in terms of the objectivity of relations rather than of quality or matter, supported by the universality of human experience and mental structures, and the determination of such universal structures by the impositions of natural energies.

In this sense, it can be said that the empirio-critical model is parallel to the model we may construct from Pound's poetics. However, the fact that these scientific discourses can be traced in Pound's metadiscourse suggests that the relation is not only parallel, analogical or metaphorical: the poetics is actually *informed* by the empirio-critical discourse.[31] I would further argue, and hope to have illustrated in the course of this chapter, that Pound's poetic practice corresponds not only to his poetics but also to the model which underwrites it and plays such a large part in its acceptability: the practice emerges as the poetic equivalent of the empirio-critical model of language.

What difference does it make to characterise Pound's poetic practice in this way? In the first place, historicising Pound's technique in terms of a *specific* scientific discourse frees us from self-validating and universalising categories of explanation that come from an ahistorical reading. It enables us to problematise the technique and to explain, to an extent, its peculiarities, especially in terms of its *authority*.

Thus, in the first place, the support of such a paradigm authorises a practice which escapes the subjectivity of idealism by effectively occluding the subject within a poetic discourse of impersonality and objectivity. As I observed at the beginning of this chapter, the poem requires the reader to decode it, to reconceive the coherence patterned in its fragmented objects (whether natural or documentary objects). If we are to do this rigorously, we have to respond to the coding which should determine the nature of its decoding. Thus it is that the poem is coded as impersonal and objective in its use of object signifiers and structured in terms of patterns which are signalled as representative of objective relations in the world, both natural and cultural. This has been symptomatically decoded in criticism very largely by the generation of analogous metaphorical guarantees of this objectivity – as we have seen in, for example, the case of Donald Davie. In other words, the poem has an authority in its very technique which determines that, as we explain it, we always tend to confirm it. This is a consequence of its objective and impersonal technique.

Secondly, Pound is enabled, by using such an objective discourse, supported by a scientific metadiscourse, to extend the range of his material. Since science is a question of method and language, having developed a scientific poetic language, based in values of precision, economy, objectivity and impersonality, there is no reason not to deal with objective material in the same scientific terms – not only the material of nature, but also, for example, history, politics and economics. Similarly, then, this coding applies to the 'curriculum' which the poem embodies. The poem presents its history according to the same technique as it uses to present its 'nature', growing, like the stones of Venice, from similar elements. The use of documents, dates and historical material generally constitutes another sort of object, presented to signify a set of historical relations. Such objects are not commented on or theorised in the text; they are juxtaposed in such a way as to imply a relation between them – a relation that predicates a specific political action in contemporary history.

The poem presents us, then, with selected and arranged objects from history, and with a conspicuous *absence* of any theory of history. Ian Bell has generalised this technique:

> Fullness is replaced by a poetics of 'things', of a non-discursive reality whereby phenomenal objects are simply given and achieve their resonance through their allusion to the full system of completeness that inhabits a ghostly meta-world of coherence, of 'rhymes', behind the text itself.[32]

This is justifiable in phenomenalism as soon as one understands that 'things' are not material objects requiring a dialectical operation of theorisation, and that such theorisation would, moreover, only be a metaphysical construction of reality, since it is based on a false assumption about the nature of reality. What we have here in Pound's 'objects' are phenomena – signifiers not of what are held to be metaphysical categories but of what are claimed to be scientific realities: necessary conceived objective relations of universal human experience imposed by the energies of nature. In other words, what is real is phenomenal structure, not object or theory, and, precisely because of this fact, the objects we construct are already signifiers of the structure which forces us to construct them: in their construction as phenomena, they already *embody* the relation to which they refer.

The fragmentary presentation of the poem's 'objects' leaves us with a difficulty in reading, a problem of access. We have to situate ourselves in the spaces between these objects in an attempted transcription of their coherence, for which the curriculum is given to us in 'notes', as Ian Bell has again demonstrated. But the objects are not presented in terms of a theory or as a random field. Their very presentation is structured in a way that predetermines their decoding. The only alternative to acceptance of that predetermination is to offer a critique of their pattern from the point of view of another theory of history which may then be characterised as 'ideological' or 'metaphysical', and embarrassed by the non-theoretical, objective character of the text.

Hence we can only decode these notes in terms of the pattern which presents them. As Bell has argued, in this way, 'by offering a series of objects in this supposedly provisional manner, it in fact traps us within the field of those objects'.[33] In order to decode their coherence, the pattern which supports their presence in the text, we have to mimic their production and reproduce their pattern. We may appear to be doing the work of decoding, but that work is already shaped for us by the aesthetic patterning: 'the instructions of the curriculum [function] as a sealed epistemology'.[34] Since the theory or conception is *in* the objects and their relations, we can only decode those objects (that is, read them) by implicitly reproducing their conception. Thus the notion of phenomenon and relation which authorises the technique commits it simultaneously to a decoding that can only repeat the structures inscribed.

This is why Pound criticism is so characteristically an exercise not only in explication but in confirmation: the text is only decipherable within the 'objective' terms of its inscription and the sealed coherence of its pattern. In this way, it is characteristically recuperated in terms of metaphors of reality, most commonly adapted from scientific discourses, or elsewhere from a modernised mysticism.[35] The only alternative is to decipher the text by constructing Pound's 'theory' of history or 'belief' in the universe in an attempt to reduce the text to a system of subjective and idealist partialities – a more or less well-intentioned 'philosophy of life'.

But such an effort is always contradicted by the text itself, which posits itself as objective and impersonal. In Pisa, Pound asks, 'Hast 'ou seen the rose in the steel dust' (74/449). This is never *a* rose. Similarly, in 'Rock Drill', the empirio-critical principle is reasserted at an important point of recuperation: ' "From the colour the nature / & by the nature the sign!" ' (90/605). Even at the point of recognition of failure, in the last Cantos, Pound wrote,

> I have brought the great ball of crystal;
> who can lift it?
> Can you enter the great acorn of light?
> But the beauty is not the madness
> Tho' my errors and wrecks lie about me.
> And I am not a demi-god,
> I cannot make it cohere.
>
>   (116/795–6)

But, crucially, with or without our supporting the formal pattern (lifting the crystal):

> i.e. it coheres all right
> even if my notes do not cohere.
>   (116/797)

It is a violence to the text to reduce it to a personal vision: that is not how it is written. To read it thus would furthermore be to deny the daring act which initiated the poem: Pound's modernist project which would make poetry more than an egoistic pastime or the arbitrary display of a particular sensibility. Yet of course it is a subjective work, however 'objective' its texture and its ambition. For this is the contradiction of phenomenalism: in projecting the subject into the object and its relations, it effectively conceals the subjective within the objective. Its safeguards against idealism are the dematerialisation of the object as apparently perceived in contemporary physics, and the assertion of the universality of human perception and conception. In short, empirio-criticism was useful in pointing out the constructive aspect of science, but at the same time it did so by collapsing matter into process and locating conception at a purely formal and universally human level. In its necessary critique of what Lenin called 'metaphysical materialism' as the dominant paradigm of nineteenth-century physics, empirio-criticism thereby also elided both matter and ideology – the key notions of the only rival contemporary epistemology which sought a scientific synthesis, dialectical materialism.[36] Without a category of ideology, both science and history become myth.

The contradiction of Pound's text comes then to this: that its *objective* signifiers can only be decoded *ideologically* – either via ideological metaphors of reality, or as a paraphrase of Pound's personal system of ultimately mystical beliefs. The text itself refuses this reduction; it signifies a real world, even though its reading ultimately reveals only the ideological movements of its occluded subject. This contradiction is constitutive of the text and a consequence of the particular path of synthesis sought in Pound's modernism, which found further authorisation in the contemporary scientific discourse of empirio-criticism – that epistemology which recuperated the crisis of subject and object in science as an alternative to dialectical materialism.

5 'The Gorilla and the Bird': Modernism and the Pathology of Language

I

Pound's modernist project for a poetry that would once again be read, without prejudice to its privileged capacities, involved a quest for techniques which would synthesise the special subjectivity of poetry with the social objectivity of 'prose'. In other words, on the one hand we have the 'Old World magic' of the poetic vision, which we have observed in terms of 'delightful psychic experience', 'the radiant world', the world of myth and of the primitive qualities of the Chinese character, relating to chosen historical moments of Classical, Romance and Oriental culture. On the other hand, we have a modern world whose dominant 'prose' discourse is that of science: modern scientific energies, psychology, and the model of the mathematician–psychologist contained in empirio-criticism. Mediating between these two worlds we have Pound's poetics and poetic practice, which we have looked at in terms of the notion of poetic energy, of the Image and the Vortex, and of the particularities of his theory of energetic grammar and metaphor.

These relations can be schematised thus:

138

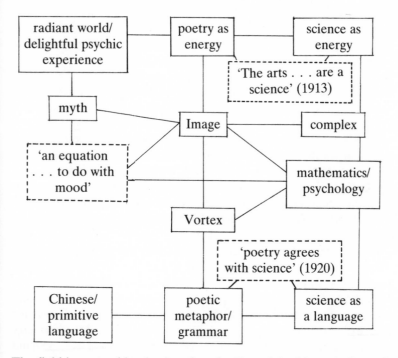

The field is secured by the fact that, for Pound (as I have indicated), myth is precisely a *primitive psychological form* for the expression of the delightful experience of the radiant world. As with the Image and the Vortex, emotion is held to determine form through the exigencies and energies of language, but here the emotion is distinguished as of a special sort of intensity, 'a vivid and undeniable adventure'. The myth appears as 'explications of mood'[1] or 'an impersonal and objective story woven out of his own emotions, as the nearest equation that he was capable of putting into words'.[2]

The connection between the Oriental language and this psychology is found in the study of the Noh plays published in 1916, where we find this drama presented, like the Image and the Classical myth, in terms of an objective form of personal psychic experience. In the first place, the Noh 'has its unity in emotion. It has also what we may call Unity of the Image',[3] achieved, as in myth, through the 'dramatization, or externalization' of the emotion.[4] The Noh plays are compared to the Greek myths in terms of their use of ghosts rather than gods:

The plays are at their best, I think, an image: that is to say, their

> unity lies in the image – they are built up about it as the Greek plays
> are built up about a single moral conviction. . . . The Greek plays
> are troubled and solved by the gods; the Japanese are abounding in
> ghosts and spirits.[5]

They thus produce what Pound calls a 'ghost psychology':[6] 'The
suspense is the suspense of waiting for a supernatural manifestation –
which comes. Some will be annoyed at a form of psychology which is,
in the West, relegated to spiritistic seances. There is however no doubt
that such psychology exists.'[7] The Noh presents a translation of the
spiritistic into the psychological – the scientifically acceptable field of
psychic experience.[8] It is in consequence not surprising that, when the
question 'whether there can be a long imagiste or vorticist poem'
arises, it is the Noh which seems to offer the first answer for a major
form.[9]

Pound's development of his technique into a long poem is clearly
more complex than its integration into a 'Noh' form – although, as we
have observed, part of the drama of *The Cantos* is the preparation for
the apparition of the gods from the sea in Canto 91. But these
developments certainly include the poetics of myth (as in the Image and
as an expression of delightful psychic experience)[10] and the primitive
linguistic capacities of the Chinese script.

If we had to summarise the technical characteristic of Pound's
practice, we might say that it concerns an operation of metonymy acting
on metaphor. The very metadiscourse implies this: the expression of
subjective perceptions and energies of transformation in terms of the
most metonymic of discourses, science. I have already shown how the
mythic technique of the Image involves 'the transformation of a
metaphor in a metonymy', how metamorphosis involves the literalisation of a metaphor, and how a basic technique of *The Cantos* is the use
of object signifiers for sensations, emotions and experiences, arranged
in analogic patterns of energetic relations. Here, the object functions
in a double sense: metaphorically, inasmuch as it is a constructed
symbol of a sensation and not, as in materialism, its cause; but also
metonymically, inasmuch as it continues at the same time to engender
its own chain of objects. The action of the metonymy on the metaphor
produces the Imagiste effects of substantiation, transformation and
harmonisation in the poem. The analogy, in its turn, is clearly a
metaphorical principle; but, because it uses objects and is coded as an
objective relation, such metaphors remain achieved in metonymies.
Metonymy hence operates dynamically with metaphor to give con-

creteness and precision to the vision, whilst the metaphoric function ensures that metonymy does not lapse back into mere description.

Implicit in my use of the terms 'metaphor' and 'metonymy' is of course a reading of Roman Jakobson's essay 'Two Aspects of Language and Two Types of Aphasic Disturbances' (1956). Herbert N. Schneidau, who has been influential in the analysis of Pound's use of metonymy, has himself taken this essay and, with a certain confessed reluctance, turned it into a literary justification of Pound's technique. He describes the 'selection-deficient aphasic', compares Pound's technique and argues 'that Ezra Pound's poetics show a surprising correlation to this aphasis'.[11] He then concludes, 'we may surmise that Pound did find a way to make his poetic speech new and primal at the same time, by embracing this fundamental pole so enthusiastically'. The keynote here is 'primal': Schneidau is drawing a three-way relation between Pound's technique, a diagnosed state of pathological disorder, and a primal poetic energy. At the same conference where this paper was originally given, the late Louis Zukofsky emphasised the creativity of the pathological question when he proclaimed of Pound's 'madness' that 'that's what genius is – in the persistence of it'.[12]

Whatever one may feel about such a problematic affirmation, at the same time one does find that reading the psychologists' reports on Pound produced at his trial is a strange experience.[13] In diagnosing him as a paranoid schizophrenic, the doctors describe his personal discourse in terms which correspond in an uncanny way to one's first impressions of his poetry. His ideas do not seem to connect; he keeps going off at a tangent; he is obsessed by economics and the American Constitution; he insists on referring everything back to Confucius; he is sometimes incoherent; he appears to suffer from delusions and has grandiose ideas (such as trying to write a twentieth-century epic poem?).

Clearly there is something in all this, and, in particular, in Schneidau's analysis. 'The lunatic, the lover, and the poet' are, in some sense, 'of imagination all compact' (*A Midsummer Night's Dream*, v.i), precisely because they are all involved in the workings of the Imaginary. So the mechanisms of poetry are bound to bear *some* relation to certain psychopathological phenomena, operating by means of displacements, condensations, projections, idealisation, catharses, and so on. Although one should beware of simplifications, studies such as Jakobson's – which has been usefully employed to elaborate theories of literary production and has an essential role in the structural anthropology of Claude Lévi-Strauss and the psychoanalysis of Jacques Lacan – do have an application to the study of literature: poetry does operate by means of the Imaginary mechanisms of a pleasure principle and not the mechanisms of logical ratiocination.

Indeed, the more one considers it, the more general the case becomes. All the techniques of poetry have clear parallels in dreams, neuroses and psychoses; and the same holds for the poetic enterprise itself. The hysteric hears voices; the dreamer annihilates distance; the psychotic produces a personal mythology. The poet does all this, and more. But does this mean that poetry is, by its nature, a pathological discourse? For the parallel threatens to lose its power to discriminate: if all poetry is 'deranged', does the parallel not become a tautology? Does it remain in any sense intelligible to draw the parallel? There would be only one test which could make the relation between poetry and pathology meaningful in this context: if it is true that all poetry is, in some analogical or non-literal sense, 'pathological', is it still possible to identify a pathological poem? – for is it not Mussolini who is reported to have said, 'I, I am not a politician; I am a mad poet!'?

In other words, it seems to me important to establish a productive discrimination between the discourse of a text and the discourse of mental disorder. This is not a question of stygmatising the latter. But it seems to me that it is not enough to say, 'All poetry is "mad" ' – as if to say, 'After all, we're all basically pretty "mad", aren't we?' Nor is it enough to be complacent about the risks run by the poet in searching for the 'new and primal' – risks which clearly rebounded on Pound. In applying studies such as Jakobson's one should not forget that the originals are studies of pathological phenomena. These phenomena do not cease to be pathological (and, one might add, associated with suffering) in being applied to the privileged texts of literature. If they do, it is because the analysis has become so metaphorical and abstract as to lose its defining rigour. I would argue that what is lacking is that test by which we could say that a text, whilst sharing the normal mechanisms of literature in relation to those of mental disorder, is actually itself in some meaningful sense pathological.

The mechanisms shared by poetry and pathology have, however, also been used to provide a general justification for art by reference not so much to symptoms of pathology as to the devices and structures of *myth*. For such mechanisms – condensation, displacement, idealisation, projection, introjection, the omnipotence of thoughts – are also found to underlie the production of myth, totem and taboo.[14] Poetry thus becomes related not to pathology, but to 'primal' mythic powers, as in Schneidau's conclusion.[15] It is certainly the case that the *technical* parallels can be drawn with respect to Pound – as I myself have sought to draw them. We find ourselves bordered, then, by the two paradigms of a romanticism of the 'mad' poet and the primal nostalgia of the poet of myth. Both are based on the incidence of similar mechanisms: a relation between the mechanisms of poetry and those of what we have come to call, in general terms, 'the unconscious'.

The modernist quest for a revitalisation of poetic discourse commonly included a recuperation of 'primitive' or 'Old World' energies perceived as primal, original powers of language, in many cases expressed in the discourses of the new sciences (among which we should include anthropology as much as physics). In this pursuit, the unconscious has been much used as an explicit or implicit resource for such powers – in the field of dreams, automatic writing or painting, myth, the naïve or primitive, or, in Pound's case, the 'complex'.[16]

Nowhere is this more the case than in Surrealism: not only implicitly in the dream-like quality of their paintings, but also explicitly in, for example, the influential manifestos of André Breton, whose Surrealism was specifically intended to open up the language of the unconscious. In pursuit of intellectual capital for this enterprise, Breton tried to enlist Freud as the 'patron saint' of Surrealism. But Freud unreservedly rejected the role. More than that, he accused the Surrealists of a 'folie': they were fetishising the unconscious, turning themselves into victims of a 'perversion' through their Imaginary fixation on a partial object.[17] Breton's use of the unconscious is, then, not Freudian, and Freud's response indicates a very different attitude to the unconscious as a resource for art.

What sort of unconscious does Breton's project suggest? It can be argued that it has much in common with Jung's and with the authority which he has given, this century, to the functions of dreams, myths, alchemy, and so on: in sum, his validation of occultism. Occultism is an epistemology which also depends on those same 'unconscious' mechanisms, as well as being an attitude which has gone hand in hand with many modernist projects. Jung himself recollects with irony an important confrontation with Freud on this subject:

> I still have a vivid memory of Freud saying to me: 'My dear Jung, promise me that you will never abandon the theory of sexuality. It is the most important thing! We must make it a dogma, an unbreachable bastion.' . . . A little astonished, I asked him: 'A bastion? –

against what?' He replied: 'Against the dark tide of . . .' – here he
paused for a moment, and added – '. . . of occultism!'[18]

This strikes me as a crucial distinction. On the one hand we have those
modernist attitudes which see in art the mechanisms of the unconscious and of myth and which celebrate those mechanisms as a positive
resource for art and, eventually, for a knowledge with which to oppose
mechanicist logic. This would be the position for which Jung is the
'patron saint'. Against this – as the only defence in this modernist
context – a Freudian, sexual theory of the unconscious.

This confrontation can be historicised. The unconscious emerged
into acceptability very slowly in England, especially before the First
World War, which is the period which most concerns us in focusing on
the crucial stage of Pound's developing modernism. It was indeed only
during the war that the therapeutic success of psychoanalytic techniques in treating cases of shell-shock greatly advanced (and transformed) its acceptability. Such was the resistance to the scientific
notion of the unconscious at the time that psychologists found that the
major problem was to establish its general acceptability as a scientific
category, rather than to specify its constitution.

Bernard Hart himself, as we have seen, contributed to the relative
acceptance of the notion, but he did so in terms of an unconscious
deprived of its sexual base.[19] An interesting contribution to the debate
was Hart's essay in a book called *Subconscious Phenomena*, edited by
Hugo Münsterberg in 1912, in which he offers a symptomatic survey of
the case for a scientific acceptance of the category itself. The work was,
in Hart's words, 'an attempt to investigate the essential nature of this
conception [the subconscious], to determine its claim to a place in the
structure of modern science, and the position which must be assigned
to it within that structure.'[20]

The need for such a debate over the very accessibility of a '*sub-*', a
'*co-*' or an '*un*conscious' to science arose because of the mechanicist
prejudice which we have already seen addressed by Hart. But it was
aggravated by the fact that the concept itself had been formed more or
less independently in a number of diverse fields – metaphysical,
mystical, poetic, physiological, pathological, philosophical and
psychological. Indeed, much of the evidence for a 'secondary consciousness' came from fields generally rejected by science. Without
dwelling here on the possible role of the nineteenth-century poets and,
in particular, mystery-story writers in the exploration of the question
of 'another' consciousness, much depended, for example, on an

assessment of the work of Mesmer and his successors, whose studies had provided material for the concept of 'suggestion' – 'the conception which may be regarded as the foundation stone of modern psychopathology', as Hart saw it.[21]

More recently, F. W. H. Myers and the Society for Psychical Research, with their studies on mediumship, hypnosis, ghost vision and so on, had provided considerable evidence in favour of concepts of suggestion, dissociation and a depth model of consciousness.[22] As William James declared in 'Frederic Myers's Service to Psychology' (1901),

> Myers has not only propounded the problem definitely, he has also invented definite methods for its solution. Post-hypnotic suggestion, crystal-gazing, automatic writing and trance speech, the willing game, etc., are now, thanks to him, instruments of research, reagents like litmus paper or the galvanometer, for revealing what would otherwise be hidden.[23]

Myers was one of the very few people to be receptive to Freud in England before the First World War. He read to the Society Freud and Breuer's first study in hysteria a few months after its publication in 1893. His researches had already led him to propound a proto-theory of the subconscious:

> Myers held that personality was composite in character, and that large areas of it were 'subliminal', i.e., below the threshold of consciousness. These subliminal regions in which symbolism was the natural language not only accounted for many abnormal phenomena . . . but also for 'supernormal' phenomena. . . . It was capable not only of telepathy, but of 'ecstasy' or 'psychic excursions'.[24]

And, as late as 1911, Freud, writing to Jung, noted with pleasure an invitation to become a corresponding member of the Society as 'The first sign of interest in *dear old England*.'[25]

So, whilst Myers was singularly receptive to Freud at both the polemical and theoretical levels, at the same time however, similar phenomena to those researched by Myers and the Society for Psychical Research were being identified not in the realm of the 'supernormal', but in that of the physiological, in terms of a strictly abnormal neuropathology. Here the subconscious was portrayed, as in the work of Boris Sidas, as bestial, primitive, crude and dangerous in its effects on conscious life. Many theorists in this physiological field in fact objected strongly to all non-materialist accounts, which they accused of being 'philosophical' or 'mystical', rather than scientific. For many such scientists, all emergent depth psychologies of a mental sort were indistinguishable from mysticism, as witness the comments of a member of the American Neurological Association in response to a paper given in 1910 by J. J. Putnam: 'It was time the Association took a stand against transcendentalism and supernaturalism and definitely crushed out Christian Science, Freudism and all that bosh, rot and nonsense.'[26]

If one considers the materials and methods on which Freud based his scientific account – hypnosis, hysteria, dreams, parapraxes, jokes – there is no reason why Myers's research should have appeared any more or less inherently invalid than that of Freud for a contemporary audience; even less so in the case of Jung. Whilst Hart combats on the one hand physiological exclusivity, and on the other seeks to relegate Myers's studies (along with those of the 'metaphysical materialist', Delboeuf) to 'speculative interpretations which do not enter into the field of science',[27] the methodological principles with which Hart introduced the unconscious into science functioned as well for the psychical researchers. I have already indicated for example William James's use of the 'science as method' argument and Lodge and Barrett's use of the inferential character of the ether. But we should also note that it is Freud himself who observed that 'The opponents of the unconscious . . . had never realized that the unconscious is something which we really do not know, but which we are obliged by compelling inferences to supply'[28] – much as Myers himself posits his 'subliminal self' as no more than a 'limiting and rationalising hypothesis'.[29] It is also worth bearing in mind that neither William James nor the positivist founder of the school of 'act psychology', William MacDougall, found their ambitions for a scientific psychology based on a depth model anything but compatible with holding the Presidency of the Society for Psychical Research.

Thus, effectively, in England and to a large extent in America, Freud was commonly rejected at this time because he was 'mystical', like Myers; in other circles, such as the Society, he was acceptable because he was 'scientific', like Myers. The middle ground, which Hart for example sought to inhabit, was very sparsely inhabited at this stage.[30]

Since Hart's own major contribution to the popularisation (and revision) of Freud was the concept of the 'complex', we might also bear in mind that, as early as 1914, Freud was saying of this word that 'None of the other terms coined by psychoanalysis for its own needs has achieved such widespread popularity or been so misapplied to the detriment of the construction of clearer concepts.'[31] By 1920, W. H. R. Rivers, an eminent English experimental psychologist, in his review of the theory of the unconscious, selected the term 'complex' as having 'so caught the general fancy that it is becoming part of popular language'.[32] He goes on to note the consequences of this popularity and misapplication, putting the responsibility on

> Bernard Hart, who more than any other English writer has made the psychology of the unconscious part of general knowledge, and has greatly extended the meaning of the term and uses it for any 'emotionally toned system of ideas' which determines conscious behaviour.[33]

He concludes,

> In fact, the word is often used in so wide and loose a sense that my own tendency is to avoid it altogether, and this course will have to be followed in scientific writing unless we can agree upon some definition which makes the term 'complex' really serviceable as an instrument of thought.

Whilst, first, we may be in a position to tell the difference between, say, William James's more extended use of the empirio-critical model and Hart's more rigorous application, they are none the less using a similar argument. The case that will admit 'purpose' or 'the unconscious' into science will admit much else besides. Secondly, but not of secondary importance, we have the fact that Hart's apparently more scientific case proves to contain its own ambiguities. Thus, remembering the contemporary status of Freud's theories, we can see that it is in fact history, ideology and the progress of science which distinguishes for us the spectrum that might go Myers→ James→ Hart → Freud, in increasing order of authentic scientific discourse. Synchronically, these distinctions are much less clear.

The abiding prejudice against mental theories, secondary consciousnesses and depth psychology meant, then, that the pressing problem was to make *a* concept of the unconscious in general scientifically acceptable. This pressure tended effectively to relegate the differential question of the scientificity of particular theories of the unconscious to a secondary level. In this way the concept remains popularly polyvalent, limited on the one hand by the normal–abnormal–supernormal continuum of the unconscious envisaged by the Society for Psychical Research (the sort of unconscious Jung was later to expound, or the sort of notion advertised by Breton – which Jean Starobinski traces away from Freud and explicitly towards Myers[34]), and on the other hand by the more disturbing unconscious posited by psychopathology as the source of abnormality and disorder. This fundamental contradiction in the constitution of the unconscious – which likewise obscures Freud's own conception from view at the time – is to a large extent effectively concealed within the contemporary debate for the acceptability of a general category of the unconscious.

What was in question was clearly a necessary revolution in the paradigm governing psychology: to establish as a science both a purely mental psychology in general and a depth psychology in particular. Such revolutions, as witness the contemporary upheaval in energetic physics, necessarily undergo a period of ambiguity before the research they permit enables its practitioners to differentiate their concepts.

Hugo Münsterberg, who, although he saw no place for a non-physiological depth psychology, was none the less aware of the problem, put the question in a most interesting way. He viewed it as a question of psychology's contemporary position as an apparent point of synthesis for the objective and subjective views (materialism/idealism), which for him in fact concealed a real contradiction:

> Psychotherapy . . . is the last word of the passing naturalistic movement; and yet in another way it tries to be the first word of the coming idealistic movement; and because it is under the influence of both, it speaks sometimes the language of the one, and sometimes the language of the other. That brings about a confusion and a disorder which must be detrimental. To transform this vagueness into clear, distinct relations, is the immediate duty of science.[35]

The collection of essays he edited (*Subconscious Phenomena*, 1912) does not, however, as I have suggested, clarify the issue in the way in which Münsterberg wished, in favour of a clear distinction between the materialist (scientific) and the idealist (philosophical) field. Rather it demonstrates the continuing range and polyvalency of the notion, synthesised in Hart's empirio-critical conclusion.[36]

Yet, as Münsterberg was, in his way, aware, the differentiation of the concept of the unconscious is of major importance. But it is important not only for psychology as a science but also indeed crucially to the destiny of modernism in all fields, at least inasmuch as it is concerned with the mechanisms of the unconscious. On this differentiation rests a decisive point about the relation between art and knowledge, between modernism and pathology.

The dilemma – towards the abnormal, or the supernormal? – is well expressed in Wyndham Lewis's lines of 1933:

Do your damnedest! Be yourself! Be an honest-to-goodness sport!
Take all on trust! Shut up the gist-nag's mouth! Batten upon report!
And you'll hear a great deal more, where a sentence breaks in two,
Believe me, than ever the most certificated school-master's darlings
    do!
When a clause breaks down (that's natural, for it's been probably
    overtaxed)
Or the sense is observed to squint, or in a dashing grammatical tort,
You'll find more of the stuff of poetry than ever in stupid syntax!

I sabotage the sentence! With me is the naked word.
I spike the verb – all parts of speech are pushed over on their backs.
I am the master of all that is half-uttered and imperfectly heard.
Return with me where I am crying out with the gorilla and the bird![37]

This primal *discours sauvage*, does it lead to lyrical transformation, or irrational distortion? Is it a return to the gorilla or to the bird? Poetry does indeed sabotage the sentence. So is it condemned to cry out with the gorilla (which, in Poe's 'Murders in the Rue Morgue' the proto-psychologist-*cum*-detective confidently identified as the bestial murderer by its *in*human language, its pastiche of the foreignness of language)? Or can we rest assured that an Orphic lyricism will arise? Must the sleep of syntax produce monsters? Or is it the liberation of creative imagination?

I believe that the answers to these questions may be found in the only place where the issue of the constitution of the unconscious was being directly confronted at the time: in the private correspondance between Freud and Jung in 1911–12. This debate is, I feel, central to the experience of this century. For it was clearly the 'bird' that our modernists, in their various versions of unconscious mechanisms (whether Freudian or, more often, not), were pursuing; the irony is that many of them, such as Pound, found themselves singing for the gorillas.

II

In 1911, as psychoanalysis was struggling out of its association with mystical non-science, Jung threatened to take it once again out of science. Freud had been meeting considerable resistance to his theory of sexuality as the material base of the psyche. Jung, in his American lectures of 1911 and in *The Psychology of the Unconscious* (1912), overcame much of the resistance, as Freud himself admitted, but only by abandoning the sexual basis.

To avoid a crude sensationalist or biological reduction, Freud had posited the term 'libido' to signify the function of sexuality in its psychic register.[38] The issue between Freud and Jung came down to the relation between libido and anxiety in their expression, particularly, in the Oedipus complex. Freud maintained that anxiety signified symptomatically the problematic presence of sexual libido. Jung reversed this relationship. Freud wrote to him on 23 May 1912, 'I believe we have held up to now that anxiety originated in the prohibition of incest; now you say on the contrary that the prohibition of incest originated in anxiety, which is very similar to what was said before the days of psychoanalysis.'[39]

Jung had maintained that the signifiers of sexuality had 'a significance that amounts to pure fantasy': 'Like the stones of the temple, the incest taboo is the symbol or vehicle of a far wider and special meaning which has as little to do with real incest as hysteria with the sexual trauma, the animal cult with the bestial tendency and the temple with the stone.'[40] He thereby established the base of the psyche not in sexuality, but in a realm of pure spirituality. As he wrote in the key chapter of *The Psychology of the Unconscious*, 'The Sacrifice',

> The sexuality of the unconscious is not what it seems to be; it is merely a symbol; it is a thought as bright as day, clear as sunlight, a decision, a step towards every goal of life – but expressed in the unreal sexual language of the unconscious, and in the thought form of an earlier stage.[41]

In sum, Jung shifted sexuality to the level of the signifier, and established some positive notion of spiritual experience at the level of the signified.

Freud's outrage at this was, presciently, total. By the end of 1912, all communication between them, except at an official level, had ceased. Freud explained the disagreement from his point of view in 1914. His main objection was that 'Jung's modification . . . loosens the connection of the phenomena with instinctual life.'[42] He argued that his former disciple was predisposed to a spiritual and religious valuation of the unconscious. Presented with the undeniable evidence of sexuality, Jung (according to Freud) was left with

only one way out: it must be that from the very first these complexes do not mean what they seem to be expressing, but bear the higher 'anagogic' meaning . . . which made it possible for them to be employed in the abstract trains of thought of ethics and religious mysticism.[43]

It is important to note that Freud does not disagree with Jung as to the *mechanisms* involved in the unconscious. His theory of the Oedipus complex, *Totem and Taboo*, also appeared in 1912; and it is clear that he and Jung identify similar mechanisms in the unconscious and in primitive thought. These are likewise the same – as they both argue – as those mechanisms which determine both the thought of the child in the narcissistic stage and the neurotic in his sickness. The difference between Freud and Jung lies entirely in the question of the evaluation of that relationship.

The primacy of religiosity or the primacy of sexuality clearly makes a major difference to the interpretation and valuation of the material. Is it the song of the bird one hears in the distortions of the unconscious – something to be cultivated for its primal spiritual values? Or is it the threat of the gorilla, of undifferentiated and unsocialised sexuality (including its sado-masochistic structures), to be repressed and sublimated for its potentially pathological character? We are offered two visions of the unconscious: from Freud, the 'night side' of mental life, requiring repression to turn it into civilisation; from Jung, 'a thought as bright as day', which only needs to be liberated as an expression of its primal spiritual value. The situation may remind us ironically of the two visions of heaven offered to Huck Finn by the widow and by Miss Watson:

Sometimes the widow would take me to one side and talk about

Providence in a way to make a body's mouth water; but maybe next day Miss Watson would take hold and knock it all down again. I judged I could see that there was two Providences, and a poor chap would stand considerable show with the widow's Providence, but if Miss Watson's got him there warn't no help for him any more. I thought it all out, and reckoned I would belong to the widow's, if he wanted me, though I couldn't make out how he was a-going to be any better off then than what he was before, seeing I was so ignorant and so kind of low-down and ornery.[44]

Our exploiters of the unconscious chose a Jungian vision of a psychic providence. But choosing the widow's would not in itself make it so. The unconscious will insist on turning out 'ignorant . . . and ornery'.

One does not want to take the metaphor too far and turn the unconscious into a veritable enemy or sort of original sin. What I mean is that many of the artists of modernism pursued a positive – as it were, innocent – vision of the unconscious, tending towards that theorised by Jung. But what so many of them came to express was a vision of the release of the unconscious more in keeping with Freud's. In other words, if Jung were right, our artists would have succeeded in restoring a primal spiritual sense to the world through their adaptation of unconscious (primitive or infantile or dream-like) mechanisms, as many sought to do. But, since he was not, they found themselves in service not of the primitive but of the barbaric.

What then of Freud's theory? As I have said, he perceived the same mechanisms at work in primitive thought, neurosis, the infantile and the dream. He elaborated the relationship by offering a genetic model of the relation between the primitive and the child which extends the psychological into a cultural analysis:

If we regard the existence among primitive races of the omnipotence of thoughts as evidence in favour of narcissism, we are encouraged to attempt a comparison between the phases in the development of men's view of the universe and the stages of the individual's libidinal development. The animistic phase would correspond to narcissism both chronologically and in its content; the religious phase would correspond to the stage of object-choice of which the characteristic is a child's attachment to his parents; while the scientific phase would have an exact counterpart in the stage at which an individual has reached maturity, has renounced the pleasure principle, adjusted himself to reality and turned to the external world for the object of his desires.[45]

But Freud continues here, 'In only a single field of our civilisation has the omnipotence of thoughts been retained, and that is in the field of art.'

So again, do we find after all a Freudian justification for art as myth, or a condemnation of art as narcissistic disorder? Although the sort of parallels established in psychoanalysis undoubtedly exist, they have tended to be seized upon in such a way as to overlook the major differences between them. Whilst primitive mechanisms correspond to narcissistic mechanisms, a primitive is not a child; a dreamer is not a neurotic; a poet is neither child, shaman, nor neurotic. As Freud also writes, 'The neuroses exhibit on the one hand striking and far-reaching points of agreement with those great social institutions, art, religion, and philosophy. But on the other hand, they seem like distortions of them. . . .'[46]

They resemble each other in terms of mechanism. But in what way do the child, the primitive, the neurotic, the dreamer, and the poet differ? The difference is found in distinguishing between *mechanism* and *function* and is dependent upon the question of *social context*. This important point is made by Freud in his analysis of the relation between dreams and jokes. Having once again drawn the parallels between the mechanisms involved in both activities, he continues,

The most important difference lies in their social behaviour. A dream is a completely asocial mental product; it has nothing to communicate to anyone else. . . . Not only does it not need to set any store by intelligibility, it must actually avoid being understood, for otherwise it would be destroyed; it can only exist in masquerade. . . . A joke, on the other hand, is the most social of all the mental functions that aim at a yield of pleasure. It often calls for three persons and its completion requires the participation of someone else in the mental process it starts. The condition of intelligibility is, therefore, binding on it; it may only make use of possible distortion in the unconscious through condensation and displacement up to the point at which it can be set straight by the third person's understanding. . . .[47]

It is altogether a question of *social conditionality*. The primitive forms which employ such mechanisms do so in a social context which gives them a rational function – as Freud wrote, 'taboo is not a neurosis but a social institution'.[48] Neurosis, on the other hand, is characteristically anti-social:

> The asocial nature of neuroses has its genetic origin in their fundamental purpose, which is to take flight from an unsatisfying reality into a more pleasurable world of phantasy. The real world, which is avoided in this way by neurotics, is under the sway of human society and of the institutions collectively created by it. To turn away from reality is at the same time to withdraw from the community of men.[49]

Thus, in the social context of the tribe, the mechanisms of the unconscious are worked up into knowledge, the animistic products of magic and myth. But those same mechanisms worked up into knowledge in the individual in capitalist society become not the social products of myth and magic but the anti-social products of delusion and neurosis.

Now, a work of art is, like the joke, a social product. It may, therefore, most certainly employ 'mythic' techniques or mechanisms, but, if it is to avoid personal or social pathology, it has to do so within the social conditionality proper to it. The poet, and the poem, no longer subsist in a social environment, such as the primitive tribe, where such mechanisms may produce knowledge. If the poem endeavours to do this, to use its mechanisms for the production of pleasure to generate knowledge, it can only produce occultism. To avoid the pathological, art must seek its social conditionality; and, if it is to avoid occultism, it must seek another conditionality than that of knowledge. As Theodor Adorno puts it, 'Art is magic delivered from the lie of being truth.'[50] Its social conditionality is that neither of knowledge nor of neurotic delusion, but of *fiction*.

Pierre Macherey offers a useful account of this specific category of fiction. In the first place, it is not, *a priori*, to be viewed as error: 'La fiction, qu'il ne faut pas confondre avec l'illusion, est le substitut, sinon l'équivalent d'une connaissance.'[51] But it uses its mechanisms of the imaginary to produce a *conditional* knowledge: 'La fiction, c'est l'illusion déterminée: l'essence du texte littéraire est dans l'institution d'une telle détermination.' The text tells us not only what it knows, but also how it knows it – the conditions under which it knows. But, because of that conditionality, the utterance of a literary text cannot take the place of science: 'La fiction n'est pas plus *vraie* que l'illusion;

on dira encore: elle ne peut tenir lieu d'une connaissance.' The conditionality which saves fiction from being merely an illusion prevents it from being a universally valid objective knowledge.

Macherey institutes three terms, separated not by a continuous progression, but by epistemological breaks:

> Il importe donc de distinguer les trois formes que donnent au langage trois usages différents: illusion, fiction, théorie. Les mêmes mots, à peu de choses près, composent ces trois discours: mais entre ces mots s'établissent des rapports incomparables, tellement séparés qu'il est impossible de passer sans rupture de l'un à l'autre.

Fiction, then, is a form of knowing that is not 'false' like illusion, nor 'true' like theory (science); it is rather a conditional knowledge, a determined illusion. To paraphrase Adorno, fiction is illusion delivered from the lie of being theory.

The simplest way of stating my case is that Pound lacks a category of fiction. His statements – 'The arts . . . are a science', and 'poetry agrees with science' – allow him to inscribe as knowledge what properly belongs in the category of fiction. Hence partial knowledges gain the status of total knowledges, the subjective passes as the objective, and products of an idealism are inscribed, using object signifiers and the discourse of science, as realism. The epistemological authority which permits such an inscription accompanies specific poetic techniques which have a parallel effect, which can be summarised as the use of 'scientific' and 'objective' procedures and 'mythic' mechanisms.

We have noted, for example, Pound's tactic of impersonality – the translation of subjective values into impersonal forms – at the levels of critical literary criteria, the metadiscourse of poetic theory, and poetic practice. We have studied his use of the radical metaphor of myth, the 'tradition of metamorphoses', and the projective signification of *The Cantos*. We have noted the use of the totalising effects of metonymy on metaphor. Finally, along with his use of a metadiscursive value of 'objectivity', we have observed Pound's use of object signifiers subordinate to a subjectivity concealed by that surface of objects. In ideological terms, we have encountered the very notion that a poem may provide historical knowledge of economics and politics in a 'scientific' manner, and the construction of an objective category of 'nature'.

The extraordinary absence of a subject as signifying presence in

Pound's poetic technique – the consequence of the required critique of the irrelevance of late nineteenth-century subjectivism – becomes an index of the absence of a category of fiction. In masking the subject *as* subject, and hence the conditional nature of his utterances, Pound determines his illusion as 'impersonal and objective'. In short, by making poetry a 'science', Pound obliterates the distinction between fiction and theory. He is then committed to employing the mechanisms of magic and sustaining the lie of their being truth.

Pound was able to do this by a narcissistic manipulation of the discourse of science: that is to say, by turning 'science' and its terms into a metaphor and a rhetorical gesture under the control of his own poetics. The incorporation of science thus gave his utterance a theoretical acceptance at the verbal level; in truth, however, it makes science an imaginary object. Such manipulation was possible because of the critical nature of the scientific discourses available at this time of epistemological transition. Empirio-criticism in particular, in abandoning the determinant of the object, and lacking the category of ideology, had opened itself for such manipulation. In its simultaneous attack on antecedent materialism and idealism and its consequent synthesis of subject and object, this epistemology had broken down the barrier between the Imaginary and the Real: if the object is an imaginary construct, then all objects, and objectivity itself, become functions of the Imaginary order, partial objects. The discourse of science, as the discourse of the Other, falls victim to that Imaginary manipulation: it becomes a phantasy object.[52]

In short, Pound uses the primitive mechanisms to produce what he codes as knowledge in a theoretical and technical phantasy of science. The text therefore becomes committed to an occultist position, in the sense that occultism is the narcissistic (Imaginary) mechanisms of primitive thought worked up into knowledge. If, as Freud argued, psychoanalysis reveals that supernatural reality was 'nothing but psychology projected into the external world',[53] in this phenomenalist science, the external world itself is nothing but the projections of psychology. What was within returns from without; or, as Adorno argues, 'Occultism is a reflex-action to the subjectification of all meaning'; it is 'subjectivity mistaking itself for its object'.[54] What is eclipsed in occultism is precisely the category of fiction, defined in terms of the conditional: 'The tendency to occultism is a symptom of regression in consciousness. This has lost the power to think the unconditional and to endure the conditional. . . . The unconditional becomes fact, the conditional an immediate essence.'[55] Occultism is not yet delusion; but nor is it, in the modern world, 'primal truth'. It is rather the epistemological formation of the primitive mechanisms existing within inappropriate social conditions.

Such occultism may be valued only in an asocial, idealist or spiritual context, such as Jung's desexualised theory of the unconscious may provide. But, once coded as knowledge, it determines the social conditionality in which it may be decoded. If *The Cantos* is 'the tale of the tribe', then it equally well seeks to construct the tribe whose tale it is telling: the subject who succeeds in reading the poem is positioned as a member of the imaginary tribe whose ideology structures the tale. It is for this reason that the potential reader is sealed within the poem's repeats and the foreclosure of its surface openness, committed to a confirmation of its metaphors. The extent to which Poundian criticism mimics Pound is a symptom of the poem's creation of a 'tribe' which is effectively a phantasy of its occluded subject, and the particular authority which it exercises. In other words, returned to the social conditionality in which the poem exists as knowledge, the picture is quite different from its potential idealisation as the lyric of personal beliefs.

It is even more different when we bear in mind that the 'tribe' which the poem sought to produce is far from satisfied in a school of criticism; its political ambition was much broader, and much more political. Thus, it may be maintained (as it often enough is) that what Pound meant by 'Fascism' was, adopting one of his metaphors, 'A thousand candles together blaze with intense brightness',[56] and that what he intended by 'jew' or 'kikery' was an economic class, not a so-called racial group, or that when he wrote that 'USURY is the cancer of the world, which only the surgeon's knife of Fascism can cut out of the life of nations',[57] his discourse did 'not mean what it seems to be expressing'. But such a restoration of spiritual ideals is given the lie by the violent literalness of history. History remains the objective test of such metaphors, supplying the irony lost in the unconditional utterance of a false knowledge.

For the fact is that the mechanisms of occultism successfully worked up into institutions in the social context not of the tribe but of late capitalism become fascism. The animistic tribe is literalised in the mythic *Volk*, organised around the all-powerful figure of the Leader and the racially based gods and demons, in pursuit of the total implementation of tribal destiny. The categories of animism at work in industrialised society generate barbaric social and international relations, organised around totems and taboos, binary power discriminations (black/white; male/female; us/them), within a totalitarian structure of authority. The objective is mystified in the occlusion of its sources, and totalitarian in the exercise of its power. Fascism may dream its ideals, but it also raises ghosts in order to persecute them. In short, the mechanisms which may be institutionalised, at a particular stage of society, in the tribe, and which, in the individual, may function asocially in the dream, when they seek implementation in institutions in the modern social context, give rise to a grotesque realisation of their pathology; or, as Adorno identified the irony so eloquently in 1935, 'In Fascism the nightmare of childhood has come true.'[58]

Pound's pursuit of a modernist synthesis develops then into the recuperation and revaluation of 'Old World' structures in 'New World' techniques and contexts, permitted by contemporary discursive conditions; the 'primal energies' of poetry are thus translated into the new energies of modern science. That energy is found in the mechanisms of what we can, post-Freud, generalise as 'the unconscious', which may be identified in terms of 'mythic' techniques or, to the extent that they share similar mechanisms, can also be referred to as 'dream' techniques. By the same token, they also resemble 'pathological' mechanisms. The point that the debate between Freud and Jung leads us to is that these are not absolute categories. To give one a privileged place and reduce the others invariably to it is part of Jung's mistake. Their variability does not, however, depend on the *incidence* of particular mechanisms; it depends rather on the social conditionality of those mechanisms.

Because Pound's discourse is self-coded as impersonal and objective and his myth inscribed in the unconditional category of knowledge, he is condemned to an occultist position. Occultism may be a workable base for social formation in a primitive society, but under late capitalism it finds its social conditionality fulfilled in the grotesque primitivism of fascism. The only escape from this is a resurrection of a category of fiction (Pound's fascism does not mean what it seems to be expressing), which is denied by the very form in which the ideology is expressed.

III

We can, therefore, if not answer our initial question categorically, at least develop its terms considerably: if we can theoretically distinguish a deranged poem from a poem which uses techniques which may be identified with their incidence in certain pathological contexts, this cannot be done simply by relating its mechanisms to certain so-called pathological phenomena. It is meaningless, for example, to call a poem 'deranged' because it employs projection. But, more important-ly, it is by the same token meaningless to claim that it has rediscovered a 'primal energy'. Technique is not the crucial variable; the variable is the function, the social conditionality of the discourse. To dream is perfectly sane; but to live one's day in the light of a dream is potentially pathological. It is one thing to recognise the survival of these mechanisms in our psyches and our social anthropology but it is quite another thing to raise them to the level of a truer form of 'reason'. In sum, if a poem employs these mechanisms to produce knowledge – as though it existed in a primitive tribal structure – then we have some justification in considering it as politically pathological: not as a matter of technique in a purely formalist sense, but of its social and historical conditionality.

Pound's tragedy is heightened by the fact that it follows from an important and admirable attempt to find a productivity for art which responded responsibly and seriously to modern conditions by pursuing the highest level of poetic efficacy in service of, rather than in reaction to, the public world. In this sense, Pound remains more important and interesting than those, such as Eliot, whose art continued, in many ways, to evade those modern questions which Pound never shirked. Yet in his work we see the effects of the contradictions which he endeavoured to overcome with such commitment. In this way, Pound remains a victim of his commitment and of his historical moment. But, in the light of his courageous and tragic calamity, we might feel entitled to ask what such mechanisms and techniques – which may be productive of what we see as 'good poetry', poetry that pleases us – may be applied to, if not to knowledge? If a poem cannot produce an 'objective' knowledge without producing occultism, what can it produce? What is its social conditionality?

Inasmuch as poetry remains committed to a pleasure principle involving the operation of mechanisms of the Imaginary order, it seems to me that the joke suggests the most interesting of the models offered by psychoanalysis which might inform the category of fiction. Unlike the occult, the delusion or the hallucination, the joke is indeed a species of fiction in that it does not predicate conviction. Unlike the dream, the delusion or the phantasy, the joke requires an audience which, moreover, participates. As a fiction addressed by someone to someone else, it is aimed at the production of pleasure in a social act, and hence, normally, its reciprocation.

If the poet, the lover and the lunatic are all functionaries of the Imaginary, then it is precisely the lunatic, and not the madman, whom the poet resembles (without ceasing to be the 'lover'). 'Lunatic' gives the idea of the Clown or Fool; a madman, in contrast, would be – like Hamlet? – a Fool who takes himself seriously. The traditional Fool does not pretend to knowledge; he leaves that to the philosopher, the priest and the politician. If he gives us wisdom, it is by using his irrationalism to subvert knowledge as a sabotage and positive corrective to the potential tyranny of science. Yet the Fool institutes himself not as a rival to knowledge, merely as representative of that necessary revolt which enables us to live with knowledge, without which we would be as rational as Houyhnhnms.

In that sense, the Fool is the complement of the King – even, or especially, the Platonic 'Philosopher King' – the authority which embodies and guarantees collective structures and the figure which demystifies that authority. Alfred Jarry's Père Ubu, the Fool turned King, illustrates the monstrosity of the confusion of realms. Pound, then, ironically directs us aright when he calls James Joyce a 'cabaret comedian' in Canto 74. And e. e. cummings is making a serious joke in his Foreword to *Is 5* (1926) when he writes,

> At least my theory of technique, if I have one, is very far from original; nor is it complicated. I can express it in fifteen words, by quoting The Eternal Question and Immortal Answer of burlesk, viz. 'Would you hit a woman with a child? – No, I'd hit her with a brick.' Like the burlesk comedian, I am abnormally fond of that precision which creates movement.[59]

For art, like the joke, celebrates and subverts language 'for its own sake'.

I offer the model of the joke as a suggestion not in the sense of a limiting model or dogma, but rather as a model with which to recall the project for a 'democratisation of art'. Once again, in present conditions, such a project cannot be realised through a commercialised market as its social condition. That would be to reduce art to a question of the mass-culture industry, in the sense in which another, rather different and more 'jocular' modernist, P. G. Wodehouse, saw the question of art. In 1924, for example, he sent the following advice to his friend W. Townend:

It seems to me that if you are to go on writing for popular magazines you will deliberately have to make your stuff cheaper. . . . You've been trying to write for magazines that aren't good enough, and you are consequently caught in two minds. You can't bring yourself to start with a cheap, tawdry plot, and yet you torture the story to suit an editor by excluding everything he objects to.[60]

When the need for productivity in a mass society is reduced to the demands of the market, democratisation collapses into commercial popularism.

So, to an extent, the project remains utopian; but not, for that reason, impossible. Besides Wodehouse's willingness to subject his art to the demands of the market (which, let it be said, rewarded him very richly for his talent for a genuine urban popularity – at least in relation to certain classes), we have also the experience of Pound, who confronted what he saw as the trivialisation of art in the face of the growing commodity market and sought to re-establish its value as a discourse every bit as 'serious' as, if not more serious than, the dominant discourses of science and technology. Central to this effort was the development and execution of standards of literary judgement by intervening in the market, as we saw in Imagisme. The other major commitment was to the idea of a control of language which would guarantee, through objective, impersonal and, one should add, musical techniques, that the reader could not but assent to its rhythmic and mythic movements. We should note then that, despite the radical difference in their attitudes, both Wodehouse and Pound keep us within the dominant question of the place of art in the modern world in terms of its function and value as a commodity for *consumption*.

Charles Ives, another contemporary modernist in an American popularist tradition, saw the challenge of the modern in another way, as his postface to *114 Songs* (1922) shows:

Everything from a mule to an oak which nature has given life has a right to that life, and a right to throw into that life all the values it can. Whether they be approved by a human mind or seen by a human eye is no concern of that right. . . . The instinctive and progressive interest of every man in art, we are willing to affirm with no qualification, will go on and on, ever fulfilling hopes, ever building new ones, ever opening new horizons, until the day will come when every man while digging his potatoes will breathe his own epics, his own symphonies (operas if he likes it); and as he sits of an evening in his backyard and shirt sleeves smoking his pipe and watching his brave children in *their* fun of building *their* themes for *their* sonatas of *their* life, he will look up over the mountains and see his visions in their reality, will hear the transcendental strains of the day's symphony resounding in their many choirs, and in all their perfection, through the west wind and the tree tops! . . . 'Various authors have various reasons for bringing out a book, and this reason may or may not be the reason they give to the world; I know not, and care not. It is not for me to judge the world unless I am elected. It is a matter which lies between the composer and his conscience, and I know of no place where it is less likely to be crowded. . . . Some have written a book for money; I have not. Some for fame; I have not. Some for love; I have not. Some for kindlings; I have not. I have not written a book for any of these reasons or for all of them together. In fact, gentle borrower, I have not written a book at all' – I have merely cleaned house. All that is left is out on the clothes line; but it's good for a man's vanity to have the neighbours see *him* – on the clothes line.[61]

There is so much here which suggests alternatives to Pound's project. Apart from the evidence of a different tradition, it is perhaps also relevant that Ives was not dependent for his livelihood on his music (indeed, very little of it was performed publically during his lifetime). What, however, seems to me to be most important here, as I finish my own house-cleaning (or at least desk-cleaning), is the focus on the democratisation of art as a question above all of *production*: 'Whether they be approved by a human mind or seen by a human eye is no concern of that right.' Ives, Jones and Duchamp all direct us, I think, towards notions of democratisation of art in terms of its production. The notion of democracy here is not that all have access to art products in a democracy of consumers, but that all have the right and capacity to produce art, *independent of* its consumption.

That approach may at least open alternatives; and, whatever their utopian or sentimental risks, they seem to me, confronted with Pound's effort and its catastrophe, to be worth reflection.[62] Whether or not the joke offers a model of social conditionality for literature, and whether or not a democratisation of the production of art is a coherent alternative to the dominant modernist traditions, the point remains that literature does need to delineate its social conditionality. One may want literature to do more, but I think that the experience of modernists such as Pound demonstrates that it cannot in that sense.

Indeed, the notion that *art* can tell us what we need to know in order to legislate the world could only have been dreamt by an intellectual alienated in his political action as a citizen. It is a seductive nostalgia for a never-was of the poet as 'legislator'; and this, as Pound proves, is a dangerous model.

If art exceeds its social conditionality, if it tries to replace science, political economy, or revolution, it is liable to backfire calamitously. In Chapter 1, I claimed that the experience of Pound leads us to a project for the 'politicisation of art', as I put it, 'in the name of art'. The point returns: 'in the name of art' because art can only ever be 'for its own sake'. That 'sake' is certainly vital to our lives and is, I think, well illustrated in Ives's model of a sociable 'showing forth' – a lending not a selling – of self. On the other hand, I would maintain that it is precisely a politicisation of art outside the condition of art which leads to Pound's calamity. If art is to have a political dimension and to discharge its power positively, it must do so within its field of possibility. That is a social question, to do with the nature of fiction, and thus returns us to the need for a democratisation of art as the only guarantee of a politicisation which does not, however honourable its intentions, end up committing violence to both politics and art.

Notes

Abbreviations of works by Ezra Pound cited in notes

ABCR   *The ABC of Reading* (1934; London: Faber & Faber, 1951).
CEP   *Collected Early Poems of Ezra Pound*, ed. Michael John King (London: Faber & Faber, 1977).
CNTJ   *The Classic Noh Theatre of Japan* (*Noh, or Accomplishment*, 1916) (New York: New Directions, 1959).
CWC   *The Chinese Written Character as a Medium for Poetry* (1920; San Francisco: City Lights, 1969).
GB   *Gaudier-Brzeska: A Memoir* (1916; New York: New Directions, 1959).
GK   *The Guide to Kulchur* (1938; London: Peter Owen, 1966).
J/M   *Jefferson and/or Mussolini* (1935; New York: Liveright, 1970).
L   *Selected Letters of Ezra Pound, 1907–1941*, ed. D. D. Paige (1950; London: Faber & Faber, 1971).
LE   *Literary Essays of Ezra Pound*, ed. T. S. Eliot (London: Faber & Faber, 1954).
P   *Personae: the Collected Shorter Poems of Ezra Pound* (1926; New York: New Directions, 1971).
SP   *Selected Prose of Ezra Pound 1909–1965*, ed. William Cookson (London: Faber & Faber, 1973).
SR   *The Spirit of Romance* (1910; New York: New Directions, 1968).
Trans.   *Translations of Ezra Pound*, ed. Hugh Kenner (London: Faber & Faber 1954).

NOTES TO CHAPTER 1. INTRODUCTION: SOME OF OUR BEST POETS ARE FASCISTS

1 'Cavalcanti: Medievalism' (1910–34), in *LE*, p. 194.
2 'Vorticism', *Fortnightly Review*, xcvi.573 (1 Sep 1914), in *GB*, p. 85.
3 *SR*, p. 168.
4 *SR*, p. 178.
5 'The Ballad of the Gibbet', *P*, p. 12.
6 Citation for the Bollingen Prize for Poetry, quoted in *Ezra Pound: The Critical Heritage*, ed. Eric Homberger (London: Routledge & Kegan Paul, 1972) p. 26.
7 Donald Davie, *Ezra Pound: Poet as Sculptor* (London: Routledge & Kegan Paul, 1965) p. 242. See also *A Casebook on Ezra Pound*, ed.

William Van O'Connor and Edward Stone (New York: Thomas Y. Crowell, 1959), which includes a selection of materials documenting the contemporary debate.

8 Peter Nicholls has recently made quite clear in what ways the *Pisan Cantos* are very much not a gesture of defeat or repentance; rather 'the "heroism" and "courage" for which the sequence has been praised often entail a holding-fast to those very ideas and principles which most critics are keen to see the poet "transcend" ' – Peter Nicholls, *Ezra Pound: Politics, Economics and Writing* (London: Macmillan, 1984) p. 163.

9 Hugh Kenner effectively launched modern Pound studies with his *The Poetry of Ezra Pound* (London: Faber & Faber, 1951). His *The Pound Era* (London: Faber & Faber, 1975), a study of modernism centred on Pound, Wyndham Lewis, James Joyce and T. S. Eliot, represented the case for Pound as modernist at the most ambitious level, as the title suggests.

10 The term 'objective correlative' was coined by T. S. Eliot, but the concept owes much to Pound's argument in *SR* – see Hugh Witemeyer, *The Poetry of Ezra Pound, 1908–1920: Forms and Renewals* (Los Angeles: University of California Press, 1969) p. 29.

11 T. S. Eliot, in *Poetry* (Chicago), Sep 1946.

12 'Vorticism', in *GB*, p. 83.

13 Letter to Harriet Monroe, 7 Nov 1913, in *L*, p. 24.

14 'Prologomena', *Poetry Review*, i.2 (Feb 1912), in *LE*, p. 9; see also, 'I Gather the Limbs of Osiris', *New Age*, x.5 (30 Nov 1911) fortnightly to x.17 (22 Feb 1912), in *SP*, p. 34.

15 Pound first published this poem as the first instalment of the series 'I Gather the Limbs of Osiris' (see preceding note); it was reprinted in the volumes *Ripostes* (1912) and *Cathay* (1915). In the first case, it was singled out by *The Times Literary Supplement* (a journal not usually responsive to Pound's verse), along with his homage to Swinburne ('Salve, O Pontifex'), as examples of what Pound may be capable of (and which he spoilt by 'vulgar gesture[s] of defiance'); the editor of the *New Age*, A. R. Orage, greeted the 1915 republication by referring to the poem as 'without doubt one of the finest literary works of art produced in England in recent years' (see *Pound: The Critical Heritage*, ed. Homberger, pp. 94 and 110).

16 'I Gather the Limbs of Osiris', in *SP*, p. 33.

17 Hugh Witemeyer provides a thorough account of this period, where he argues that 'Pound's personae combine his concern for revitalizing history with his concern for portraying dramatic ecstasy . . . in other words, they stand somewhere between Browning's dramatic monologues and Yeats's masks' (Witemeyer, *Poetry of Pound*, p. 60; see the full discussion in his fourth chapter).

18 Interview with Donald Hall, *Paris Review*, 28 (1962), in *Writers at Work*, 2nd ser. ed. George Plimpton (New York: Viking, 1963) p. 33.

19 The distinction between 'symptomatic' and 'donative' facts and writers is made by Pound in 'I Gather the Limbs of Osiris', *SP*, p. 25.

20 *Writers at Work*, ed. Plimpton, p. 36.

21 Arthur Symons, *The Symbolist Movement in Literature* (1899; rev. 1908, 1919; New York: E. P. Dutton, 1958) p. xix.

22 Ford Madox Ford, in *Critical Writings of Ford Madox Ford*, ed. Frank

MacShane (Lincoln, Nebr.: University of Nebraska Press, 1964) p. 154. Ford was related to the Pre-Raphaelites through his maternal grandfather, the painter Ford Madox Brown, who was also the father of William Michael Rossetti's wife (Madox Brown's daughter by a previous marriage). Pound to an extent works out his relations with Dante Gabriel Rossetti in his translations of the *Sonnets and Ballate of Guido Cavalcanti* (1912), which Rossetti had himself translated in an influential edition. See the discussion in David Anderson, *Pound's Cavalcanti: An Edition of the Translations, Notes, and Essays* (Princeton, NJ: Princeton University Press, 1983) pp. xvii–xviii.

23 Ian F. A. Bell, *Critic as Scientist: The Modernist Poetics of Ezra Pound* (London: Methuen, 1981) p. 229. I make considerable use of this book throughout the present work. I also rely on its most thorough discussion of Pound's poetics (rather than his practice) and its relations to fields of science which are not embraced by my own work. Bell selects four familiar keynotes of the poetics: 'his analogies from geometry and electromagnetism, his campaign for the seriousness of the artist, his conceptions of the "vortex" and of "tradition" ' p. 3). He contextualises Pound's model of diagnosis, the luminous detail and the *virtù*, lines of force, the Vortex itself, the ideogram, tradition and historicity, the 'repeat', myth and metamorphosis, the palimpsest, etymologies, a language of objects, pattern, design and harmony of process, in terms of a poetic model of transcendentalism and scientific models of, mainly, atomic physics and biology. Besides the clearer dependencies, what will be less visible is the extent to which Ian Bell's work has informed and assisted my own beyond what can be indicated by direct reference.

24 The anxiety is even present for Stephen Daedalus in Joyce's *Ulysses*: 'Who ever anywhere will read these written words?' – Joyce, *Ulysses* (1922; Harmondsworth: Penguin, 1969) p. 54. There is, of course, much talk of the death of literacy, but one might note that the novel still manages to survive more happily than poetry – even to the point, in more recent times, of adapting itself to the commercial dominance of television and cinema by providing texts for, or of, series and films.

25 There is of course the case of the Georgian poets and their (especially commercial) popularity. This success in relation to the modern reading public is, however, very much achieved at the cost of a marginalisation of the scope of poetry, reduced to a rather parochial pastoral mode dependent on sustaining a myth of 'England', most of which was destroyed (as we know, all too literally) by the First World War. It is none the less curious how many contemporary poets have recently returned to the sort of attention to place (as opposed, for example, to Pound's internationalist perspective) as is encountered in the work of the best of the Georgians, such as Edward Thomas. Despite the fact that many of them also acknowledge or exhibit the influence of Pound, the work of poets such as Basil Bunting (*Briggflatts*, 1965), Geoffrey Hill (*King Log*, 1968; *Mercian Hymns*, 1971), Seamus Heaney, Jeremy Hooker, Ronald Johnson and Jonathan Williams also demonstrates a recuperation of this alternative response to the fate of poetry in the modern world.

26 Paul Valéry, 'Existence du Symbolisme' (1938), *Oeuvres*, I (Paris: Pléiade, 1962) 689–90.

27 Pound discharged, as it were, his debt to the religious cult of the Symbolists in his homage to Swinburne ('Salve, O Pontifex'), in which the poet is represented as a high priest, addressed here by an acolyte. The poem, first published in *Ripostes* (1912), was not reprinted in Pound's subsequent collections. Likewise, in 'Prologomena' (1912), Pound also acknowledges how Swinburne and Yeats, and their concept of 'pure art', had managed to restore musical values to a poetry otherwise decayed into rhetoric, a 'post-chaise for transmitting thoughts poetic or otherwise' (*LE*, p. 11). The problem with which they leave him appears to be that of enabling this musical art to display *intelligent* thought – hence his contemporary experimentations with translating Cavalcanti 'more for sense than for music' (see Pound's letter to *The Times*, published 5 Dec 1912, quoted in Anderson, *Pound's Cavalcanti*, p. xviii).

28 Symons, *The Symbolist Movement*, p. 94.

29 *The Context of English Literature: 1900–1930*, ed. Michael Bell (London: Methuen, 1980) p. 18.

30 'Plotinus', *CEP*, p. 36.

31 'Vorticism', in *GB*, p. 85.

32 Paul Valéry, 'Dialogue ou nouveau fragment relatif à M Teste', *M Teste* (1946; Paris: Gallimard, 1969) p. 97.

33 Valéry, 'La Soirée avec M. Teste' (1896), ibid., p. 28.

34 'Masks', *CEP*, p. 34.

35 'Psychology and Troubadours' (1912), in *SR*, p. 92.

36 'Affirmations, I: Arnold Dolmetsch', *New Age*, XVI. 10 (7 Jan 1915), in *LE*, p. 431.

37 Ibid.

38 'The Tree', *P*, p. 3.

39 For Pound's notion of 'delightful psychic experience', see 'Psychology and Troubadours' (*SR*), 'Cavalcanti: Medievalism' (*LE*) and the 'Postscript to *The Natural Philosophy of Love* by Remy de Gourmont' in *Pavannes and Divagations* (New York: New Directions, 1958). See also Witemeyer, *Poetry of Pound*, ch. 2.

40 'La Fraisne', *P*, p. 4.

41 'Piere Vidal Old', *P*, p. 32.

42 'Cino', *P*, p. 6.

43 'Na Audiart' (introductory note), *P*, p. 8.

44 'Au Salon', *P*, p. 52.

45 'The Flame', *P*, p. 50. What Pound had inherited from the end of the previous century was, amongst other things, to a large extent the restriction of poetry to lyric in evermore sophisticated forms of the exquisite. He believed however that the comparable technical excellence of the Troubadours was not a mere aestheticism, unavoidably condemned to the ineffectuality of a lyric cult of love and beauty. Rather, he believed that this accomplished love poetry was written in a coded language, the language of the 'trobar clus' – see 'Troubadours – their Sorts and Conditions' (1913), in *LE*, p. 94. The Troubadours offer themselves as an alternative to the

Symbolists and Aesthetes of the 1890s because the elaborateness and obscurity of their lyric did in many cases – Pound believed and would have us believe – serve a real and active political purpose (cf. 'Near Perigord'). This code indeed went further, referring obscurely not only to contemporary politics, but also, as he argues in 'Psychology and Troubadours', to what he saw as the survival of a pre-Christian, pre-Humanist Classical vision which, transmitted by the Troubadours, eventually issued in Dante's epic. In this way, the Troubadours appear as a resource which does not sacrifice the musical excellence and sophistication of the Aesthetes but which sustains political and mythic dimensions in alternative to their self-regarding escapism.

46 'De Aegypto', *P*, p. 18.
47 'Famam Librosque Cano', *P*, p. 14.
48 'Prologomena', in *LE*, p. 9.
49 Such a question was clearly present in discussions with Pound's literary colleagues, such as the editor of the *New Age*, A. R. Orage, and Ford Madox Ford, who both devoted much attention to the question of audience. Orage used his column in the paper to elaborate a model of reader and language which is characterised by a doctrine of 'common sense' and 'idiom', whilst Ford, in his essays 'Impressionism – Some Speculations' (1911) and 'On Impressionism' (1912), reprinted in *The Critical Writings of Ford Madox Ford*, ed. MacShane, took issue with Tolstoy's model of the peasant, in favour of 'homines bonae voluntatis' of the contemporary urban environment, such as 'the cabmen round the corner' (p. 49).
50 'I Gather the Limbs of Osiris', in *SP*, pp. 32–3.
51 'The Serious Artist', *New Freewoman*, i.9 (15 Oct 1913) to i.10 (1 Nov 1913), in *LE*, p. 49.
52 'Mr Hueffer and the Prose Tradition in Verse', *Poetry*, iv.3 (June 1914), in *LE*, p. 371.
53 'Prologomenon', in *LE*, p. 12.
54 'Psychology and Troubadours', in *SR*, p. 87.
55 'I Gather the Limbs of Osiris', in *SP*, p. 34.
56 'The Serious Artist', in *LE*, p. 44.
57 Ibid., p. 42.
58 'I Gather the Limbs of Osiris', in *SP*, p. 23.
59 Walter Lippman, *A Preface to Politics* (London: Fisher & Unwin, 1909) pp. 49–51. See also, for example, Graham Wallas, *Human Nature in Politics* (London: Constable, 1908), of which Lippman made considerable use. Wallas, a professor at the London School of Economics, was close to the radical Liberals, and to the *New Age* circle.
60 'The Serious Artist', in *LE*, p. 43.
61 The contrast between the poetic universe as inherited from the later Romantics and the counter-imperatives of the 'prosaic' world may be illustrated from Thomas De Quincey's eloquent defence of poetry in his essay 'The Poetry of Alexander Pope' (1848). De Quincey distinguished between what he calls the function of the 'literature of power' and that of the 'literature of knowledge', exemplifying the superiority of the former by contrasting 'poetic justice' with 'common forensic justice' to the extent to

which the former '*attains* its object, . . . is more omnipotent over its own ends, as dealing, not with the refractory elements of earthly life, but with the elements of its own creation, and with materials flexible to its purest preconceptions'. Clearly, any engagement of notions of poetic justice with the 'earthly' materials of society is bound to prove difficult. Just how difficult is shown by the confusion which constitutes Pound's economic theory in general, and his theory of 'just price' in particular. See Martin A. Kayman, 'Ezra Pound: The Color of his Money', forthcoming in Paideuma.

62 Compare, for example, Eliot's response in 1942 to a solicitation for a poem to be included in a volume entitled *London Calling*. He declines to write a war poem, arguing,

> War is not a life: it is a situation,
> One which may neither be ignored nor accepted,
> A problem to be met with ambush and stratagem,
> Enveloped or scattered.

> The enduring is not a substitute for the transient,
> Neither one for the other. But the abstract conception
> Of private experience at its greatest intensity
> Becoming universal, which we call 'poetry',
> May be affirmed in verse.

– 'A Note on War Poetry', in *The Complete Poems and Plays of T. S. Eliot* (London: Faber & Faber, 1969) p. 201.

63 'A Visiting Card' (1942), in *SP*, p. 297.

64 See Julian Cornell, *The Trial of Ezra Pound: A Documentary Account of the Treason Trial by the Defendant's Lawyer* (London: Faber & Faber, 1967), and also a recent, rather more sensationalist account, which none the less includes new material: E. Fuller Torrey, *The Roots of Treason: Ezra Pound and the Secrets of St Elizabeth's* (London: Sidgwick & Jackson, 1984).

65 Peter Nicholls glosses many specific references to the theory and recent history of fascism in his *Pound: Politics, Economics and Writing*, pp. 163ff.

66 Charles Olson, in *Charles Olson and Ezra Pound: An Encounter at St Elizabeths*, ed. Catherine Seelye (New York: Grossman, 1975) pp. 19–20.

67 ' "Beauty is truth, truth beauty" – that is all / Ye know on earth, and all ye need to know' (Keats, 'Ode on a Grecian Urn', 1819). Popularised readings have tended to forget the inverted commas around the quotation, reducing Keats's text to a crass aestheticist hedonism.

68 George Orwell, 'Politics and the English Language' (1946), in *'Inside the Whale' and Other Essays* (Harmondsworth: Penguin, 1962) p. 143.

69 Ibid., p. 152.

70 Orwell, 'Politics versus Literature' (1946), ibid., p. 139.

71 A symptomatic case occurred at the very beginning of the modern period of Pound studies, in the early numbers of the *Pound Newsletter*. In October 1954, in response to a review of a recent work on Pound, Thomas Parkinson asked, 'how long can a responsible – yes, responsible – criticism

remain silent on the question of Pound's Fascism?' (*Pound Newsletter*, 4, p. 8). Amongst the various, largely evasive replies, we find this, from Hugh Kenner: 'I should say that "Pound's Fascism" (whatever that is; does Mr Parkinson imply that he was a member of some party?) would be part of his biography' – *Pound Newsletter*, 5 (Jan 1955) 27. Things have not improved much since then (Peter Nicholls's admirable *Pound: Politics, Economics and Writing* being one of the honourable exceptions), and new impetus for evasion has recently been granted by Daniel Pearlman's pseudo-provocative 'Ezra Pound: America's Wandering Jew', *Paideuma*, 9.3 (Winter 1980), an unconvincing psychological account of Pound's anti-semitism which, to my mind, rather misses the acuteness of the irony in Jean-Paul Sartre's *Anti-Semite and Jew* (on which it unconfessedly depends).

72 Walter Benjamin, 'The Work of Art in the Age of Mechanical Reproduction' 1936, in *Illuminations* (London: Fontana, 1970) p. 243.

73 Geoffrey Hartman, *The Fate of Reading* (Chicago: University of Chicago Press, 1975) p. 258.

74 David Jones, 'Art and Democracy' (1947), in *Epoch and Artist*, ed. Harman Grisewood (London: Faber & Faber, 1959) p. 85.

75 *Dialogues with Marcel Duchamp*, ed. Pierre Cabane (1967), tr. Ron Padgett (New York: Viking, 1971) p. 16.

76 David Jones, 'Preface to *The Anathemata*' (1951), in *Epoch and Artist*, ed. Grisewood, p. 108.

77 In this respect, it is worth bearing in mind Edward Dorn's critique of 'the concept of absolutism in terms of style'. He argues that 'that's the whole point of democracy – that it demands style' – *Edward Dorn: Views*, ed. Donald Allen (San Francisco: Four Seasons Foundation, 1980) p. 20. The conclusion that I would draw from his remarks is that not only is style power, but the right to personal styles (as opposed to the commodity of fashion: 'When diminished expectations are sold as a commodity, you get Governor Brown and Linda Ronstadt' – p. 23) is a component of democracy.

78 Jones, in *Epoch and Artist*, ed. Grisewood, p. 108.

79 David Jones himself came dangerously close to admiration for the fascists late in the 1930s. The danger of such a collapse may be owing in part to his religious framework – which always threatens to enter into contradiction with the social implications of his aesthetic attitudes – and in part to his actual politics: his involvement, with Eric Gill and others, in communities which owed much to Guild Socialism – a 'modernist' politico-aesthetic ideology with which A. R. Orage was also associated. In other words, the 'socialism' to which his aesthetic theory led him was thought in mediaevalist and religious terms and could not be thought in materialist terms.

NOTES TO CHAPTER 2. HOW TO WRITE WELL AND INFLUENCE PEOPLE: POUND AND IMAGISME

1 The debate between Basil Bernstein and William Labov over questions of class and linguistic codes – see Labov's 'The Logic of Nonstandard English' (1969), in *Tinker, Tailor . . .: The Myth of Cultural Deprivation*, ed. Nell Keddie (Harmondsworth: Penguin, 1973) pp. 21–66 – and the work of the University of London's Institute of Education, and the Schools' Council in England (in particular the contributions of educationalists such as James Britton and Harold Rosen) have, more recently, challenged a monostylistic model of language use in schools, whilst the Open University Course Team ('Society, Education, and the State') led by Roger Dale has studied the power functions of the educational system as a whole. But it would, I think, be an exaggeration to claim that they have liberated the educational system in general or the teaching of English in particular from its function of transmitting a particular set of criteria – as it would equally well be a simplification to say that they have provided an entirely unproblematic and operational alternative. In any case, the counter-attack of the 'core curriculum', 'vocational' and functional approaches tends to return us to a model of pragmatic efficiency based on a uniform communication model. In sum, it is important to note that there is a serious political question at play in debates over 'standards of English' in schools and the models of language implicit in the various positions.

2 Kenner, *The Pound Era*, p. 186.

3 'Vorticism', in *GB*, p. 83.

4 This orthodoxy is fairly common in general literary histories, and is argued most clearly and specifically in Samuel Hynes's Introduction to his edition of *Further Speculations of T. E. Hulme* (Minneapolis: University of Minnesota Library, 1955); in Alun R. Jones, 'Imagism: A Unity of Gesture', *American Poetry* (London: Arnold, 1967); and in Peter Jones's Introduction to *Imagist Poetry* (Harmondsworth: Penguin, 1962). The original suggestion came from F. S. Flint, 'History of Imagism', *Egoist*, II.5 (1 May 1915) 70–1.

Pound's denials of influence are plentiful enough. The best known is 'This Hulme Business', *Townsman*, II.5 (Jan 1939), repr. in Kenner, *The Poetry of Ezra Pound*. Also important are the articles in the series 'Affirmations' in the *New Age*, 1915 (esp. the fourth in the series, 'As for Imagisme', repr. in *SP*); 'Vorticism', *Fortnightly Review* (1 Sep. 1914); and 'On Criticism in General', *Criterion*, I.3 (Jan 1923).

The most reliable demystifications of Hulme's influence appear in the texts by Kenner already cited, plus Herbert N. Schneidau, *Ezra Pound: The Image and the Real* (Baton Rouge: University of Louisiana Press, 1969); Stanley K. Coffman, *Imagism* (New York: Octagon, 1972); Christophe de Nagy, *Ezra Pound's Poetics and Literary Tradition* (Bern: Franke Verlag, 1966); and Wallace Martin, *'The New Age' under Orage* (Manchester: University of Manchester Press, 1967).

5 Alun Jones, *American Poetry*, p. 122.

6 F. S. Flint, 'Verse Chronicle', *Criterion*, xi.45 (July 1932) 686.

7 De Nagy, *Pound's Poetics*, p. 70.

8 'This Hulme Business', in Kenner, *The Poetry of Ezra Pound*, p. 308.

9 'Ford Madox Ford (Hueffer): obit', *Nineteenth Century and After*, cxxvi.750 (August 1939), in *SP*, p. 431. See also 'On Criticism in General' (*Criterion*, 1939); 'The Prose Tradition in Verse' (1914), in *SP*; 'Analysis of the Decade', *New Age*, xvi.15 (11 Feb 1915); and 'Status Rerum', *Poetry*, i.4 (Jan 1913).

10 'Ford Madox Ford (Hueffer): obit', in *SP*, p. 431.

11 'The Prose Tradition in Verse', in *LE*, p. 371.

12 Coffman, *Imagism*, p. 154.

13 'The Prose Tradition in Verse', in *LE*, p. 373.

14 'Ford Madox Ford (Hueffer): obit', in *SP*, p. 431.

15 'The Prose Tradition in Verse', in *LE*, p. 377. Cf. Pound's own project for 'great art': 'I find I mean something like "maximum efficiency of expression" ' ('The Serious Artist', in *LE*, p. 56).

16 De Nagy, for example, suggests that the movement might have more suitably been known as 'sciencism' or 'mot justism' (*Pound's Poetics*, p. 67).

17 'Vorticism', in *GB*, p. 85.

18 Ibid., p. 89.

19 'The Book of the Month', *Poetry Review*, i.3 (Mar 1912) 133.

20 For this reason, 'The logical end of impressionist art is the cinematograph. . . . Or, to put it another way, the cinematograph does away with the need of a lot of impressionist art' ('Vorticism', in *GB*, p. 89). I discuss the manner in which science proposes itself as something more than 'description' in Chapter 3.

21 'Status Rerum', *Poetry*, i.4, p. 125.

22 Ibid., pp. 123–5.

23 Ibid.

24 'Vorticism', in *GB*, p. 84.

25 The 'Doctrine of the Image' was first articulated in Pound's article 'A Few Don'ts By an Imagiste', *Poetry*, i.6 (Mar 1913), in *LE*, p. 4. I have emphasised Imagisme as a problematic of metaphor since I feel that this aspect of the movement focuses most clearly the sort of issues raised by its innovations at the most inclusive levels: that is, in terms of the relation of subject to object. But it would be an error to argue that this was all that Imagisme was. Its 'critical hygiene' in relation to questions of diction and rhythm is also of key importance. The former issue is, I think, implicit in the Ford-based critical movement. The question of Pound's contribution to the question of free-verse rhythms is, of course, matter for another book.

26 'A Few Don'ts by an Imagiste', in *LE*, p. 5.

27 'Prologomena', in *LE*, p. 12.

28 *CWC*, p. 15.

29 *CWC*, p. 28.

30 'A Girl', *P*, p. 62.

31 Pound had written in 1910, 'I use the term "comparison" to include metaphor, simile (which is a more leisurely expression of a kindred variety of thought), and the "language beyond metaphor", that is, the more

compressed or elliptical expression of metaphorical perception' (*SR*, p. 158). In 1914 he wrote, 'The point of Imagisme is that it does not use images as *ornaments*. The image is itself the speech. The image is the word beyond formulated language' ('Vorticism', in *GB*, p. 88). Neither of these statements is finally very helpful in understanding the Image; but they do at least point us towards Pound's sense of higher, more intensive levels of metaphor. In this sense, Marianne Korn is right to put Imagisme in the context of Pound's earliest poetic projects, as 'the culmination, in Pound's theory, of his old search for the Longinian sublime and its thunderbolt effect' in adequately modern forms – *Ezra Pound: Purpose/Form/Meaning* London: Pembridge Press, 1983) p. 83.

32 'Doria', *P*, p. 67.
33 'Liu Ch'e', *P*, p. 108.
34 William Carlos Williams, 'The Young Housewife', in *Collected Earlier Poems of William Carlos Williams* (New York: New Directions, 1938) p. 136.
35 'A Few Don'ts By an Imagiste', in *LE*, p. 4. Compare Pound's gloss on his poem 'In a Station in the Metro': 'In a poem of this sort one is trying to record the precise instant when a thing outward and objective transforms itself, or darts into a thing inward and subjective' ('Vorticism', in *GB*, p. 89); or his distinction between the 'subjective' Image ('External causes play upon the mind, perhaps; if so, they are drawn into the mind, fused, transmitted, and emerge in an Image unlike themselves') and the 'objective': 'Emotion seizing up some external scene or action carries it intact to the mind; and that vortex purges it of all save the essential or dominant or dramatic qualities, and it emerges like the external original' – 'As for Imagisme' (1915), in *SP*, p. 345. For a discussion of the Image as a 'psychological event', see Korn, *Pound: Purpose/Form/Meaning*, ch. 3; and, for a gloss on the scientific support of the notion of the 'complex', Martin A. Kayman, 'A Context for Hart's "Complex": A Contribution to a Study of Pound and Science', *Paideuma*, 12.2–3 (Fall–Winter 1983) 223–35.
36 Jonathan Culler, *Structuralist Poetics* (London: Fontana, 1974) pp. 180–1.
37 Ernst Cassirer, *Language and Myth*, tr. Susanne Langer (1946; New York: Dover, 1953) pp. 86–8.
38 Ibid., p. 91.
39 Claude Lévi-Strauss, *The Strange Mind* (1962; London: Weidenfeld & Nicholson, 1966) p. 106.
40 'Ortus', *P*, p. 84.
41 Marianne Korn again offers us a useful account of the technique in her summary comment that 'the Image . . . tended to place two representational elements in a non-representational contiguity' (*Pound: Purpose/Form/Meaning*, p. 87). However, as I hope my account makes clear, I believe that the technique is a little more complex and considerably more ambitious than such an otherwise effective description would lead us to feel.
42 What I mean here is that, without Pound's rigour and ambition for the radical effects of his complex Image, the contribution of the movement, in the work of poets such as Flint and Lowell, is largely reduced to a model of short lines and short poems, a slightly discontinuous and provocative

juxtaposition of largely visual images (in the more traditional sense of the word), a not particularly disciplined or exigent free verse, and, at times, a dislocated atmosphere (the Oriental, and so on), conveying moments of sensitivity and the perpetual 'dying fall'. Such short informal poetry has of course been extremely common in contemporary verse throughout the century. I imagine that there is some autobiography in this assertion. But this too has a curious literary history. F. S. Flint tells us, in his 'History of Imagism', that his innovatory group experimented much with the haiku and other intensive poetic forms (and, indeed, this is characteristic of most Imagiste poems). At the Perse School in Cambridge, as a young student of English, I too was encouraged to write in such forms, including the haiku. The creative-writing component in the course was a characteristic of its tradition of English teaching (based on the 'Mummery' classroom), which dated from the early years of the century. It was then with particular satisfaction that I discovered, in reading through the *New Age* files for the Imagiste years, similar short, intensive, Imagistic poems (albeit generally rhymed) written by schoolboys from the Perse School – the *New Age*, XIV.11 (15 Jan 1915) 335–6. It is my conviction that the Flint–Lowell line of Imagisme without Pound's Doctrine of the Image is not easily distinguishable, at least technically, from the sort of thing that one wrote as an adolescent or that other adolescents, under the excellent influence of Caudwell Cook (founder of the Mummery system), were writing at the same time – or that many adolescents (and non-adolescents) continue to write. It is, however, incapable of development to the level of poetic achievement exemplified by writers such as Pound and William Carlos Williams.

43 F. S. Flint, 'Verse Chronicle', *Criterion*, xi.45 (July 1932) 686–7. His examination of French verse appeared as 'A Review of Contemporary French Poetry' in a special number of *Poetry Review*, I.8 (Aug 1912).

44 Letter dated November 1917, quoted in Kenner, *The Pound Era*, p. 178.

45 See note 4, above.

46 The problem with a retrospective discussion is that the relativities become blurred at a distance. For example, as regards poetics, Pound and Hulme certainly had more in common with each other than they had with their predecessors (such as the Aesthetes) or contemporaries such as the Georgians. In that sort of context one is bound to discover certain similarities. Since the context of theory is that of generalisation, the difficulty, in this case, becomes even greater. It is for this reason that I maintain that the precise discrimination of difference is best achieved through an attention to the actual circulation of the *signifier*, rather than the signified (the theory).

47 Coffman, *Imagism*, p. 4. Harriet Monroe is quoted on p. 145.

48 Richard Aldington, *Life for Life's Sake* (New York: Viking, 1941) p. 135.

49 For the relations between Pound, H. D. and Aldington, see Vincent Quinn, *Hilda Doolittle (H. D.)* (New Haven, Conn.: College and University Press, 1967); Kenner's chapter on 'Imagism' in *The Pound Era*; and Brigit Patmore, *My Friends when Young* (London: Heinemann, 1968).

50 'Status Rerum', *Poetry*, I.4, p. 126; letter dated Oct 1912, in *L*, p. 11.

Indeed, Monroe must have been surprised and somewhat disconcerted by this reference: the editor of a new journal of poetry who had not heard of what would seem to be an important new European movement – above all, one that had the contemporary literary mystique of a French name. In fact, Pound had sent her a poem ('Middle-Aged') in August, published in *Poetry*, I.1 (Oct 1912), which he described for her as 'an over-elaborate post-Browning "imagiste" affair' (*L*, p. 10); but neither the poem nor the note explains much. In the November issue (I.2), Monroe took a chance on explaining Imagisme. She informed her readership that its practitioners were a group of 'ardent Hellenists' who 'attain in English certain subtleties of cadence of the kind which Mallarmé and his followers have studied in French'. It was only when she received the 'Imagisme' article for publication in March 1913 that Monroe was able to correct this impression; her note introduced the article with the observation that '*Imagism* is not necessarily associated with Hellenic subjects, or with *vers libre* as a prescribed form' – *Poetry*, I.6 (Mar 1913).

51 Quoted in Quinn, *Hilda Doolittle (H. D.)*, p. 22.

52 Letter to Harriet Monroe, Oct 1912, in *L*, p. 11.

53 See Pound's letter to William Carlos Williams, 21 Oct 1908, in *L*, p. 6. See also 'I Gather the Limbs of Osiris', in *SP*; 'Prologomena', in *LE*; and 'Imagisme' and 'A Few Don'ts by an Imagiste', *Poetry*, I.6, in *LE*. The 'three principles' published in 'Imagisme' were as follows: '1. Direct treatment of the "thing" whether subjective or objective. 2. To use absolutely no word that does not contribute to the presentation. 3. As regarding rhythm: to compose in the sequence of the musical phrase, not in sequence of a metronome' (*LE*, p. 3).

54 'Patria Mia' and 'America: Chances and Remedies' were both originally published in instalments in the *New Age*: 'Patria Mia', from XI.19 (5 Sep 1912) to XII.2 (14 Nov 1912); and 'America: Chances and Remedies' from XIII.1 (1 May 1913) to XIII.6 (5 June 1913). In June 1913 Pound prepared a synthesis for book publication. For commercial reasons, the book did not appear until 1950, as '*Patria Mia' and 'The Treatise on Harmony'* (London: Peter Owen, 1950). Although Pound again redrafted the articles for this edition – which is the text used here – it agrees in most important areas with the 1912–13 articles. For the discussion of the magazines, see pp. 24–8; for the advice to the young poet, p. 28; for the question of wealth, p. 50; for subsidies, p. 73; and for the 'super-college', p. 62.

55 *L*, pp. 11–27.

56 For Pound's relations with Amy Lowell, the attempts to purchase a magazine, and the fight over the movement's title, see Coffman, *Imagism*, p. 44; and *L*, pp. 31–3 and 38. For the idea of the college, see Pound's letter to Harriet Shaw Weaver, 12 Oct 1914, in *L*, p. 41, where the prospectus is printed as a footnote.

57 Patricia Hutchins, *Ezra Pound's Kensington* (London: Faber & Faber, 1965) p. 15.

58 The draft article and corrections were published as 'Some Imagism Documents', ed. Christopher Middelton, in the *Review*, 15 (Apr 1965) 30–51.

59 F. S. Flint, 'Imagisme', repr. as part of 'A Retrospect', in *LE*, p. 3.
60 The terms are Harriet Monroe's, from her introductory note in *Poetry*, I.6 (Mar 1913).
61 Introduction to 'The Complete Poetical Works of T. E. Hulme', *P*, p. 251.
62 Letter to Flint, 2 July 1915, quoted in 'Some Imagism Documents', ed. Middleton, *Review*, 15, p. 41; Flint, letter to Pound, 3 July 1915, ibid.
63 Martin, *'The New Age' under Orage*, p. 145; Coffman, *Imagism*, p. 4. The Club had arisen following the publication of *For Christmas MDCCCCVIII*, a pamphlet of poems by members of Hulme's 'Poets' Club', and Flint's attack on it in the *New Age*. After a lively correspondence, Flint and Hulme became fast friends, and founded the new Club in 1909 as a secession from the old.
64 Letter from Edward Marsh to Rupert Brooke, 22 June 1913, quoted in Noel Stock, *The Life of Ezra Pound* (London: Routledge & Kegan Paul, 1970) p. 139. The point is that this does exist as a group, but it is significant that Marsh does not identify it as a group of the 'School of Images' or 'Imagistes'.
65 Letter to Flint, 7 July 1915, in 'Some Imagism Documents', ed. Middleton, *Review*, 15, p. 44; Flint 'History of Imagism', *Egoist*, II.5 (1 May 1915) 70.
66 *Further Speculations of T. E. Hulme*, ed. Hynes, pp. 72–3.
67 As Marianne Korn points out, 'there is a remarkable poverty of visual imagery in [Pound's] own verse of the period' (*Pound: Purpose/Form/ Meaning*, p. 76).
68 Martin, *'The New Age'*, ch. 9 *passim*, esp. pp. 163–4. Martin's entire account of the *New Age* and Pound's relations with the journal and its circle is essential for a precise understanding of the Imagiste years.
69 Flint, 'Verse Chronicle', *Criterion*, XI.45, p. 687.
70 'Des Imagistes', *Glebe*, I.5 (Feb 1914) 1–63, and subsequently as a book (New York: Albert and Charles Boni; and London: Poetry Bookshop, 1914). A testimony to the opportunistic nature of the anthology came from one of its contributors, Allen Upward, in the letter of protest he wrote to the *Egoist* in reply to Flint's 'History of Imagism', offering his experience in relation to the 'movement':

> My own poems I did not produce:
> They were sent back to me by the *Spectator* and the *English Review*.
> I secretly grudged them to the Western devils.

> After many years I sent them to Chicago, and they were printed by Harriet Monroe. (They were also printed in THE EGOIST.)
> Thereupon Ezra Pound the generous rose up and called me an Imagist. (I had no idea what he meant.)
> And he included me in an anthology of Imagists.

> This was a very great honour.
> But I was left out of the next anthology.
> This was a very great shame.

And now I have read in a history of Imagism
That the movement was started in nineteen hundred and eight
By Edward Storer and T. E. Hulme.

– from 'The Discarded Imagist', *Egoist*, II.6 (1 June 1915) 98.
71 *J/M*, pp. 15–16.
72 'Vorticism', in *GB*, p. 82.
73 Wyndham Lewis, Introduction to the catalogue for the *Wyndham Lewis and Vorticism* exhibition at the Tate Gallery, London, July–Aug 1956.
74 In relation to the more direct relation between values of 'opportunism' and notions of political authority, particularly in reference to Pound's relation to Mussolini, see Peter Nicholls's chapter 'Pound and Fascism' in *Pound: Politics, Economics and Writing*, where he comments (p. 98),

> Gramsci's distinction between the manufactured philosophy of the state and its true one, realised in its historical actions, is very much to the point here. 'Gentile's system', he observed, 'is really only the captious camouflaging of the political philosophy better known as opportunism and empiricism.' Pound, I think, never penetrated beneath this 'camouflage', largely because it presented itself to him as the public expression of precisely those principles upon which his own methodology was based.

75 See note 50, above, and Pound's somewhat tetchy later comment in 'As for Imagisme' (*SP*, p. 344),

> The term 'Imagisme' has given rise to a certain amount of discussion. It has been taken by some to mean Hellenism; by others the word is used most carelessly, to designate any sort of poem in *vers libre*. Having omitted to copyright the word at its birth I cannot prevent its misuse. I can only say what I meant by the word when I made it.

NOTES TO CHAPTER 3. 'THE DRAMA IS WHOLLY SUBJECTIVE': POUND AND SCIENCE

1 As in the crisis of scientific materialism I describe below, industrial capitalism was finding itself confronted with its own consequences at this time: increasingly dramatic cycles of boom and unemployment, major financial crises, conspicuous urban poverty alongside technological development, and diminishing returns at the margins of colonisation. The major change, in English terms, began with the Liberal Party victory of 1906 and Lloyd George's 'People's Budget' of 1909, which precipitated a major constitutional crisis, provoked by the radical rebellion of the Tories. The story is masterfully told in George Dangerfield, *The Strange Death of Liberal England: 1910–1914* (1935; New York: G. P. Putnam's Sons, 1961). We find here 'not a record of personalities but of events; and not of great events but of little ones, which, working with the pointless

industry of termites, slowly undermined England's parliamentary structure until, but for the providential intervention of a world war, it would certainly have collapsed' (pp. 71–2). Apart from the problems caused by the Tory rebellion, the consensus was under attack from Militant Suffrage, Ireland, and massive industrial agitation, mainly in the mines, docks, shipping fleets and transport system. If the First World War represents a major crisis in industrial capitalism and a new stage of imperialism in the wake of nineteenth-century expansion, it did not, of course, resolve more than the immediate crisis which caused it. It did, however, give rise to a number of modernist proposals which sought to restore forms of order through models for the synthesis of those forces responsible for confrontation. These 'solutions', too – such as the pseudo-organicism of fascism or the welfare economics associated with Keynesianism and the New Deal – only postponed, for shorter or longer periods, the disorderly effects of the contradictions they concealed.

2 Walter Baumann, 'Old World Tricks in a New World Poem', *Paideuma*, 10.2 (Fall 1981).

3 Letter to Homer L. Pound, 11 Apr 1927, in *L*, p. 210.

4 Bell, *Critic as Scientist*, p. 1; see also the same author's 'The Phantasmagoria of Hugh Selwyn Mauberley', *Paideuma*, 5.3 (Winter 1976), and 'Mauberley's Barrier of Style', in *Ezra Pound: The London Years, 1908–1920*, ed. Philip Grover (New York: AMS Press, 1978).

5 'I Gather the Limbs of Osiris', in *SP*, p. 21.

6 Ibid., pp. 22–3.

7 Ibid., p. 34.

8 Ibid.

9 'The Wisdom of Poetry', *Forum*, xlviii.4 (Apr 1912), in *SP*, p. 330. The title of this essay and much of the matter of its text refer to Hudson Maxim's *The Science of Poetry and the Philosophy of Language* (1910), an empirio-critical theory of poetry, which Pound reviewed in *Book News Monthly*, xxxix.4 (Dec 1910) 282.

10 'The Serious Artist', in *LE*, p. 49.

11 'A Few Don'ts by an Imagiste', in *LE*, p. 4.

12 'Vorticism', in *GB*, p. 92.

13 'As for Imagisme', in *SP*, pp. 344–5.

14 'The Serious Artist', in *LE*, p. 48.

15 Ibid., p. 50.

16 'Psychology and Troubadours', in *SR*, p. 93.

17 Schneidau, *Pound: the Image and the Real*, pp. 124–5; see also his important essay, 'Pound and Yeats: the Question of Symbolism', *Journal of English Literary History*, 33 (1965) 220–37.

18 Pound's project for synthesising the contradictions of inherited traditions is nowhere clearer than in the way in which he structured his apprenticeship. We have already seen his dialectic of Yeats and Ford – the one for music and aesthetic effect, the other for a contemporary diction and concreteness. Likewise his two largest bodies of systematic translation, which run side-by-side through 'I Gather the Limbs of Osiris': the canzoni of Arnaut Daniel and the sonnets and ballads of Guido Cavalcanti. In his discussion of the former (the subject, for example, of

the second chapter of *SR*, entitled 'Il Miglior Fabbro'), it is clear that, without denying the value of the content of the canzoni, Pound's interest in Daniel is rather more in terms of a resource for musical experimentation, especially in rhyme structures. On the other hand, the Introduction to the Cavalcanti translations makes clear that, although, once again, Cavalcanti's rhythmic structures are worthy of study, Pound is here rather more interested in experimentation of forms which convey intelligent thought, for precision of expression (*Trans.*, p. 18). For, as he says following a discussion of Daniel's musicality in 'I Gather the Limbs of Osiris', 'it is not until poetry lives again "close to the thing" that it will be a vital part of contemporary life' (*SP*, p. 41). It is for this reason that, as we have seen (Ch. 1, note 27), Pound did not challenge Rossetti's more musical translations of Cavalcanti. The crux of Pound's governing project at this time is given in the Introduction to the Cavalcanti translations (*Trans.*, p. 23):

> I believe in an ultimate and absolute rhythm as I believe in an absolute symbol or metaphor. The perception of the intellect is given in the word, that of the emotions in the cadence. It is only, then, in perfect rhythm joined to perfect word that the two-fold vision can be recorded.

It is then precisely the Image's synthesis of 'intellectual and emotional' presentation in musical rhythms which achieves the 'two-fold vision' as one.

19 *Trans.*, p. 18.
20 'I Gather the Limbs of Osiris', in *SP*, p. 28.
21 *Trans.*, p. 18. Note how this 'something more substantial' (*SP*, p. 28) is a 'property' of a 'substance or person'. The nature of this 'property' is that of 'potency' or efficiency: that is to say, an energetic tension.
22 'Cavalcanti: Medievalism', in *LE*, pp. 154–5.
23 'Affirmations: Vorticism', *New Age*, xiv.11 (14 Jan 1915) 277–8.
24 Yvor Winters, *The Function of Criticism* (1957), quoted and debated in Davie, *Pound: Poet as Sculptor*, p. 217.
25 Ibid., p. 220.
26 *GK*, p. 152; quoted in Davie, *Pound: Poet as Sculptor*, p. 219.
27 Davie, *Pound* (London: Fontana Modern Masters, 1975) pp. 63–4.
28 Ibid., p. 65.
29 Ibid., p. 66. Compare a similar process in Kenner, *The Pound Era*, *passim*, but esp. the chapter 'Knot and Vortex' (for example, p. 153).
30 Davie, *Pound*, p. 67.
31 *CWC*, p. 28.
32 Gaston Bachelard, *Le Rationalisme appliqué* (Paris: Presses Universitaires de France, 1975) p. 153. The following account has been considerably influenced by Bachelard's theory of science, which I consider to offer the most sophisticated answer to empirio-criticism in providing a coherent dialectical materialist epistemology. At the same time I should like to acknowledge a debt to Baudoin Jourdant, of the University of Strasbourg, whose seminars at the University of York in 1974 were of invaluable assistance in this area.

33 Martin A. Kayman, 'Ezra Pound: A Model for his Use of "Science" ', in *Ezra Pound: Tactics for Reading*, ed. Ian F. A. Bell (London: Vision Press, 1982) pp. 79–102. The theory of acceptability is related to Jean-Pierre Faye's use of the concept in *Langages totalitaires* (Paris: Hermann, 1972) and *La Critique du langage et son économie* (Paris: Éditions Galilée, 1973) pp. 45–63. As one might gather from the title of his major work, Faye uses the concept to considerable effect in dealing with the specific languages of fascism and nazism.

34 Max Nänny, *Ezra Pound: Poetics for an Electric Age* (Berne: Franke Verlag, 1973). Nänny argues, for example, that 'Pound, following the subliminal mandate of the electric age with its instant speed of information movement, replaced the slow and serial logic of literacy and print by the intuitive mosaic of instantaneous communication' (p. 89).

35 'Affirmations: Vorticism', *New Age*, xiv.11 (14 Jan 1915) 277.

36 'Vorticism', in *GB*, p. 91. In his hierarchy of mathematical languages, arithmetic corresponds to 'ordinary common sense'; algebra, in expressing 'underlying similarity', corresponds to 'the language of philosophy', whilst in Euclidean geometry one has pictures and 'criticism of form'; lastly, there is the analytical geometry of creation. It seems to me significant, especially when one comes to consider the question of form in relation to economics and to history, that Pound stops here, and does not move on to the differential calculus. Rather than a language of difference and change, we have 'The statements of "analytics" ' as ' "lords" over fact. They are the thrones and dominations that rule over form and recurrence' (ibid.), which come to govern 'The repeat in history' (see note 3, above).

37 See Ch. 2, note 19; and the definition of the Image, *LE*, p. 4.

38 'The Wisdom of Poetry', in *SP*, p. 332.

39 Ibid., p. 331.

40 *SR*, p. 14.

41 'Arnold Dolmetsch', in *LE*, p. 431.

42 'Vorticism', in *GB*, p. 92.

43 Trevor I. Williams, *The Biographical Dictionary of Science* (London, 1969), entry for James Clerk Maxwell.

44 G. H. A. Cole, in C. B. Cox and A. E. Dyson, *The Twentieth Century Mind*, i (London: Oxford University Press, 1972) p. 267.

45 Henri Poincaré, *The Value of Science* (1908), tr. George Bruce (New York: Dover, 1958) ch. 8.

46 Lenin provides a fairly full survey of the range of reactions in *Materialism and Empirio-Criticism* (1908, rev. 1920; Moscow: Progress Publishers, 1970). A good example of the vitalist argument is found in the works of Edward Carpenter, who is throughout an interesting contrast to Pound – see, for example, his 'The Science of the Future', in *Civilisation, its Causes and Cures* (London: Methuen, 1912). T. E. Hulme also uses an attack on the contradictions of science to justify his Bergsonian intuitivism – see *Speculations*, ed. Herbert Read (London: Kegan Paul, 1924), the posthumous edition of Hulme's more important writings.

47 Kayman, in *Pound: Tactics for Reading*, ed. Bell, pp. 85–7.

48 Gustave LeBon, *The Evolution of Forces*, ed. F. Legge (London: Kegan Paul, 1908) p. 350.

49 J. Arthur Thomson, *An Introduction to Science* (London: Williams & Norgate, 1911) p. 191.

50 Ibid., p. 174.

51 Ibid., p. 180.

52 Ibid., p. 186.

53 Sir William Barrett, *On the Threshold of the Unseen* (London: Kegan Paul, 1917) p. 107. Barrett tells us in the Preface that he wrote the book before the outbreak of war, but decided to hold it over for the time being, which explains the later publishing date. See also his *Psychical Research*, whose contemporary seriousness is reflected in the fact that it also warranted a volume in the Home University Library series (London: Williams & Norgate, 1911).

54 William James, 'What Psychical Research has Accomplished' (1896), in *William James on Psychical Research*, ed. Gardner Murphy and Robert O. Ballou (New York: Viking, 1973) p. 47. See also his 'Frederic Myers' Service to Psychology' (1901), in same collection.

55 Thomas Szasz, Introduction to Ernst Mach, *The Analysis of Sensation* (1897; New York: Dover, 1959) p. ix.

56 John Losee, *A Historical Introduction to the Philosophy of Science* (London: Oxford University Press, 1972) p. 169.

57 Karl Pearson, *The Grammar of Science* (London: Walter Scott, 1892) pp. 103–4.

58 Ernst Mach, *Popular Scientific Lectures* (1894–8; La Salle, Ill.: Open Court, 1943) p. 199.

59 Ibid.

60 Pearson, *The Grammar of Science*, p. 81.

61 Ibid., p. 77.

62 Mach, *Popular Scientific Lectures*, pp. 200–1.

63 Pearson, *The Grammar of Science*, p. 44.

64 Ibid., p. 56.

65 Thomson, *An Introduction to Science*, p. 40. The fact that this volume (serving as the privileged general introduction to science in a major series of popularisation, comparable to our more recent Pelican-style pocketbooks) manifests an empirio-critical paradigm is suggestive of the influence exercised by the epistemology at the time.

66 Poincaré, *The Value of Science*, p. 37.

67 Mach, *Popular Scientific Lectures*, p. 205.

68 Poincaré, *The Value of Science*, p. 77.

69 Ibid.

70 Mach, *Popular Scientific Lectures*, p. 250.

71 Ibid.

72 Poincaré, *The Value of Science*, p. 26.

73 Ibid., p. 136.

74 Ibid., p. 140.

75 Ibid., p. 80.

76 Pearson, *The Grammar of Science*, p. 132. Pearson's own career demonstrates his commitment to the model: as Francis Galton Professor

of Eugenics at University College, London, he continued Galton's work on the application of statistics to heredity and psychology.

77 Mach, *Popular Scientific Lectures*, p. 17.

78 Mach, *The Analysis of Sensation*, p. 341.

79 Mach, *Popular Scientific Lectures*, p. 17.

80 Ibid., p. 210.

81 Mach, *The Analysis of Sensation*, p. 341.

82 Bernard Hart, *Psychopathology, its Development and its Place in Medicine* (London: Cambridge University Press, 1927) pp. 22–3.

83 Ibid., p. 46.

84 Ibid., p. 45.

85 Ibid., p. 4. Cf. Pound: 'A god is an eternal state of mind. . . . It is better to perceive a god by form, or by the sense of knowledge, and after perceiving him thus, to consider his name or to "think what god it may be" ' – 'Religio' (1918), in *SP*, pp. 47–8. The empirio-critical model provides bases for arguing that gods are conceptual entities for a science of 'states of consciousness'.

86 Hart, *Psychopathology*, p. 47. This is the fundamental epistemological paradigm of the Society for Psychical Research, similarly based on an exploitation of concepts such as the ether – as Sir Oliver Lodge (inventor of the radio coherer and ardent psychical researcher) observes: 'entities which cannot be expressed in terms of matter and motion are common enough without going outside the domain of physics. Light, for instance, and Electricity' and the ether – *Raymond, or Life and Death* (London: Methuen, 1916) p. 286. Cf. William James (see note 54, above).

87 Bernard Hart, in *Subconscious Phenomena*, ed. Hugo Münsterberg (New York and London: Rebman, 1912) pp. 116–18.

88 Ibid.

89 Bernard Hart, *The Psychology of Insanity* (London: Cambridge University Press, 1912) p. 62. It is to be noted that the scientists in the Society for Psychical Research were also careful to maintain and exploit this relation: see, for example, William Barrett's rejection of the physical analogy of 'brain waves' as anything more than a useful metaphorical manner of accounting for the none the less scientifically sustainable hypothesis of telepathy (*Psychical Research*, pp. 107–8).

90 *CWC*, p. 28.

91 *CWC*, p. 26.

92 *CWC*, p. 23.

93 *CWC*, p. 10.

94 *CWC*, p. 12. Cf. Henry Adams: 'Ernst Mach . . . admitted but two processes in nature – change of place and interconversion of forms. Matter was Motion – Motion was Matter – the thing moved' – *The Education of Henry Adams* (London: Constable, 1918) p. 453.

95 *CWC*, p. 15.

96 *CWC*, pp. 12, 8, 9.

97 *CWC*, p. 8. It does not seem to me that Pound is arguing an entirely naïve theory of immediacy in the Chinese script. No more than the empirio-critics would he collapse the argument back into a theory of simple reflection. It is rather a question of the relation of the convention to the continua that nature 'imposes' on us. In contrast to abstract and falsifying

Western 'logical' forms, the Chinese model is a convention simply closer to the energetic processes of nature, bearing their mark more conspicuously.

98 Compare Poincaré: 'there is not a single model which is imposed upon [the mind]; it has *choice*; it may choose, for instance, between the space of four or space of three dimensions. What then is the role of experience? It gives the indications following which the choice is made' (Poincaré, *The Value of Science*, p. 72). The Chinese script, uniquely, follows those indications.

99 *CWC*, p. 10.

100 *CWC*, p. 12.

101 Ibid.

102 Poincaré, *The Value of Science*, p. 79. Note Poincaré's relation of the notions of mathematical equation and 'image'.

103 *CWC*, p. 19.

104 *CWC*, p. 9.

105 *CWC*, p. 28. Pound calls the formula 'The cherry tree is all that it does', 'The true formula for thought'.

106 *SR*, pp. 158–9.

107 *CWC*, p. 19.

108 See *CWC*, pp. 13–14 and 20.

109 *CWC*, pp. 21–2.

110 Ibid.

111 Ibid.

112 *CWC*, p. 23.

113 *CWC*, p. 28.

114 *CWC*, p. 23.

115 *CWC*, pp. 24–5.

116 I do not deal in any detail with the ideogram because I believe that it does not alter the basic analysis of the Image as radical metaphor (the totalising relation), but rather expands the notion in harmony with the 'luminous detail' as a more generalised methodology. A look at the simplest explanation of the 'Ideogrammic Method, or the Method of Science' (*ABCR*, pp. 22–6), should illustrate the point and show how the ideogram is a sort of radical metaphor in which every part becomes the whole and is informed by the whole.

117 Cf. Mach, *Popular Scientific Lectures*, p. 192:

The economy of language is augmented, of course, in the terminology of science. With respect to the economy of written intercourse there is scarcely a doubt that science itself will realize that grand old dream of the philosophers of a Universal Real Character. That time is not far distant. Our numeral characters, the symbols of mathematical analysis, chemical symbols, and musical notes, which might easily be supplemented by a system of color-signs, together with the phonetic alphabets now in use, are all beginnings in that direction. The logical extension of what we have, joined with a use of the ideas which the Chinese ideography furnishes us, will render the special invention and promulgation of a Universal Character wholly superfluous.

118 Albert Einstein, quoted in Thomas Szasz's Introduction to Mach, *The Analysis of Sensation*, p. xiii.
119 Ibid., p. xiv.

NOTES TO CHAPTER 4. 'AND . . .': READING *THE CANTOS*

1 There are 116 complete Cantos, four 'fragments' at the end, and two (72 and 73 – the most explicitly fascist ones) have been suppressed, never appearing in any collection of Cantos. The on-going work was originally published in the following sections: *A Draft of XVI Cantos for the Beginning of a Poem of some Length* (Paris, 1925) and *A Draft of Cantos 17–27* (London, 1928), both subsequently subsumed under *A Draft of XXX Cantos* (Paris, 1930); *Eleven New Cantos, XXXI–XLI* (New York, 1934); *The Fifth Decad of Cantos: XLII–LI* (London, 1937); *Cantos LII–LXXI* (London, 1940); *The Pisan Cantos: LXXIV–LXXXIV* (New York, 1948); *Section: Rock-Drill, 85–95 de los Cantares* (Milan, 1955); *Thrones de los Cantares* (Milan, 1959); and *Drafts and Fragments of Cantos CX–CXVII* (London and New York, 1969).
2 'Date Line' (1934), in *LE*, p. 86. Pound also refers to the epic in terms of the 'tale of the tribe' (*GK*, p. 194). The latter expression appears to have two main sources: Mallarmé and Rudyard Kipling. In terms of the provenance and consequences of this definition, see Michael A. Bernstein's admirable study, *The Tale of the Tribe: Ezra Pound and the Modern Verse Epic* (Princeton, NJ: Princeton University Press, 1980).
3 The remark is Yeats's, reported by Pound in a letter to Sarah Cope, 22 Apr 1934, in *L*, p. 257.
4 Hugh Kenner, 'Art in a Closed World', *Virginia Quarterly Review*, 38 (Autumn 1966). See also Marianne Korn's discussion of Pound's 'purpose' and his 'conception of a poetry which communicates educationally but not didactically' (Korn, *Ezra Pound: Purpose/Form/Meaning*, p. 53).
5 'Vorticism', in *GB*, p. 86.
6 Eva Hess, Introduction to *New Approaches to Ezra Pound*, ed. Hess (London: Faber & Faber, 1969) p. 42.
7 Boris de Rachewiltz, 'Pagan and Magic Elements in Ezra Pound's Works', ibid., p. 196.
8 Ibid., p. 182.
9 Davie, *Ezra Pound: The Poet as Sculptor*, p. 231.
10 De Rachewiltz, in *New Approaches to Pound*, ed. Hess, p. 175.
11 Kenner, *The Pound Era*, p. 367.
12 See, for example, Walter Baumann's masterly analysis of Canto 4 in his *The Rose in the Steel Dust: An Examination of the Cantos of Ezra Pound* (Miami: University of Miami Press, 1970) pp. 19–53.
13 Kenner, in *Virginia Quarterly Review*, 38.
14 Many of the terms of analysis here are based on the model offered by Samuel Levin in *Linguistic Structures in Poetry* (The Hague: Mouton, 1973).

15 *CWC*, p. 9. Note also Pound's emphasis on the Chinese tendency towards compounding (p. 10).
16 'The Wisdom of Poetry', in *SP*, p. 332.
17 'Religio', in *SP*, p. 47.
18 'Arnold Dolmetsch', in *LE*, p. 431.
19 *CWC*, p. 28.
20 *CWC*, p. 18.
21 *New Approaches to Pound*, ed. Hess, p. 29. The resources of this submarine world are announced in poems such as 'Sub Mare' (1912), where the poet 'gropes', as yet, towards these 'familiars of the god' (*P*, p. 69).
22 The importance of Vorticist sculpture for Pound can be observed in his essays 'The New Sculpture', *Egoist*, I.4 (16 Feb 1914) 67–8; 'Brancusi', *Little Review*, VIII.1 (Autumn 1921) 3–7; and, of course, *GB*. Likewise, in Canto 90, at a point of climax in the poem, we find the lines, 'Templum aedificans, not yet marble, / "Amphion!" ' (90/605), which recuperate the Temple for which Sigismundo Malatesta was so valued in Cantos 8–11. See also Walter Baumann's discussion of the Amphion motif in 'Ezra Pound and Magic: Old World Tricks in a New World Poem', *Paideuma*, 10.2. For a general understanding of the importance of sculpture for Pound, Davie's *Pound: The Poet as Sculptor* is clearly crucial.
23 'Cavalcanti: Medievalism', in *LE*, p. 154.
24 The schema is reprinted in *Paideuma*, 2.2 (Fall 1973) 201.
25 Davie, *Pound: The Poet as Sculptor*, pp. 126–9.
26 The raft motif is important. Eventually, Odysseus is shipwrecked from his raft, to be saved by Leucothea: ' "my bikini is worth your raft" ' (91/616). Christine Brooke-Rose uses Kenner's article 'Leucothea's Bikini: Mimetic Homage', *Texas Quarterly*, x.4 (Winter 1967), to argue that 'Language and memory are Leucothea's bikini' – *A ZBC of Ezra Pound* (London: Faber & Faber, 1971) p. 145. But is Leucothea's bikini language and memory? That is to say, for most of the poem, the traveller–hero voyages through history and culture on his raft – which is already his language travelling through the medium of language. When he is shipwrecked, he is saved by another language. As Peter Nicholls has pointed out, there is a major shift around the time of Pisa, whereby Pound raises his language to a higher, more metaphysical level (Nicholls, *Pound: Politics, Economics and Writing*, p. 181). Whatever the issue of the debate, it is clear that the complex of images of the fluid, the raft and the bikini mediates central linguistic values in the poem and the metaphors involved must be considered with special attention.
27 'A Few Don'ts by an Imagiste', in *LE*, p. 7.
28 Two contemporaries offer interesting comparisons. Edward Carpenter's prose is built on similar scientific materials to Pound's, but is committed to an explicit Vitalism. Similarly, his poetry is aggressively idealist: 'I weave these words about myself to form a seamless web' – *Towards Democracy* (1881–2; London: George Allen, 1912) p. 32. In this text, natural objects are always used either in relation to abstract values, or in obvious processes of idealisation by an ever-present subject: 'I am the spray'; 'I now descend into materials.' The idealist form does not, however, limit the text to

solipsism, precisely because it marks its distance: 'And the fall of a leaf through the air and the greeting of one that passes on the road shall be more to you than the wisdom of all the books ever written – and of this book' (p. 110).

Paul Valéry's idealist poetics likewise borrows much from science, but in a radically rationalist mode, and his verse technique – which has nothing in common with Carpenter's – expresses most of all the subject, this time in terms of his capture within language. The subject only escapes from the circle of language by an action outside the text, as at the end of 'Le Cimetière Marin' (1920): 'Brisez, mon corps, cette forme pensive! . . . Le vent se lève! . . . Il faut tenter de vivre! / L'air immense ouvre et referme mon livre. . . .' – *Charmes ou Poèmes*, ed. Charles Whiting (London: Athlone Press, 1973) p. 42.

29 If the elements of the universe are not totalised in the imagination or ideology of a present subject, the process of projection requires the establishment of a total 'outside' (of which one is, of course, also part): Natura. However, the same process of projection is bound to totalise inimical as well as affectionate elements: Usura. This projective process is hence not irrelevant to Pound's antisemitism.

30 New persuasive readings of Pound have recently emerged in a phenomenological context: for example, Korn, *Ezra Pound: Purpose/Form/Meaning* (1983); and Eric Mottram, 'Pound, Merleau-Ponty and the Phenomenology of Poetry' in *Ezra Pound: Tactics for Reading*, ed. Bell (1982). Indeed, Peter Nicholls also argues for a phenomenological openness in Pound's technique in the early sections of *The Cantos*, which closes up with his increasing involvement with fascism. Such phenomenological readings are interesting and fruitful, but they still tend to rely on the proposal of a modern scientific reality which is presented, in some sense, as the twentieth-century condition. This is particularly the case in the clearest exposition of such a reading, that of Eric Mottram. However, it seems to me that the fact that Pound and, say, Merleau-Ponty (or, for that matter, Derrida) share a similar modern 'condition' is not in itself a sufficient base for relating them in this way. There are similarities to be observed, but not at the time of the formation of Pound's poetics, which, as I hope to have shown, do have a contemporary correlative. Furthermore, phenomenology, whilst it has some roots in empirio-criticism, contains important differences in relation to it. In short, such comparisons, precisely because they do share a 'twentieth-century condition', have to be discriminated historically with some precision.

31 One cannot, of course, evade the question of how much of the empirio-critics Pound actually read. It is clear that he took a fairly keen interest in science in general (as Ian Bell has shown in his *Critic as Scientist*) and that he read at the very least the Machist Hudson Maxim and Bernard Hart. But this is not, for me, the major problem.

I am trying to deal here with what I see as a specifically modernist phenomenon of which Pound is, again, typical: the use of a scientific discourse as a validation for poetics. This is a question not so much of influence as of appropriation. Science is a validating discourse not because it is more true than verse, but because it is the acceptable language of mass modernity. The new problematic that one needs to confront is the question of that appropriation in an age of mass media and intellectual popularisation.

In an age of mass popularisation, it is not easy to determine what precisely is read, and, particularly, under what conditions it is encountered: in a scholarly work, a popular series, in public lectures, or in a café. The more dispersed the materials, the harder it is both to identify the text and to specify the reliability of its appropriation. In short, it is characteristic in modernism, where our access to science increases almost in proportion to our ignorance of its real meaning, for the non-scientist's appropriation of science for his own purposes to be informed more by popular acceptance – that is, historical misunderstandings – than by scholarly certainty.

In face of this problem, rather than rely on a generalised history of ideas, I have sought to make the connections more concrete by trying to identify crucial discursive articulations which appear, in their different ways, in the otherwise distinct contexts of poetics and science.

32 Bell, *Critic as Scientist*, p. 239. The theory of the 'subject-rhyme' comes from Pound himself, although it is traceable to Emerson, and has been much used by Pound critics: see Ian Bell, 'Pound, Emerson and "Subject-Rhyme" ', *Paideuma*, 8.2 (Fall, 1979). In relating elements on this basis, one runs the risk of concealing more difference than one actually denotes similarity. As a principle for structuring historical material, it is particularly dangerous. But, if we recall the harmonisation of the natural and the cultural in Venice, as discussed above, we can see how the principle of 'rhyme' follows from the technique we have been analysing. Precisely what permits the harmonisation is a technique which unifies 'objects' which would otherwise be discrete. That is to say that in a materialist paradigm – of the object as much as of history – elements are marked by difference, rather than by a principle of harmonisation, such as that permitted by Mach's notion of analogy and Pound's poetic practice.

33 Bell, *Critic as Scientist*, p. 243.

34 Ibid.

35 Where Davie and Kenner effectively directly endorse the metaphor, others have offered validating models from, for example, Emerson or Goethe (see Hess, introduction to *New Approaches to Ezra Pound*, p. 19). Alternatively, we have, for example, Daniel Pearlman's endorsement of a parallel philosophical theory of 'holism': *The Barb of Time* (New York: Oxford University Press, 1969) p. 42. In the end, however, the closure captures the reader in nothing less than a totalising universe in which the very cosmos is invoked in order to sustain its concealed coherence. As a more striking and radical example of the lengths of endorsement or confirmation to which Pound critics may be carried by his discourse, I quote the following, from A. D. Moody, 'The Pisan Cantos: Making Cosmos in the Wreckage of Europe', *Paideuma*, 2.1 (Spring–Summer 1982) 146:

the total process, as I have traced it in Canto LXXXI, and as it could be traced through *The Cantos* as a whole, progresses beyond metonymy to the discovery of necessary natural relations and essential identity: 'man, earth: two halves of the tally' – when one has learnt one's place in the green world. And this perception of identity gives rise to a new conception of the self. The function of the discontinuities has been to break down conventional perceptions and received ideas, such as that Man is the master of nature. It is a deliberate rejection of the Western idea of the supremacy of the 'rational self', and of its works. But this rejection is on behalf of a reconstruction of the world and the self upon the basis of the one life that is in all things. That is the positive and active Subject of *The Cantos*, and what makes Cosmos in them.

Peter Nicholls succinctly observes that Pound's 'methodology is, like any ideology, premised on the assumption of its own correctness' (*Pound: Politics, Economics and Writing*, p. 99). But that will not in itself explain why so many of his critics establish a discourse with such a degree of endorsement.

36 The debate is illustrated, as I have already indicated, in Lenin's *Materialism and Empirio-Criticism* – which has the further interest of being effectively contemporary. The theory of empirio-criticism becomes in a sense unnecessary when theory catches up with its discoveries. It has, however, continued to be influential, as it generated modern epistemologies which continue to defend themselves against the claims of dialectical materialism. Its proposals had considerable influence in the development of logical positivism, in the sense that the latter studies our categorisations of the universe as determined by and manifest in language. It can also be traced through to the sociological relativism of Thomas Kuhn and to the ideological relativism of Karl Popper. On the other hand, it has played a part in the development of certain tendencies in phenomenology. Its commitment to a model of man as an instrument of sensation (which is, of course, only one part of its model), has been influential in the development of behaviourism as a study of stimulus-response mechanisms. Although in many senses superseded by the various more coherent paradigms that it has given rise to, empirio-criticism continues to be an important, and inadequately studied, modernist epistemology, whose ideological consequences, if they are not clear from Lenin's analysis, may be indicated by their working-out in these developments of aspects of the theory.

NOTES TO CHAPTER 5. 'THE GORILLA AND THE BIRD': MODERNISM AND THE PATHOLOGY OF LANGUAGE

1 'Psychology and Troubadours', in *SR*, p. 92.
2 'Arnold Dolmetsch', in *LE*, p. 431. One might note the transition in Pound's discourse from a language which presents the sources of the poem in mystical terms ('mood', 'psychic experience') or, occasionally, as in 'Prologomena', in metaphysical terms (a semi-Bergsonian 'impulse'), to that in which 'emotion' becomes identifiable with the causal 'law' of the

poem. The intervention of Hart's psychological discourse helps account for this development.

3 *CNTJ*, p. 27.

4 *CNTJ*, p. 115.

5 *CNTJ*, p. 37.

6 *CNTJ*, p. 12.

7 *CNTJ*, p. 36.

8 Pound's critique of 'spiritism', allied to his defence of the psychological verity of such experiences, again locates his model within the field outlined or illustrated by the Society for Psychical Research: precisely the place for the scientific study and expression of such phenomena, as jealous of its scientific credentials as it was of its faith in the existence of verifiable phenomena.

9 'Vorticism', in *GB*, p. 94.

10 Cf. George Dekker's distinction of 'Two Aspects of Myth in *The Cantos*': 'myth as [im]moral fable' and 'myth as the record of delightful psychic experience', in *Sailing After Knowledge: The Cantos of Ezra Pound* (London: Routledge & Kegan Paul, 1963) p. 62.

11 Herbert N. Schneidau, 'Wisdom Past Metaphor: Another View of Pound, Fenollosa, and Objective Verse', *Paideuma*, 5.1 (Spring–Summer 1976) 26.

12 Louis Zukofsky's comment was made at the Ezra Pound Symposium held at the University of Maine at Orono in June 1975, and reported in *Paideuma*, 4.3 (Winter 1975).

13 See Cornell, *The Trial of Ezra Pound*.

14 I have already argued that the Image relates to Cassirer's theory of totem; we might observe that totem is indeed a unique phenomenon in that it is, by definition, one in which 'the natural object' is in fact the 'proper symbol' by means of the process of totalisation he describes. The ideogram, as opposed to the deductive pyramid of Western logic (as Pound characterises it) also theoretically shares this fusion of thing and symbol inasmuch as its meaning is inseparable from the thing, and *vice versa*.

15 Max Nänny has developed his study of Pound in relation to 'primitive' forms (such as the oral epic) through an application of Schneidau's thesis. See, for example, Nänny, 'The Oral Roots of Ezra Pound's Methods of Quotation and Abbreviation', *Paideuma*, 8.3 (Winter 1979).

16 Pound does not concern himself explicitly with a notion of the unconscious as such. Indeed, it is a concept which would be difficult to assimilate to his value of the will. But this does not alter the fact that his values of 'race consciousness' (linked to tradition), his mystical biology (from Remy de Gourmont and Louis Berman – see Bell, *Critic as Scientist*, pp. 211ff.), his notions of absolute rhythms and symbols, of the complex and of myth, as well as his invocation of anthropology, all relate to some form of 'other' psychological vitality, in some sense more reliable or creative than the purely conscious mind, residing in a semi-physiological unconscious (de Gourmont) or in primitive cultures. Cf. 'Poetry only does consciously what the primitive races did unconsciously' (*CWC*, p. 23).

17 Jean Starobinski, 'Freud, Breton, Myers', *La Relation critique* (Paris: Gallimard, 1972) p. 324.

18 Carl Jung, quoted ibid., p. 341.
19 See Martin A. Kayman, 'A Context for Hart's "Complex" ', *Paideuma*, 12.2–3 (Fall–Winter 1983) 235; and L. S. Hearnshaw, *A Short History of British Psychology: 1840–1940* (London: Methuen, 1964) p. 167. The sources that Hart himself gives, in the Introduction to *The Psychology of Insanity*, are precisely Jung, Pierre Janet, Karl Pearson and Krafft-Ebing. Freud is not mentioned.
20 Hart, 'The Conception of the Subconscious', *Subconscious Phenomena*, ed. Münsterberg, p. 103.
21 Hart, *Psychopathology*, p. 11.
22 See Alan Gauld's account of the work of the Society in *The Founders of Psychical Research* (London: Routledge & Kegan Paul, 1968). See also F. W. H. Myers's *Human Personality and its Survival of Bodily Death* (London: Longman, Green, 1901; rev. and abridged, 1927).
23 *William James on Psychical Research*, ed. Murphy and Ballou, p. 218.
24 Hearnshaw, *A Short History of British Psychology*, p. 160.
25 Freud, letter to Jung, 17 Feb 1911, *The Freud/Jung Letters*, ed. William McGuire, tr. Ralph Manheim and R. F. C. Hull (Princeton, NJ: Bollingen Press, 1974) p. 396.
   The only 'psychoanalysts' working in England at this time were Hart, M. D. Eder (a friend of A. R. Orage and D. H. Lawrence, and hence a sometime member of the *New Age* circle) and Ernest Jones, Freud's biographer. Jones was, however, working in Canada between 1908 and 1913. Eder in fact read a paper on Freud to the British Medical Association in 1911. In striking contrast to the receptivity shown by the Society for Psychical Research on the occasion of Myers's presentation in 1893, the members of the Association present listened politely until the end and then all silently walked out.
26 Joseph Collins, quoted in Nathan G. Hale, Jr, *Freud and the Americans* (New York: Oxford University Press, 1971) p. 275.
27 Hart, in *Subconscious Phenomena*, ed. Münsteberg, p. 140.
28 Sigmund Freud, *Jokes and their Relation to the Unconscious* (1905), tr. James Strachey (Harmondsworth: Penguin Freud Library, 1976) p. 218.
29 Myers, *Human Personality and its Survival of Bodily Death*, abridged edn, p. 17.
30 Münsterberg, in his Introduction to *Subconscious Phenomena*, effectively excludes such a middle ground. He identifies three basic fields for current theory: the 'laymen', who are most responsive to Myers's theories, in which the subconscious was seen as part of a 'psychical stream of a full real personality' (p. 19); the 'physicians', or neuropathologists, who, he claims, see the subconscious as a set of discontinuous, pathological phenomena; and the 'psychologists', who hold that 'the subconscious that underlies the abnormal facts is the same that underlies the ordinary processes of memory, attention, etc., it is not psychical at all, but a physiological brain process' (p. 20). Such a division (even if it were accurate – the position of Pierre Janet, a psychopathologist, proves it not so) would actually exclude Hart himself. Münsterberg represents a school of physiology-based functionalism, influential in the later development of behaviourism.

31 Sigmund Freud, *On the History of the Psychoanalytic Movement* (1914), tr. James Strachey (London: Routledge & Kegan Paul, 1960) pp. 29–30.
32 W. H. R. Rivers, *Instinct and the Unconscious* (London: Cambridge University Press, 1920) p. 85.
33 Ibid.
34 Starobinski, 'Freud, Breton, Myers', *La Relation Critique.*
35 Hugo Münsterberg, *Psychotherapy* (London: T. Fisher Unwin, 1909) p. 3.
36 See note 30, above.
37 Wyndham Lewis, 'The Song of the Militant Romance', *One Way Song* (London: Faber & Faber, 1933) p. 30.
38 Freud, 'Three Essays on the Theory of Sexuality' (1905), *Complete Psychological Works*, standard edn, vii (London: Hogarth Press, 1953) p. 135.
39 *The Freud/Jung Letters*, ed. McGuire, p. 507.
40 Carl Jung, *The Psychology of the Unconscious* (1912), tr. Beatrice M. Hinkle (London: Kegan Paul, Trench, Trubner, 1946) pp. 388 and 506.
41 Ibid., p. 239.
42 Freud, *On the History of the Psychoanalytic Movement*, p. 60.
43 Ibid., p. 62.
44 Mark Twain, *The Adventures of Huckleberry Finn* (1884; New York: Harper, 1931) p. 16.
45 Sigmund Freud, *Totem and Taboo* (1912) tr. James Strachey (London: Routledge & Kegan Paul, 1960) p. 90.
46 Ibid., p. 73.
47 Freud, *Jokes and their Relation to the Unconscious*, pp. 237–8.
48 Freud, *Totem and Taboo*, p. 71.
49 Ibid., p. 73.
50 Theodor Adorno, *Minima Moralia*, tr. E. F. M. Jephcott (London: New Left Books, 1974) p. 222.
51 Pierre Macherey, *Pour une théorie de la production littéraire* (Paris: Maspero, 1974) pp. 80–1.
52 The vocabulary here is that of Jacques Lacan, who divides psychic activity into three fields: the Imaginary, the Symbolic, and the Real. The Symbolic is governed by the concept of the 'Other' (elsewhere characterised as 'The-Name-of-the-Father' or 'Paternal Metaphor'): the place from which the subject appears as an object. This place is, in epistemological terms, occupied by the 'Supposedly-Knowing-Subject' ('sujet supposé savoir'). The 'other', with a lower case 'o', represents the world as manipulated through narcissistic phantasy, under the control and towards the formation of the subject's ego. In this sense, whereas the 'other', which is the object of the Imaginary order, is a result of our subjective control, the 'Other', which dominates the Symbolic order, places *us* in the position of objects. The best account of Lacan's thought continues to be Anthony Wilden's *The Language of the Self* (Baltimore: Johns Hopkins University Press, 1968).
53 Sigmund Freud, *The Psychopathology of Everyday Life* (1901; Harmondsworth: Penguin Freud Library, 1975) p. 258.
54 Adorno, *Minima Moralia*, p. 240.
55 Ibid., p. 238. Jean-Pierre Faye notes a similar process of literalisation in

two of the key discursive operations of fascism in Italy. Faye notes a transition in Mussolini's use of 'totalitario', a transition from its originally conditional utterance ('they say that we are . . .', 22 June 1925) to 'l'énoncé sans condition' (3 Jan 1925), by which time the party had fulfilled what had before been effectively an irony. See Jean-Pierre Faye, *La Critique du langage et son économie*, p. 81; and also his *Théorie du récit* (Paris: Herman, 1972), pp. 57ff.

56 'A Visiting Card' (1942), in *SP*, p. 276.

57 'What is Money for?' (1939), in *SP*, p. 270.

58 Adorno, *Minima Moralia*, p. 193.

59 e. e. cummings, *Complete Poems 1913–1962* (New York: Harcourt, Brace, Jovanovich, 1980) p. 223.

60 P. G. Wodehouse, letter to W. Townend, 2 Oct 1924, in *Wodehouse on Wodehouse* (Harmondsworth: Penguin, 1981) p. 260.

61 Charles Ives, 'Postface to *114 Songs*' (1922), in *'Essays Before a Sonata' and Other Writings*, ed. Howard Boatwright (London: Calder & Boyars, 1969) pp. 128–30.

62 The distinction between the production and consumption of art and literature relates to the sometimes problematic distinction between 'popular culture' and 'mass culture': the one produced by communities usually for their own consumption; the other produced by an industry for consumption by a class distanced and dislocated from the act of its production.

   To give a general idea of the sort of areas that I am indicating, we might consider the move towards the teaching of writing in schools and some universities as a supplement to an otherwise largely consumption-oriented reading-course. This is an interesting field of experimentation, especially in the perspective of educationalists such as James Britton, who describes literature as 'a written form of language in the role of spectator and so related to the spoken form, gossip about events' – *Prospect and Retrospect: Selected Essays of James Britton*, ed. Gordon Pradl (London: Heinemann, 1982) p. 49 – although one perceives the ambiguities of the situation when confronted with the boom in the publication and sale of students' or children's writing – or with the expectation of students on 'creative writing' courses that the production of good work itself merits publication. On the other hand, the emergence of community publishing co-operatives (such as Centerprise and QueenSpark in London and Brighton), and of feminist and ethnic groups, has also given many people access to their own 'showing-forth'. Of particular interest, then, is the development of a literature of working-class autobiographies and women's writing, most often under the auspices of this type of co-operative. For an account of the experience of such groups, see *The Republic of Letters: Working Class Writing and Local Publishing*, ed. Dave Morley and Ken Worpole (London: Comedia Publishing Group, 1982). One does not wish to be overnaïve about this, nor does one underestimate the capacity for recuperation of the culture industry and educational system, nor does one view the word-processor and personal video necessarily as revolutionary elements. None the less, inasmuch as the condition of modern culture is that its 'massification' passes through its integration into a particular form of commercial market, one can offer a notion of culture based in personal and communal production as an alternative to the otherwise disturbing two-sided alienation represented by 'mass culture' and 'high culture'. The examples I have given here are indications, albeit some more problematic than others, of the fact that the project does have some concrete possibilities which have been or are being explored.

Index